VIOLENCE AGAINST QUEER PEOPLE

VIOLENCE AGAINST QUEER PEOPLE

Race, Class, Gender,
and the Persistence of
Anti-LGBT Discrimination

DOUG MEYER

RUTGERS UNIVERSITY PRESS
New Brunswick, New Jersey, and London

Library of Congress Cataloging-in-Publication Data

Meyer, Doug, 1980
Violence against queer people : race, class, gender, and the persistence of anti-LGBT
discrimination / Doug Meyer.
pages cm
Includes bibliographical references and index.
ISBN 978–0-8135–7316–8 (hardcover : alk. paper)—ISBN 978–0-8135–7315–1
(pbk. : alk. paper)—ISBN 978-0-8135–7317–5 (e-book (epub))—ISBN
978–0-8135–7318–2 (e-book (web pdf))
1. Gays—Violence against—United States. 2. Hate crimes—United States. 3. United
States—Race relations. 4. Social classes—United States. I. Title.
HV6250.4.H66 M492015
362.88086'64—dc23
2015004939

A British Cataloging-in-Publication record for this book is available from the British
Library.

Visit our website: http://rutgerspress.rutgers.edu

Manufactured in the United States of America

CONTENTS

ACKNOWLEDGMENTS

First and foremost, I would like to thank Victoria Pitts-Taylor and Barbara Katz Rothman, both of whom helped improve this project tremendously through their invaluable support and guidance. Their dedication to the project helped me grow as a researcher, scholar, and feminist. For giving me space when I wanted it, but also feedback when I needed it, I thank them. This work would also not have been possible without the participation of the people I interviewed. They deserve my deepest thanks for sharing their experiences. I remain indebted to them, as I learned a lot through their openness and kindness. I would also like to thank the many organizations that allowed me to place recruitment flyers in their lobby or waiting room; for making that process run smoothly, I am grateful.

Colleagues at multiple institutions helped improve this project. Mimi Schippers has provided crucial guidance throughout my academic career and deserves special thanks. Joshua Freilich has also been incredibly helpful and supportive, and I thank him for his feedback on this project at various stages. At the Graduate Center of the City University of New York (CUNY), Hester Eisenstein helped me tremendously through my early years of graduate study. For listening to my ideas and responding with a supportive but critical ear, I also thank Maria Biskup, Kara Van Cleaf, Ali Salerno, Soniya Munshi, Nomvuyo Nolutshungu, Ron Nerio, Julie Lavelle, Ken Nielsen, Hilary Burdge, and Mitra Rastegar. I am grateful to Jes Peters for helping with some of the transcriptions and Andrew Stewart for providing advice on my work. At the College of Wooster, Christa Craven provided enormously helpful feedback and support; I thank her tremendously. I also thank Anne Nurse, Setsuko Matsuzawa, Olivia Navarro-Farr, Michael Forbes, Craig Willse, David McConnell, Thomas Tierney, Heather Fitz Gibbon, Nick Kardulias, and Pam Frese. At the University of Virginia, I benefited from the feedback and support of many colleagues: Charlotte Patterson, Andre Cavalcante, Denise Walsh, Corinne Field, Lisa Speidel, Kath Weston, Amanda Davis, Miranda Waggoner, and Sabrina Pendergrass.

The funding agencies that supported this project provided crucial support. Particular thanks go to the Williams Institute on Sexual Orientation Law and Public Policy at the UCLA School of Law, the Ford Foundation Award from the CUNY Graduate Center, and the Professional Development Funds from Queens College and the College of Wooster. Their generous support helped me to complete this project. My research assistants, Lily Vela and David Hirsch, as well as Gina Christo and Jacob Danko, also deserve thanks. At academic conferences, I benefited from the feedback of several people, including Eric Anthony Grollman, Salvador Vidal Ortiz, Patrick Grzanka, Emily Mann, and Molly Merryman. Although I have written *Violence against Queer People* in a more accessible way than my work in various academic journals, some of the data from this text have appeared elsewhere. Some of chapters 3 and 4 has appeared in *Gender & Society* as "An Intersectional Analysis of Lesbian, Gay, Bisexual, and Transgender (LGBT) People's Evaluations of Anti-Queer Violence" (2012, 26(6): 849–873). Parts of chapter 6 have appeared in *Sociology* as "Evaluating the Severity of Hate-Motivated Violence: Intersectional Differences among LGBT Hate Crime Victims" (2010, 44(5): 980–995), and sections of chapter 5 have appeared in *Race, Gender & Class* as "Interpreting and Experiencing Anti-Queer Violence: Race, Class, and Gender Differences among LGBT Hate Crime Victims" (2008, 15(3–4): 262–282). A few paragraphs from this text were published in *Critical Criminology* as "Resisting Hate Crime Discourse: Queer and Intersectional Challenges to Neoliberal Hate Crime Laws" (2014, 61(4): 453–470). I thank the editors and reviewers of these journals for their critical, but extraordinarily useful, feedback.

Peter Mickulas, my editor at Rutgers University Press, helped improve this project tremendously. For his helpful feedback and unwavering support, I am grateful. Special thanks to John Raymond for his extremely useful help with copyediting, and Carrie Hudak for her help with production. Finally, I would like to thank my family members for all of their support—A. J. Meyer, Mike Meyer, Howard Meyer, and Sharron Meyer; I could not have completed this project without all of your love. Most important, I would like to thank my husband, Alberto McKelligan, whose selflessness and kindness continues to move me. He has made this project infinitely better through not only his helpful comments and suggestions but also his love and support. His advice has always been tremendously useful, as he has read much of my work and listened to me talk about this project many times. For helping me in infinite ways, I thank him dearly.

VIOLENCE AGAINST QUEER PEOPLE

1 • INTRODUCTION

Social Inequality and Violence against LGBT People

On a hot summer day in 2006, Latoya, a fifty-year-old Black lesbian, was holding hands with her girlfriend on the streets of New York City.[1] As the lesbian couple walked and held hands, a man began whistling at them. When the couple ignored him, he approached Latoya's girlfriend, Brianna, a Black woman Latoya described as "very girly." The man, whom Latoya described as Black and heterosexual, then asked Brianna for her phone number because he "wanted to get in on that." As he insisted, repeating "come on" several times, Latoya stepped between Brianna and the man and said, "Listen, she's not interested, she's with me." He then became agitated and grabbed Brianna's arm; this action caused Latoya to pull on the man's shirt and insist, "Let her go." He grasped Brianna's arm tighter, causing her to scream in pain, but then he let go as Latoya yelled louder. As Brianna fell backward onto the ground, the man motioned toward Latoya as if he was going to hit her, but instead said that she should "take that white shit home" and nodded toward Brianna, saying, "You know that she just needed a dick." Latoya laughed and said that "no woman would touch" him because he was "disgusting." This comment prompted the man to punch Latoya's arm and refer to her as a "dumb bitch." As Brianna checked to see if her girlfriend was hurt, the man left the area.

Kevin, a sixty-two-year-old Black gay man, also experienced violence related to his sexuality. While in his forties, Kevin was approached after leaving a department store by two white male police officers who said that they had a report of someone who "matched his description" stealing something from the store. Kevin had not stolen anything—the officers did not find any merchandise on him—but he had some crack cocaine in his

1

pockets, which resulted in him being arrested. At the police station, one of the police officers questioned Kevin in an interrogation room. Initially, Kevin said that the officer was trying to learn about his drug supplier, but then the questions turned to Kevin's gender performance, as the policeman asked, "Why do you talk like that?" and "Why do you act like that?" Kevin said that he "wanted to go all ballistic," but just kept "sitting there laughing." The officer elevated his insults to the point of asking Kevin if he was "one of those faggots who liked to take it up the ass." When Kevin said, "Wouldn't you like to know?" the officer rose from his chair and slammed Kevin's head into the table. The policeman then pushed over Kevin's chair, causing him to fall backward onto his wrists, which were handcuffed together. Kevin spent the night in jail with what he thought was a broken nose and broken wrist. When receiving medical care three days later, he learned that his wrist was indeed fractured. He did not report the police officer's violence to anyone, believing that his version of the events would not be believed and fearing that he would then experience more police violence during his time in jail.

Latoya's and Kevin's experiences reveal that some forms of violence occur because of prejudice and discrimination against lesbians and gay men—often referred to as "homophobia." Indeed, it is possible—likely, even—that Latoya and Kevin would not have experienced violence had they been heterosexual. The man in the first incident became upset when a lesbian woman said that her girlfriend was not interested in him, while the police officer in the second incident used homophobic language to insult Kevin, referring to him as "one of those faggots who liked to take it up the ass." Moreover, both Latoya and Kevin viewed the men as homophobic—as "having issues with gay people," as Kevin described it. At the same time, Latoya's and Kevin's violent experiences were also considerably more complex than simply reflecting homophobia. In particular, racism and sexism were deeply implicated in their experiences. Sexism structured Latoya's experience: gender norms in the United States permit men to approach and sexualize women in public space, and the man's reference to Latoya as a "dumb bitch" reflects misogyny—hatred of women. Reversing the gender identities of the people involved demonstrates the role of gender: imagine a heterosexual woman approaching two gay men and insisting that one of the gay men give the woman his phone number. In the United States, that interaction seems very unlikely to occur, even though it is exactly what happened between the man and this lesbian couple. Further, racism likely played a role in Kevin's experience, as Black men face the unwarranted suspicion of theft to a much greater extent than white men. The suggestion that he "fit a description" is racially coded—a statement a white LGBT person would be unlikely to hear and an indication that Kevin was approached by the police officers largely because of his race. Kevin's racial identity, then, set the stage for the entire encounter. He likely never would have been arrested or ended up at the police station if he had been white. In this sense, racism and sexism make some forms of antigay violence possible.

This book focuses on incidents such as those experienced by Latoya and Kevin, which are based on interviews conducted with forty-seven people who encountered violence for being perceived as lesbian, gay, bisexual, or transgender (LGBT). Although most emphasis on anti-LGBT, or anti-queer, violence has focused on homophobia, many LGBT people confront violence based on other aspects of their identity, including race, class, and gender.[2] Homophobia certainly plays a role in many forms of anti-queer violence, yet other dimensions of inequality are often equally significant. Many lesbians experienced forms of rape and sexual assault—violence undoubtedly shaped by their status as women in a male-dominated society. Moreover, lesbians were frequently called misogynistic insults such as "bitch" or "whore"—in fact, more lesbian respondents described being called these insults than homophobic ones such as "dyke"—and lesbians frequently spoke about violence as violating their sense of safety as women. Thus, given that sexism and misogyny are essential to many forms of anti-lesbian violence, homophobia offers an incomplete picture of lesbians' violent experiences (Denissen and Saguy 2014; Perry 2001). Further, for many LGBT people of color, racism was as important as homophobia in shaping their violent experiences. To focus only on homophobia would obscure the racial dynamics of anti-queer violence; police violence against Black LGBT people cannot be understood solely through the lens of homophobia, since racism undoubtedly plays a role.

Although *Violence against Queer People* focuses on LGBT people, this book is written for readers hoping to learn about inequality based on race, class, gender, and sexuality. The overlap, or intersection, of these institutional power structures is especially important to consider. What are we to make of Latoya's experience of being told to "take that white shit home" by a Black heterosexual man? These ideas stem from the association of homosexuality with whiteness. This association, however, can only be understood by examining the overlap of race and sexuality. Examining race on its own or sexuality by itself would prove insufficient—both need to be examined at the same time. I emphasize these intersections throughout this text, as I show that racism, sexism, and social class inequality continue to affect what individuals encounter in their daily lives, including forms of violence. In this regard, social inequality remains deeply embedded in the United States, as one's social position—one's location in society with regard to institutional power structures—shapes one's life experiences. My social position, for instance, as a white and middle-class gay man affects what I encounter in my life, and these experiences are different from what other social groups face. Undoubtedly, one's social position has a profound effect on a wide range of phenomena, including where one grows up, how likely one is to attend college, and whether one encounters violence (Jones 2010; Lareau 2003). Indeed, one of the main ideas of this book is that race, class, and gender profoundly affect individuals' experiences and perceptions of violence. As such, I emphasize that the opportunities granted to LGBT people differ in significant ways based on where they are located in society and, more broadly, that racism, sexism, and homophobia continue to play an important role in the United States, as individuals encounter different experiences depending on their social position.

THE PRIVILEGING OF WHITE AND MIDDLE-CLASS GAY MEN'S VIOLENT EXPERIENCES

Evidence suggests that gay men experience higher rates of physical violence than lesbian and bisexual people, yet rates of violence do not explain which LGBT people's violent experiences have been emphasized (Ahmed and Jindasurat 2014; Herek 2009). Instead, power relations—the privileging of some groups over others—are considerably more important. To be sure, although significant evidence indicates that transgender people experience higher rates of violence than lesbians and gay men, much more attention has focused on homophobic violence.[3] Moreover, as little emphasis has been placed on homeless LGBT people—who undoubtedly experience higher rates of violence than many other queer people—the frequency of anti-LGBT attacks explains relatively little about whose experiences have been emphasized (Gibson 2011). Rather, some LGBT people's experiences—primarily those who are white, male, and middle class—have been emphasized more than others because these identities remain the most privileged in LGBT communities. The most privileged LGBT people have been favored by traditional understandings of anti-queer violence, while marginalized LGBT people, many of whom experience violence at higher rates, have been excluded. This trend, of course, reflects the privilege granted to white and middle-class men's experiences in the dominant U.S. society, as whiteness, maleness, and middle-class positions are privileged throughout the United States. Thus, LGBT communities are not unique in privileging white and middle-class men, but reflect the norms of mainstream U.S. society.

While *Violence against Queer People* highlights the experiences of LGBT people marginalized in multiple ways, white and middle-class gay men's experiences have figured most prominently in traditional understandings of anti-queer violence. Indeed, ideas about homophobic hate crime—that is, violence motivated by bias or hate—associate victims with white and middle-class gay men. The case of Matthew Shepard, the most famous and well-known antigay hate crime, occurred in 1998 and involved the brutal murder of a white and gay male college student. This case reflects the privileging of white and middle-class gay men's experiences, as a Black transgender woman murdered several weeks prior to him received no comparable media attention (Spade and Willse 2000). More recent mainstream media representations have continued to position white and middle-class gay men as the victims of antigay bullying. Even though some media coverage has focused on gay teens of color such as Carl Joseph Walker Hoover, lesbian and transgender people have rarely featured in these media representations. The most high-profile victims of antigay bullying, including Tyler Clementi, have been gay men, who are often white and middle class as well, and fictional representations, including on the TV show *Glee*, have also focused largely on white gay men. This emphasis does not reflect the frequency with which LGBT people encounter violence, as considerable evidence indicates that white and middle-class gay men experience violence at lower rates than transgender people and low-income gay men (Ahmed and Jindasurat 2014; Kosciw et al. 2012; Stotzer 2008, 2009).

White and middle-class gay men certainly experience homophobia; my point is not to deny this reality. Nevertheless, traditional understandings of anti-queer violence have privileged this group's experiences by viewing anti-queer violence as resulting from homophobia. According to this line of thinking, anti-queer violence occurs because the perpetrator "hates" lesbians or gay men. This perspective serves the interests of white, middle-class gay men, whose violent experiences occur largely because of homophobia and do not typically experience racist, sexist, or classist violence. For less privileged queer people, forms of inequality other than discrimination based on sexuality and gender identity are equally important, as their violent experiences are frequently implicated in more than homophobia.

Although white and middle-class gay men's violent experiences have undoubtedly been privileged, a very particular formulation of their experiences has been advanced. Matthew Shepard, for example, was HIV positive at the time of his murder, yet many individuals remain unaware of this aspect of the attack because it went largely unreported (Loffreda 2000). Most likely, this detail has not been widely reported because it complicates his status as an ideal gay subject. In this sense, stigmatized aspects of LGBT people such as being HIV positive are frequently hidden from public view, while normative aspects such as being white, male, and middle class become part of the representation. When many people think of Matthew Shepard, they think of a white gay man, not an HIV-positive white gay man. Thus, representations of LGBT people do not simply focus on a particular type of victim—usually male, white, and middle class—but omit aspects considered less than ideal, such as being HIV positive, from the representation. Unfortunately, these depictions create types of violence that are viewed as the most worrisome and create categories of victims that are viewed as the most legitimate. Consequently, individuals with less privileged identities— poor, transgender, Black and Latino, and gender-nonconforming people— are less likely to be viewed as "real" victims, given that their experiences and identities do not align with the traditional representation.

Through informal discussions with other LGBT people, I have heard others defend this emphasis on the violent experiences of white and middle-class gay men by arguing that it is beneficial to show that even the most privileged LGBT people experience homophobic violence. According to this perspective, focusing on the most privileged LGBT people sells the seriousness of anti-queer violence to mainstream society; that is, homophobic abuse is clearly a widespread problem because even the most privileged gay subjects experience it. Presumably, if white and middle-class gay men such as Matthew Shepard experience violence, one can only imagine what is happening to less normative LGBT people. The problem with this approach is that it produces gains for a relatively small segment of LGBT people. This approach challenges homophobia, while privileging other characteristics—whiteness and maleness—that are already privileged. As a result, by emphasizing the experiences of white and middle-class gay men, dominant U.S. race, class, and gender norms remain in place. Whiteness, maleness, and middle-class respectability are still positioned as ideal.

I am critical of approaches that privilege white and middle-class gay men's experiences, yet in many ways I embody, as a blue-eyed, white gay man in his thirties, the very identity so frequently privileged in LGBT communities. Consequently, even though I experience homophobia that white and middle-class heterosexual men do not confront, I remain privileged in comparison to many other LGBT people. It is my hope that by reading this text other LGBT people, as well as more general readers interested in social inequality, will think about their own privileges and work to challenge multiple forms of discrimination, not simply the one that affects them the most. Black and Latina lesbians have been calling for greater attention to inequality within LGBT communities for quite some time now (Hull, Bell-Scott, and Smith 1982; Lorde 1984; Moraga and Anzaldúa 1983); it would be ridiculous if these calls were only paid attention to now that a comparatively privileged white gay man such as myself has started making them. At the same time, *Violence against Queer People* should be viewed as contributing to this scholarship calling for more serious consideration of racism, classism, and sexism within LGBT communities (Carbado 2013; Hanhardt 2013; Moore 2011; Ward 2008). If advocacy and scholarly work hopes to benefit LGBT people in the broadest sense possible—not simply promoting lesbians and gay men who are already the most privileged in queer communities—then we must push beyond frameworks that focus solely on homophobia and instead emphasize the experiences of queer people who are marginalized in multiple ways.

While sexism, racism, and social class inequality continue to shape individuals' life experiences, sociologists have described the appeal of colorblindness, in which individuals are discouraged from pointing out differences in opportunity based on race (Bonilla-Silva 2006; Gallagher 2003; Steinbugler 2012). This tendency to ignore racial differences remains widespread, even though racial disparities continue to exist in nearly every arena of American society, from health and education to job opportunities and treatment in the criminal justice system (Alexander 2010; Bonilla-Silva

2006). I argue that a similar process is happening with regard to sexuality—the rise of sexuality blindness—in which it is becoming increasingly frowned upon to point to unequal conditions based on sexual orientation. According to this line of thought, the struggle for gay rights has largely been accomplished and the tide of history has swung in favor of LGBT equality. I argue, in contrast, that the lives of many LGBT people—particularly those of the most vulnerable—have improved very little, if at all, over the past thirty years and that research can dispel these myths of equality by focusing on the lives of the most marginalized LGBT people. Although it has become less acceptable to express homophobia publicly, the larger structures of society continue to privilege heterosexuality. Thus, conditions have undoubtedly improved for LGBT people who benefit from the decline of public homophobia, but for LGBT people who must also concern themselves with racism, classism, and sexism it is much more debatable as to whether challenges to homophobia have substantially improved their lives.

At times, challenges to homophobia have reinforced racism and classism. Under these frameworks, discrimination against LGBT people has been characterized in negative terms because it is practiced by marginalized race and social class groups; that is, homophobia is bad because "certain groups" engage in it. These groups, not coincidentally, are often already marginalized by mainstream society: antigay prejudice and discrimination has been attached disproportionately to low-income heterosexual people and to Black, Latino, and Muslim Americans.[4] Such strategies, while challenging homophobia, reinforce racism, classism, and Islamophobia. Although challenging homophobia while simultaneously reinforcing these other forms of inequality may benefit white and middle-class gay men, it does not help—and typically hurts—Black, Muslim, and Latino LGBT people. Homophobia certainly should be opposed, but doing so at the expense of marginalized race and social class groups is not helpful in combating inequality.

The point is not simply to include more low-income people of color into existing narratives but to pay attention to how race, class, and gender are already built into common sense understandings of anti-queer violence. When hearing of homophobic violence, most people probably think of street violence or bullying in schools. The victim that comes to mind is frequently a white and middle-class gay man. Yet the perpetrator is often raced and classed in problematic ways as well. In particular, ideas about homophobic violence typically focus on public attacks perpetrated by strangers.

Hate crime, especially, calls forth notions of "stranger danger," in which an implicitly innocent person is suddenly and randomly attacked by a highly prejudiced, out-of-control stranger. Hate crime is thought to occur because the perpetrator "hates" the victim's social group. Race and social class are fundamental to these ideas: the victim, merely going about his or her business, has "not done anything wrong," and is therefore associated with an innocent, implicitly middle-class white person, while the perpetrator is supposedly prejudiced, disruptive, and disorderly. Since low-income people of color, particularly poor Black men, have routinely been constructed as unruly and out-of-control throughout U.S. history, hate crime discourse reproduces problematic race and social class politics (Collins 2000; Hanhardt 2013; Mogul, Ritchie, and Whitlock 2011).

Focusing on LGBT people of color's experiences of hate crime will not help to alleviate these concerns, as any discourse that emphasizes the wild, irrational, or demented aspects of the perpetrator will inevitably reinforce existing social hierarchies by encouraging the punishment of poor Black and Latino people (Alexander 2010; McCorkel 2013; Rios 2011). The bodies of Black men in particular have been pathologized as "naturally violent," and hate crime discourse relies on classist and racist ideas of an excessively violent perpetrator to gain its meaning (Hanhardt 2013; Richardson and May 1999; Tomsen 2006). In this regard, traditional understandings of anti-queer violence have reproduced troubling ideas that low-income people of color should be feared and, consequently, controlled. People across racial lines commit homophobic violence, of course, but hate crime discourse encourages people to associate this abuse with low-income people of color. Thus, abandoning the idea of homophobic hate crime is necessary because the entire concept reproduces notions of white victims and low-income perpetrators of color. The goal is to change how individuals think and speak about anti-queer violence, not simply to include a more diverse group of people into current thinking.

Most forms of anti-queer violence are undoubtedly intraracial—where the victim and the perpetrator are the same race—and yet a few of the most high-profile acts of antigay violence have been interracial, with a heterosexual perpetrator of color and a white victim. The suicide of Tyler Clementi, a white gay man at Rutgers University, and the subsequent prosecution of Dharun Ravi, an Indian American heterosexual student at the same university, garnered the most media attention of the suicides by gay teens in late

2010. Many other forms of interracial violence remain hidden from public view. Although Black gay men and transgender people of color in this study experienced police brutality, in which a white police officer perpetrated the abuse, these experiences are rarely associated with anti-queer violence. This absence is due largely to the exclusion of LGBT people of color from mainstream society: most lesbians and gay men receiving media attention have been white, and police brutality has largely been associated with Black heterosexual men. Police violence against this group is undoubtedly a widespread problem, but Black LGBT people experience these forms of abuse at high rates as well (Mogul, Ritchie, and Whitlock 2011; Spade 2011).

In addition to overlooking race and gender, much of the previous work on anti-queer violence has not given serious consideration to social class.[5] Its absence is particularly surprising given that poverty exposes low-income LGBT people to constraints that middle-class queer people do not face. Low-income transgender women—people who identify as women but were categorized as male at birth—frequently experienced violence in homeless shelters, where they were housed with men due to policies that divide residents based on birth sex rather than gender identity. In these contexts, transgender women sometimes "chose" to live on the streets to escape abuse they faced in homeless shelters. Lela, a forty-eight-year-old Black transgender woman, described her decision to become homeless by arguing that it was safer than being housed with men in a homeless shelter: "I couldn't escape [the violence]. . . . They'd just tell me how I had to be with the men. . . . I thought I'd die. It got so bad that I just had to leave [and become homeless]." The challenges confronting transgender people differ to a significant degree from those facing lesbians and gay men; consequently, forms of antitransgender violence must be viewed on their own terms, as separate from homophobic attacks. Certainly, transgender people faced violence in which they were constructed as objects—as inhuman "things"—because they transitioned from one gender to another, which are ideas that lesbians and gay men do not face.

Although this book focuses primarily on differences among LGBT people, respondents spoke about violence in some similar ways. Indeed, low-income gay men also faced barriers in escaping violence, as they regularly experienced abuse in group homes or homeless shelters. Jayvyn, a thirty-three-year-old Black gay man, described constant harassment he faced in a group home during his twenties: "For the first two, three, four years, I never fought back. I would just take it. They would hit me with shit, throw shit at me, I would be the pit of all the jokes. I would just feel so low. There were points I was sitting there, I was just thinking, 'I want to die.'" As poverty and social class constraints lead to many forms of anti-queer violence—Jayvyn felt as if his only option in escaping this abuse was to live on the streets, as the staff members of the group home refused to help him—LGBT people do not confront violence to the same extent. Instead, some queer people, disproportionately those who are poor, are more likely to face abuse than other LGBT people. Respondents' violent experiences were also generally quite difficult to listen to, as they spoke of the pain they felt. Both Lela and Jayvyn mentioned their own death: Lela said, "I thought I'd die," while Jayvyn said, "I want to die." Of course, middle-class LGBT people may also have suicidal thoughts and face extreme hardship, but the point is that poverty makes it harder for low-income queer people to escape these contexts, as middle-class LGBT people can use their financial resources to avoid living in a group home or homeless shelter.

When many people in the United States think of homophobic violence, the experiences of Lela and Jayvyn are probably not what come to mind, yet they are exactly the sort of experiences described by low-income LGBT people in this study. These incidents have been excluded in large part because anti-queer violence has been viewed through the lens of homophobia—racism, sexism, and social class inequality have been an afterthought. White and middle-class gay men tend to experience violence primarily based on their sexuality, but many other LGBT people are marginalized in multiple ways—not only based on their sexuality but also based on their race, class, and gender identity. Middle-class white lesbians are marginalized based on gender and sexuality, and middle-class Black gay men are oppressed based on sexuality and race. These dynamics become even more complex when taking multiple dimensions of inequality into account at the same time. The violence confronting low-income Black lesbians differs from that confronting their male counterparts—low-income Black gay men—and both of these groups are likely to encounter different experiences than white, low-income lesbians. Still, all of these groups are marginalized under frameworks that focus solely on homophobia.

Mainstream media representations are likely to be extraordinarily slow to focus on the challenges confronting low-income LGBT people of color, yet my frustration lies as much with supposedly progressive queer communities that have continually ignored the concerns of socially marginalized queer subjects, including those who are poor and homeless. Many low-income LGBT people described violence that occurred in homeless shelters or group homes. These violent experiences were frequently perpetrated by strangers; yet, as mainstream gay rights advocacy has largely ignored the concerns of low-income queer people, these incidents have been overlooked (Hanhardt 2013; Ward 2008). Further, police brutality against queer people of color has frequently gone unnoticed due to LGBT political advocacy that privileges the experiences of white and middle-class gay men and fails to take seriously racism and social class inequality. Hate crime invokes particular images and thoughts, and yet these representations are not the forms of violence that most LGBT people face, much less the forms of abuse confronting low-income people of color. Rape, police brutality, and parents kicking children out of their home are rarely considered under the rubric of "hate crime." Pointing to these institutionalized forms of violence—against women, people of color, and homeless LGBT people—would underscore that racism, sexism, and homophobia continue in American society. In contrast, emphasizing public, stranger-based attacks shifts attention away from these more pervasive forms of abuse that minority groups confront.

Violence in the home has also been overlooked as attention has focused on public, stranger-based attacks. As feminist analyses of domestic violence have pointed out, the home is frequently not a safe space for marginalized groups, especially women (M. Johnson 2006; Richie 1996). In fact, many women are the least safe on dates, in families, and in relationships. Women are much more likely to be raped on a date than by a stranger and considerably more likely to experience violence from someone they know than from someone on the street (Hlavka 2014; Madriz 1997). Thus, the construction of family life as "private" and "safe" frequently serves men's interests, relegating domestic violence to a private matter and obscuring the many forms of violence women face in the home. Similarly, families have frequently served as an arena where LGBT youth face rejection rather than support from their family members. Critiques of family life, however, have remained marginal to traditional analyses of anti-queer violence; public attacks from strangers have been emphasized most frequently (Horn, Kosciw, and Russell 2009). This emphasis is unfortunate to the extent that it obscures domestic violence and homophobic abuse in the home. Ignoring familial violence against LGBT people leaves in place dominant norms that associate family life with safety. Nevertheless, for many LGBT people the family is the primary arena where they experience violence, rejection, and ostracism. Public attacks certainly do occur, yet violence in the home, often hidden from public view, is undoubtedly more common (Barton 2012; Kenagy and Bostwick 2005).

Throughout this book, I focus on LGBT people's violent experiences that do not fit neatly into traditional understandings of anti-queer violence; my focus includes forms of abuse that have been overlooked in mainstream discourse. Although I describe some public, stranger-based attacks, *Violence against Queer People* shifts attention toward a wider range of LGBT people's violent experiences, emphasizing the role of power dynamics in these forms of abuse. Indeed, this book reveals that queer people—and, by implication, other groups as well—are privileged and disadvantaged in significant ways based on their social position. As such, attempts to reduce anti-queer violence that ignore race, class, and gender do so at their own peril, as such approaches are likely to aid only the most privileged gay subjects. Instead, by emphasizing marginalized queer people's perspectives, scholarly and advocacy work can dispel the myth that LGBT people experience violence uniformly and aid a broad range of queer people, including those who experience racism, classism, and sexism, rather than simply attending to the needs of white and middle-class gay men.

ORGANIZATION OF THE BOOK

Subsequent chapters focus on LGBT people's violent experiences, collected from in-depth interviews with forty-seven people in New York City from 2006 through 2011 (see the appendix for a description of the research methods). In chapter 2, I provide examples of LGBT people's violent experiences rooted in racism, classism, and sexism, shifting attention from a unitary analysis of homophobia toward a more complex analysis that includes the role of other systems of inequality. I first provide examples that seem clearly rooted in homophobia, such as a gay man who was hit after making out with his boyfriend on the street. Still, these incidents, which were among the most obviously homophobic of the people in this study, were not based solely on homophobia. Instead, these experiences were implicated in the overlap of gender and sexuality, as the physical violence was typically directed against the person who performed gender in nontraditional ways. Thus, multiple systems of inequality are taken into account to reveal the limits of homophobia in explaining anti-queer violence.

Chapter 3 focuses on how LGBT people perceived their violent experiences differently along racial lines: Black and Latino respondents viewed anti-queer violence as having racial implications; white respondents, in contrast, did not view their experiences in this way. Indeed, LGBT people of color perceived forms of anti-queer violence as suggesting that they had inappropriately represented their racial communities. One respondent, a fifty-year-old Black lesbian, thought that she was being punished for "making Black people look bad." Conversely, white LGBT people did not emphasize the importance of race, due to their white privilege. These differences reflect racial inequality in the United States, whereby white people are allowed to represent themselves rather than their broader racial community, while people of color are held accountable for representing their racial or ethnic group. Consequently, LGBT people of color are not granted the privilege of whiteness and, therefore, are made to think about their actions in relation to their racial and ethnic communities. These racial differences also overlapped with gender, as Black and Latina lesbians differed from gay men of color in important ways.

In chapter 4, I compare respondents' evaluations of physical and verbal violence. This chapter shows that lesbian and transgender women were more likely than gay male respondents to emphasize the severity of physical violence because the former viewed these forms of abuse as suggesting that sexual assault might occur. Lesbian and transgender women described violent incidents in which a sexual component was introduced into the encounter, while gay men occasionally described violence that was designed to prevent an encounter from becoming sexual. Further, sexualized forms of violence were viewed differently by women and men, even when the violence was similar in some ways: forms of abuse did not produce the same amount of fear in gay men because they did not have to think about how physical violence might lead to rape. Indeed, even in the few cases where the possibility of a sexual assault was made explicit, gay men did not necessarily think that rape would occur.

Chapter 5 focuses on how LGBT people of color sometimes found it difficult to determine that anti-queer violence was based on their sexuality because they could not be certain whether racism or sexism had also played a role. White perpetrators often mixed racist insults with homophobic or transphobic ones, which then made it difficult for LGBT people of color to determine the cause of the violence. Conversely, white gay men made comments such as "it happened because I'm gay" or "it happened because of my sexuality." In stark contrast to the uncertainty expressed by LGBT people of color, white gay men almost always perceived their violent experiences as rooted in homophobia.

In chapter 6, I reveal that middle-class respondents were more likely than low-income LGBT people to perceive their violent experiences as severe. At the same time, low-income participants described the most experiences of physical violence. The group, then, reporting the most physical abuse— low-income LGBT people—was also the least likely to perceive their experiences as severe. These social class differences depended on LGBT people's reference groups—the groups with which they compare themselves. In particular, respondents were the most likely to emphasize the severity of their violent experiences when comparing themselves with someone they perceived as having experienced relatively little violence. Since low-income LGBT people were typically friends with individuals who had encountered a lot of violence, and middle-class respondents were not, the latter were more likely than the former to perceive their violent experiences as severe.

Chapter 7 focuses on a neglected area of study—homophobic abuse in the family. Much of media and scholarly attention has focused on extreme manifestations of anti-queer violence—hate crime, in particular—and has overlooked more common and insidious forms, especially those that occur in the home. Indeed, verbal abuse from family members, described by all of the people in this study, is marginalized under frameworks that focus on public, stranger-based attacks. Moreover, stereotypical representations of anti-queer violence frequently reinforce social inequality, as homophobic perpetrators have often been classed and gendered as low income and male, while victims have been constructed as white and middle-class gay men. These representations marginalize the experiences of low-income LGBT people and reproduce existing social class divisions.

With chapter 8, I conclude by challenging hate crime laws and arguing that anti-queer violence must be examined through the lens of race, class, and gender. Focusing on only homophobia privileges the experiences of LGBT people who encounter violence primarily based on their

sexuality—most likely, white and middle-class gay men, who do not typically experience racist, sexist, or classist violence. Such an approach is inad-
equate, given that it reproduces the interests of the most privileged LGBT
people—arguably those who need the least help—and marginalizes the
experiences of LGBT people who are the least privileged. Additionally,
given that many forms of anti-queer violence are not shaped solely, or even
predominantly, by homophobia, scholarship on anti-queer violence must
account for other systems of oppression, taking into consideration the
experiences of marginalized groups, including low-income LGBT people of
color.

2 · MORE THAN HOMOPHOBIA

The Race, Class, and Gender Dynamics of Anti-LGBT Violence

Lesbians' violent experiences are sometimes very obviously related to their sexuality. Take the experiences of Jetta, a twenty-eight-year-old Black lesbian who described a violent incident on the subway in which a male stranger started harassing her when she was holding hands with her girlfriend. Jetta described the man as "looking at me like he wanted to kill me," before muttering something under his breath, which she thought was directed toward her. Jetta then asked the man, "Is there a problem here?" to which he responded by muttering, slightly louder, "Stupid dyke." She then said, "I'm not afraid of you" and told him to "mind his own business." In response, the man kicked her shin, bruising her in the process. Lesbians were not the only respondents to describe these types of experiences. Gay men also encountered forms of violence that seemed directly related to their sexuality. Kevin, a sixty-two-year-old Black gay man, described several violent incidents, one of which occurred after making out with his boyfriend on the street. Moments after kissing, a group of teenage boys yelled "faggot" at him; Kevin responded by sticking up his middle finger at one of the boys. Several minutes later, this boy rammed his knee into Kevin's back, pushing him to the ground. As he gathered his things, several of the boys laughed, before running away.

The experiences of Jetta and Kevin were undoubtedly rooted in homophobia, as two heterosexual people who had engaged in the same behavior would probably not have encountered a negative response. The same act, in other words, such as kissing or holding hands, can result in different consequences depending on the gender and sexual orientation of the people involved. Still, despite the centrality of homophobia to the experiences described above, LGBT people's violent experiences frequently have as much to do with race, class, and gender norms as with sexuality-based ones. Indeed, forms of anti-queer violence often cannot be fully understood through the lens of homophobia, as the violent experiences of many LGBT people are shaped by racism, classism, and sexism. The incidents described above cannot be explained entirely by the respondents' sexuality. Reducing these incidents to a form of homophobic violence leaves many questions unanswered: Why did Jetta rather than her girlfriend experience the brunt of the violence and harassment? Why did the boys in the second incident choose to single out Kevin rather than his boyfriend? The answer to these questions can only be understood by examining gender, in addition to sexuality. Certainly, Jetta and Kevin both thought that they were targeted instead of their partners, both of whom were also Black, because they performed gender in less traditional ways than their significant other—that is, because they appeared as gender-nonconforming in their presentation of self.[1] Thus, even the experiences of Jetta and Kevin, which were among the most obviously homophobic of the people in this study, were not solely based on homophobia.

THE OVERLAP OF GENDER AND SEXUALITY

Given the strong cultural connection between homosexuality and gender nonconformity, gender and sexuality norms are implicated in most forms of anti-queer violence (Collier at al. 2013; Mogul, Ritchie, and Whitlock 2011). Indeed, the close connection between gender and sexuality in the contemporary United States makes it difficult to separate them from one another, as people tend to judge someone's sexual orientation based on their gender performance (Tomsen and Mason 2001). In this context, stigmatized sexualities such as lesbianism and male homosexuality are associated with nonconforming gender displays; heterosexuality, on the other hand, is linked with gender conformity. Andre, a self-described androgynous Black gay man, addressed this dynamic when arguing that others have judged his sexuality by examining the way he performs gender: "I didn't even know I was gay [when I was in high school], but I was feminine, so I guess they equated that with gay. They kind of put them both on the same spectrum." Andre was presumed to be gay because others perceived him as feminine; his gender nonconformity signaled to others that he might have been queer. Moreover, during this time, he experienced homophobic violence not because he identified as gay but because others identified him as gay based on his gender performance. The way he performed gender, then, marked him as visibly "out," even though he did not publicly identify as gay. In these situations, LGBT people, as well as gender-nonconforming heterosexual people, may experience violence for violating gender norms rather than for disclosing their sexuality.

Respondents generally perceived themselves as gender-nonconforming: lesbians frequently identified as "butch" or "aggressive," while gay men typically appeared feminine in their gender presentations of self. Several of the gay men came to the interview carrying a purse or wearing eyeliner, and women and men described incidents where perpetrators mentioned their gender performances during the attack. For instance, Jasmine, a forty-four-year-old Black lesbian, was spat on by a man when holding hands with her girlfriend, a woman whom Jasmine described as "very feminine." On the street, several men began to taunt the couple, with one of the men telling Jasmine's girlfriend, "Come on, I could do more for you than she can." When the women ignored the comments, this same man told Jasmine, "Don't start walking like a dyke, trying to show your manhood, you're still a woman." Jasmine then told the man that he was "just jealous" because he "couldn't get laid." In response, the man said, "I'm not worried, you can't please her, you don't have a dick," and then spat on her. Here, Jasmine violated gender norms by supposedly "walking like a dyke" and "trying to show [her] manhood." The man's suggestion that she could not "please" her girlfriend because she does not "have a dick" also reinforces male-centered ideas that only men are capable of sexually satisfying women. Gender norms played a central role in situations such as these, as lesbian respondents described being punished for engaging in behavior traditionally associated with men.

While lesbians frequently encountered violence for appearing as gender-nonconforming, their violent experiences were also shaped by sexism and misogyny. Judy, a forty-three-year-old Latina lesbian, was sexually assaulted at a party when she was twenty. Judy said that she is usually perceived as a "big dyke" and that straight men view her as "intimidating" because she is "fat and tall." At the party, Judy was socializing with a group of friends when several people left to pick up alcohol, leaving Judy alone with another man, whom she barely knew. The man then asked Judy several questions about her sexuality, moving closer to her on a couch. As he began to invade her space, Judy said that she "felt uncomfortable" in the situation and "began to fear for [her] safety." She stood up from the couch, telling him that she was going to look for something to eat. When she tried to leave the apartment, he leaped from the couch, grabbed her by the hair, and pushed her to the ground. He then began sexually assaulting her, grabbing her breasts and tearing open her T-shirt. When he could not forcibly remove her pants because Judy was holding on to her belt, he told her, "All I want to do is fuck you and I bet you'll come back straight." As he continually tried to remove her belt, he called her a "bitch" and a "whore." Before he could remove her belt, another woman entered the apartment. As Judy and the woman yelled at the man, he ran out of the room.

Judy's violent experience illustrates the difficulty of unpacking sexist and homophobic forms of violence from one another. It is difficult to determine where the line for one begins and the other ends. Would Judy have been sexually assaulted had she been a heterosexual woman? Was her attacker trying to punish her for what he saw as a deviant sexuality? Did he actually believe that he could make her "come back straight," as he stated? Or was her lesbianism merely the most readily available discourse that he could draw upon to justify his own behavior while simultaneously shifting blame onto her? These questions might be impossible to answer, as it seems unlikely that even the attacker could explain all of his unconscious thoughts and feelings at the moment of the assault. While these questions may be unanswerable, my research suggests that lesbians often ask themselves such questions as they struggle to make sense of their violent experiences. Indeed, after the sexual assault, Judy wondered why she had been singled out. Examining the violence approximately twenty-three years later, she concluded: "I can't be sure if it occurred because of my sexuality or just because I'm a woman. Both probably played a role."

Judy described other experiences that involved misogyny and homophobia. One of these experiences occurred when she had an argument with one of her brother's friends on the street. The argument began with the man saying that Judy "wanted to be a man." Judy, in contrast, suggested that she was "happy being a woman," but that she "liked to dress this way." The argument intensified when she said that he was "uncomfortable with his own sexuality" and he told her to remember that she was "just a dyke, not a man." They nearly fought each other, as he said, "If you want to be a man, you should learn to fight like a man." In response, Judy said that she could "probably beat [his] ass," which caused him to push her and say, "The only reason you're like that is because you haven't had a good man. Nobody has fucked you right."

Gay men did not typically describe statements such as those outlined by Judy; lesbians confronted these experiences in large part because of institutional sexism. Statements such as "you're only like that . . . because you haven't had a good man" establish lesbians' sexuality as shaped by men. Further, if lesbians' sexuality occurs because they "haven't had a good man," then their sexuality can only be understood by referring to men. These statements establish lesbians' sexuality as resulting from negative experiences with men, or at least the absence of positive ones; as the man crudely puts it, lesbianism supposedly occurs when "nobody has fucked you right." Gay men may also confront suggestions that their sexuality has occurred because of negative events, yet they are not typically assumed to be gay because a woman "hasn't fucked them right." Moreover, even though lesbians and straight men are both sexually attracted to women, suggesting that heterosexual men are straight "because they haven't had a good man" would likely seem absurd to most people in the United States. Many lesbians, however, described these sorts of statements.

Viewing lesbians' sexuality as the result of negative experiences with men clearly reflects homophobia to the extent that it reinforces ideas about homosexuality as abnormal and unnatural—as something that occurs under negative conditions. At the same time, ideas about women's sexuality are deeply implicated in these experiences, as sexism encourages women to think about their sexuality in passive terms (Garcia 2012; Tolman 1994). The language used to describe heterosexual sex even varies based on gender: men's sexuality is usually constructed as active—they "fuck," so to speak—while women's sexuality is more frequently described in passive terms—they "are fucked," supposedly. Thus, the sexuality of men, gay and straight alike, is not typically viewed as dependent on women because men's sexuality is viewed as active and stable. In this sense, lesbians' experiences of violence and harassment were often male-centered, as they reported being asked questions such as "why don't you like men?" or "have you tried being with a man?"; eleven of the fifteen lesbian respondents described one of these questions, while none of the gay men in this study described being asked similar questions about women. These differences are due in large part to sexism: in a society where men are more valued than women, lesbians must explain their partner choice more frequently than gay men because the assumption is that a rational human being would desire men. Indeed, violence against lesbians and gay men frequently reproduces hierarchies based on gender, placing more value on masculinity, and those characteristics traditionally associated with men, than on femininity and those characteristics traditionally associated with women (Pascoe 2007; Perry 2001).

While lesbians described male-centered questions, they also perceived many of their violent experiences as attempts to punish them for "converting" another woman—usually their girlfriend—into lesbianism. Approximately half of lesbian respondents perceived at least one of their experiences in this way. When doing so, they described situations in which perpetrators treated lesbian partners differently based on their gender performances, labeling one lesbian "masculine" and the other as more "feminine." Judy described several violent experiences that occurred when she was with her girlfriend, Tiara, a Black woman whom Judy described as "regular, like the kind of girl [straight men] think they can sleep with." Their different gender performances shaped an incident of verbal harassment that occurred at the house of Tiara's brother. A friend of Tiara's brother, a man in his late twenties, was also there. Judy said that this man asked Tiara "all of these really annoying questions" such as "what made you that way?" and "what did [Judy] do to you?" Judy laughed when describing his questions, saying that the man was acting "like if I wasn't with [Tiara], she'd want to be with him." Judy found the suggestion that Tiara would want to be sexually involved with this man laughable. Butch lesbians often mocked individuals for suggesting that they had "converted" their girlfriends into lesbianism, rejecting such ideas in the process.

Notions that butch lesbians "recruit" feminine women into lesbianism reinforce traditional gender ideology by constructing masculine women as active (they are "doing" the changing) and feminine women as passive (they are changed), while also stereotyping lesbians as either corrupting and controlling or flighty and complicit.[2] Indeed, defining lesbians in these dichotomous terms creates an oppressive structure for them, as they become associated with negative characteristics regardless of whether they are labeled as masculine or feminine. Further, lesbian respondents did not necessarily view their own relationships in such dichotomous ways, sometimes arguing that their gender identities were more fluid than the labels of "masculine" and "feminine" would suggest.[3] Still, lesbians often thought that their perpetrators had viewed them as masculine or feminine, even in cases when they did not perceive themselves in that way. That is, lesbian respondents sometimes felt as if heterosexual labels—where one lesbian was viewed as "the man" and the other as "the woman"—had been mapped onto them.

On the other hand, about half of the lesbians in this study involved in a romantic relationship described one of the women as more masculine or feminine than the other.[4] When making these arguments, lesbians noted that they experienced violence differently depending on their gender presentation of self. Describing violence against a lesbian couple, they said that physical violence was usually directed against the supposedly more "masculine" woman, while the more "feminine" woman was constructed as susceptible to others' influence. Tamika, a fifty-three-year-old Black lesbian woman who said that she was usually viewed as feminine, argued that physical violence was directed against her girlfriend: "*Always* toward her. Because they see her as more masculine. They mostly leave me alone because they see me as the feminine one; the kind of girl they think would sleep with them." Given that the same woman could be perceived as masculine in one situation and feminine in another, these categories of "masculine" and "feminine" must be understood to represent the labels attached to a lesbian during a particular situation rather than the property of an individual woman. At the same time, these findings suggest that lesbians are likely to experience violence and harassment differently depending on how they perform gender.

These differences in how lesbians confronted violence cannot be fully understood through the lens of homophobia, as gendered power relations clearly played an important role. Of course, depending on the context, forms of antilesbian violence will relate to gender and sexuality to different degrees, yet accounting for both of them typically provides for a better understanding of LGBT people's violent experiences than does viewing anti-queer violence as rooted in only one of these power structures. Undoubtedly, viewing anti-queer violence as emanating solely from homophobia overlooks the ways in which gender is implicated in many of its forms (Pascoe 2007; Perry 2001). Moreover, approaches that privilege gender over sexuality are equally problematic, as the violent experiences of many LGBT people cannot be reduced to sexism or misogyny.

The overlap of gender and sexuality also played an important role in structuring violence against gay men. In particular, gay male respondents frequently described being harassed for engaging in activities stereotypically associated with women. Daniel, a twenty-six-year-old Black gay man, described several experiences during his childhood when his mother would beat him for playing with dolls. Later, when he "came out" to her at the age of eighteen, she told him, "I don't care what you are, just don't be acting feminine." Here, she explicitly condemned femininity from men rather than homosexuality. At times, then, gay men may be chastised more harshly for identifying as feminine than for identifying as gay. Certainly, masculinity norms in the United States encourage men to repudiate behaviors traditionally associated with femininity (Klein 2012; McCormack 2012; Pascoe 2007). In this regard, antigay violence is a social control mechanism designed to police masculinity norms. Still, Daniel interpreted his mother's comment as related to his sexuality when he said, "She was trying to tell me to keep it hidden, like I shouldn't be open about it." On the surface, his mother's comment appeared as if it was primarily related to gender, but Daniel believed that it had homophobic implications as well. Indeed, even though she said that she did not care about his sexuality, her suggestion that he should not "be acting feminine" could also be viewed as a statement meant to discourage him from being open about his sexuality. The close connection between gender and sexuality means that statements concerning one will also generally relate to the other.

Reactions to anti-queer violence are even implicated in this overlap, as respondents frequently mentioned how heterosexual people whom they had told about the violence implied that it had occurred because they had been "too open" or "too obvious" about their sexuality or gender identity. The implication was that LGBT people should have been "less open" or "less obvious." Respondents frequently perceived these remarks as suggestions that they should perform gender in a more traditional way. For instance, Daniel described an occasion when he told his minister about being assaulted by a white male police officer. Daniel described the police officer as being "very condescending" in telling Daniel to move from a street corner. Daniel was not sure why he was being told to leave, except that maybe the police officer had assumed he was a sex worker. When Daniel told the officer "it's a free country" and "I can stand where I want to stand," the cop pushed Daniel's face against the side of a building, referring to him as a "smart-ass faggot." Describing this incident to his minister, Daniel said that the minister suggested that he should "not be so obvious" about his homosexuality and should deepen his voice to avoid "sounding weak." The minister said that Daniel should change his voice to sound "more like [rappers] DMX and Ja Rule" and less "like Michael Jackson." The comment struck Daniel as ironic, given that a minister was encouraging one of his congregation members to emulate two rappers.

Notice here that the minister constructed Daniel's feminine-sounding voice—an aspect of gender nonconformity—as the attribute that he should change. Indeed, when describing incidents of victim blaming, lesbians and gay men typically described confronting reactions that they should avoid gender nonconformity, which potentially signals their homosexuality, rather than reactions telling them not to be gay or lesbian. According to these views, identifying as lesbian or gay may be acceptable, or at least tolerable, as long it is hidden and accompanied by gender conformity. For this reason, heterosexual people may experience anti-queer violence when violating gender norms, and LGBT people may avoid this abuse when conforming to them. At the same time, heterosexuality remains privileged in the United States because of its association with gender conformity. As a result, heterosexual victims of violence are unlikely to confront reactions where the abuse is blamed on their open display of heterosexuality. Imagine heterosexual people experiencing violence and having others suggest that it had occurred because they had been "too open" or "too obvious" about their sexuality. That response seems very unlikely to occur in large part because of the society we live in, where heterosexuality and gender conformity are constructed as normal and ideal. Being "too straight" or "obviously heterosexual" does not carry the same weight as being "too gay" or "obviously lesbian" does.

RACE AND SOCIAL CLASS IMPLICATIONS

Although some forms of anti-queer violence appear obviously rooted in homophobia, many LGBT people's violent experiences are considerably more complex. The experiences of Gideon, a twenty-five-year-old Black gay man, reflect this complexity, as he referred to the area in which he lived as a relatively "dangerous area" of the Bronx. Gideon, who occasionally wore

eyeliner and carried a purse, said that heterosexual men in his neighborhood did not "mess with" him because they knew that he could defend himself. He had, however, experienced several physically violent experiences
in the past. One of these experiences involved a man in his neighborhood
calling him a "cocksucker" at a deli. Gideon responded to this insult by saying, "That's right, and I suck better dick than you'll ever get." This response
led the man to claim that Gideon should "get that nasty white shit out of
here," or the man would "beat [Gideon's] ass." Gideon then said, "Let's
go," and put up his fists as if he was ready to fight. This encounter ended at
that moment, but several days later the same man, along with three other
men, approached him on the street. As the men approached Gideon, they
made homophobic comments, calling him a "faggot" who "deserved to be
taught a lesson." Gideon said very little, but he did take out a knife as the
men moved closer, intensifying their insults. The four men then attacked
Gideon, punching and kicking him. Defending himself with the knife, he
cut one of the men on his arm. As a result of the attack, Gideon experienced significant bruising on his face and body. He did not go to the hospital because he did not have health insurance, although he now admitted, "I
probably should have, I was in pain all over."

Gideon's violent experience cannot be understood very well by focusing
on gender and sexuality to the exclusion of race and social class. Examining his experience only through the lens of homophobia, or even through
the lens of gender and sexuality, would produce a limited understanding of
the incident. Being told to "get that nasty white shit out of here" has more
to do with the overlap of race and sexuality than the overlap of gender and
sexuality. Indeed, as scholarship has shown, homosexuality has historically
been linked with whiteness (Cohen 1999; Collins 2004). This association of
homosexuality and whiteness, while not unique to Black communities, has
led to notions of authenticity whereby the most "authentic" Black identities have become constructed as exclusively heterosexual (P. Johnson 2001;
Thomas 2001). Moreover, white LGBT communities and Black heterosexual communities have often reinforced the whitening of homosexuality to
present their social group as "respectable" to mainstream society (Moore
2011). Black communities, confronting institutional racism, have sometimes
encouraged Black people to conceal negative aspects of themselves. As a
result, LGBT people of color confront pressures to keep their sexuality or
gender identity hidden because of notions that they should represent their

racial groups in a positive way. White LGBT people, in contrast, do not face these pressures due to their racial identity. By examining forms of anti-queer violence exclusively through the lens of homophobia, research would miss these racial differences, as Black LGBT people's violent experiences could be collapsed with those of white gay men.

Social class as well as race played an important role in shaping Gideon's experience. Without understanding his social class position, the choices he made might make little sense. When describing these results to others, I have often been struck by the number of people, primarily middle class, who seem surprised that gay men such as Gideon would verbally respond to being called a homophobic name. In contrast, many low-income gay men argued that verbally responding to homophobic insults was necessary and justified. This response was likely informed by masculinity norms, which encourage men to retaliate against someone who causes them harm, yet for many low-income gay men "pushing back" also seemed to be a matter of survival. Gideon argued that he had little choice but to respond to homophobic insults: "I could either learn how to fight [and] protect myself, no longer be gay, or die. Those were my choices." Framing his options in this way, Gideon implied that his choice was obvious: he had to learn how to fight and protect himself. His neighborhood, coupled with his feminine gender presentation of self, meant that he could probably expect to encounter homophobic insults for the foreseeable future, even if he chose not to respond to them. Thus, he most likely could not escape verbal harassment, short of moving, which would have been difficult since he was unemployed and living with his sister. His social class position, then, limited his options in escaping homophobic insults. In contrast, middle-class gay men can usually afford to live in an environment where they are not exposed to the potential hardships that come with widespread poverty and unemployment; indeed, Gideon's neighborhood and social class position led him to confront forms of violence that most middle-class LGBT people would be unlikely to experience in their own neighborhoods.

Gideon also noted that the violence directed against him usually escalated: "If a guy calls you a faggot one day, what if he calls you ten faggots the next day? If it gets physical then what are you gonna do?" This escalation of violence suggested to Gideon that he had to defend himself by not letting heterosexual men call him homophobic names in the first place. Deciding to respond to homophobic insults, he began to carry a weapon—a pocketknife with a five-inch blade. Given that the violence had decreased over time, he concluded, "When they know you can defend yourself, they won't mess with you." As evidence of this conclusion, he described a more recent experience in which a group of men began to taunt him and he thought that they were going to physically attack him, but then the men "backed off and ran away" when they saw that he carried a weapon.

Other low-income gay men found themselves in similar, although arguably not quite as dire, situations. Most gay men in this study carried weapons, particularly those living in neighborhoods they perceived as relatively violent or dangerous. Several of these respondents showed me their weapons during the interview, which ranged from a small pocketknife to a seven-inch switchblade. Most gay men had not used their weapons to injure someone, but a majority had used them to fend off perpetrators. These respondents, in many ways, seemed to contradict stereotypes of passive gay men, as they often spent a considerable amount of time describing how they had actively responded to homophobic violence. At the same time, they were unabashedly feminine, refusing to hide their sexuality or to perform gender in line with cultural expectations.

Despite the particular challenges confronting low-income LGBT people, little attention has focused on their violent experiences, even though they likely encounter anti-queer violence more frequently than their middle-class counterparts.[5] Instead, public attention has typically focused on violence against middle-class LGBT people, many of whom are also white gay men (Halberstam 2005; Moran 2000). The case of Matthew Shepard involved an attack on a college student, and cases of anti-gay bullying involving middle-class students have received the most media attention. Indeed, some of the most commonly referenced cases of anti-gay harassment have been those that have occurred on college campuses. College, however, is an opportunity that middle-class Americans have greater access to than those from poor families. Moreover, even when cases of violence against low-income LGBT people have received media attention, experiences such as Gideon's have not been emphasized. Certainly, Gideon's experience of escalating violence is similar in some ways to forms of antigay bullying that have received mainstream media attention, yet because gay men have often been associated with whiteness and middle-class income levels, violence against low-income LGBT people of color has remained largely absent from mainstream media coverage.

To focus on low-income LGBT people's violent experiences would per-haps shed light on a dark side of U.S. society, where poor communities—with few jobs, deficient housing, and underfunded schools—tend to produce comparatively high rates of crime (Collins 2004; Jones 2010). These rates of violence may affect low-income LGBT people to a greater extent than their heterosexual counterparts, as the more marginalized members of these communities are likely to bear the brunt of the hard-ship.[6] As a result, efforts to enhance the social safety net could potentially benefit low-income LGBT people more than other social groups. Nev-ertheless, since mainstream gay rights organizations have typically con-structed poverty as a social problem that is "not a gay rights issue," efforts to improve the conditions of low-income LGBT people have remained marginal to the conventional gay rights movement (Spade 2011; Ward 2008). This mainstream advocacy approach not only marginalizes the concerns of poor and working-class LGBT people but also produces gains for high-income queer people, who arguably need the least amount of support.

The social class politics of anti-queer violence are also important in other ways. As considerable criminological research has shown, random forms of street violence perpetrated by strangers are rare (Best 1999; Gar-land 2001; Wacquant 2009). Although the media have focused consider-able attention on victims who are suddenly and randomly attacked, this notion of "stranger danger" is largely a media exaggeration. Instead, peo-ple who experience violence are much more likely to know their perpetra-tor or to quarrel with the perpetrator before the violence occurs.[7] Indeed, although some of the LGBT people who participated in this project were attacked without previously knowing their perpetrator, the violence usually began with an argument or involved someone they knew. These "stranger danger" myths have a social class component; the assumption of these narratives is often that a middle-class person is being attacked by a low-income, implicitly "unstable," person. These narratives are one of the ways that poor people are presented as pathological and demented; they also keep attention off the forms of violence that low-income people more commonly face. Most violence is perpetrated against low-income, not middle-class, people. As a result, although random attacks remain rare, violence in low-income communities is a serious social problem, worthy of public attention.

BEYOND THE OPPRESSION OLYMPICS

While examining race and social class is necessary to understand many forms of anti-queer violence, forms of inequality should not be viewed as competing with one another—gender vs. sexuality or race vs. social class—as these approaches tend to foster endless debate over which social group has the most oppressive experiences. Under these frameworks, which have been deemed the "Oppression Olympics," minority groups are constructed as competing to establish which group is the "most oppressed" (Hancock 2007, 250). Students in my courses, for example, have a hard time discussing race and sexuality at the same time without ranking one as "worse" than the other. In these situations, I have heard students argue that homophobia is worse than racism because LGBT people "have fewer rights" than Black heterosexual Americans (e.g., marriage rights, legal protection from discrimination in the workforce) and I have heard other students argue that racism is worse because sexuality is less immediately visible than race (e.g., "homosexuality can be hidden"). I find both of these arguments, while perhaps factually accurate, nevertheless misguided.

The problem with ranking one form of inequality over another is that it forces individuals who are oppressed in more than one way to downplay an aspect of themselves. Constructing racism or homophobia as more significant than the other would require Black gay men—oppressed based on their race and their sexuality—to downplay some of their oppressive experiences. Viewing homophobia as worse than racism would necessitate Black gay men to minimize the role of racism in structuring their experiences, while constructing racism as more important than homophobia would require downplaying the importance of sexuality in their lives. These analyses that construct one form of inequality as predominant also overlook important contextual differences in how systems of oppression operate. Black LGBT people confront racism more often than homophobia in white LGBT communities, while facing homophobia more frequently in Black heterosexual communities. Depending on the situation, then, different aspects of one's identity become more salient. Indeed, racism, sexism, and homophobia all operate in different ways, and attempts to construct one form of inequality as the most powerful inevitably ignore these contextual differences.

Since individuals always belong to multiple social groups, their social position cannot possibly be reduced to any singular aspect of their identity. Many Black LGBT and feminist scholars have also argued against notions of individuals being asked to privilege aspects of their identity. Audre Lorde (1981, 15), a renowned Black lesbian feminist, said in an interview: "There's always someone asking you to underline one piece of yourself, whether it's Black, woman, mother, dyke, teacher, etc.—because that's the piece they need to key into. They want you to dismiss everything else. But once you do that, then you've lost because then you become acquired or bought by that particular essence of yourself, and you've denied yourself all of the energy that it takes to keep all those others in jail. Only by learning to live in harmony with your contradictions can you keep it all afloat." Other scholars have named this process of being asked to choose between different aspects of themselves as "a kind of psychic suicide," whereby marginalized people are required to privilege one aspect of their identity at the expense of another (Thomas 2001, 332).

Undoubtedly, it is difficult to discuss inequality without also describing hierarchies. Some differences—such as shoe size and left-handedness—are not made socially significant in the same way as other differences—such as race, class, and gender. Furthermore, not everyone experiences oppression to the same degree or in the same way. Black Americans experience racial oppression in ways that white Americans do not, and women encounter more discrimination than men with regard to gender inequality. Nevertheless, these power relations become exceedingly complex when considering the experiences of people who are oppressed in multiple ways. For instance, the experiences of low-income Black lesbians—oppressed based on their race, class, gender, and sexuality—cannot be understood very well through the lens of only one form of inequality. To focus exclusively on sexuality would collapse their experiences with those of white lesbians and white gay men, and to privilege gender would link their experiences with those of heterosexual women. The challenges, however, confronting low-income Black lesbians differ in important ways from those confronting other social groups. Paying attention to these differences reveals some of the ways privilege and oppression operate, illustrating that forms of inequality work in different ways and yet also draw upon and reinforce one another.

Scholarship on privilege has shown that individuals tend to remain largely unaware of the benefits granted to them by their privileged status (McIntosh 2004). Members of minority groups, on the other hand, are frequently mindful of the disadvantages facing them because of their marginalized standing. Thus, individuals are likely to view those forms of inequality in which they have experienced discrimination as the most important, since they have a history of being marginalized based on those status markers and may not be aware of the discrimination facing other minority groups. Little good, then, can be accomplished from constructing one form of inequality as more important than another; this strategy is likely to lead to defensiveness rather than acknowledgement that others' oppressive experiences are as severe as one's own. This problem with ranking forms of inequality can be seen in individual encounters: telling others that you have encountered more painful or traumatic experiences than they have is unlikely to result in their acknowledging that what you have said is true—even if it is—but to result in their becoming defensive and resisting the implication of your statement. This argument also applies on a societal level, where marginalized groups are likely to alienate other communities by equating different systems of oppression. Mainstream LGBT organizations have alienated many Black Americans by comparing modern gay rights with the civil rights movement of the 1950s and 1960s. Referring to "gay rights as the new civil rights," after all, implies that inequality based on race is largely a thing of the past—a statement that many people of color, heterosexual and LGBT alike, are likely to dispute.

A widely circulated newspaper column by Dan Savage (2008), a prominent gay rights advocate, illustrates the degree to which some LGBT-movement leaders have tried to construct homophobia as worse than racism. In response to polling data released after the passage of Proposition 8, which banned gay marriage in California, Savage chastised Black heterosexual Americans for their seemingly extensive homophobia: "I'm done pretending that the handful of racist gay white men out there—and they're out there, and I think they're scum—are a bigger problem for African Americans, gay and straight, than the huge numbers of homophobic African Americans are for gay Americans, whatever their color." While homophobia in Black communities is an important issue facing Black LGBT people, Savage constructs homophobia in Black communities as a bigger problem than racism in white LGBT communities. Indeed, to construct homophobia as more urgent than racism, he compares "a handful" of racist gay white men with "the huge numbers" of homophobic Black Americans. This framework, in which Savage is speaking for Black LGBT people as well as himself, constructs white gay men and Black heterosexual people as competitors. Black LGBT people, presumably, are left to pick a side, with the implication being that the fight against homophobia is the more important one.

The problem with Savage's argument is that it requires LGBT people of color to accept that racism is a relatively minor problem in LGBT communities. Nevertheless, mainstream gay rights organizations have frequently marginalized the interests of low-income LGBT people of color, particularly low-income Black and Latina lesbians, by excluding them from leadership positions and constructing their views as the least reputable (Ward 2008). Mainstream gay rights organizations have also been criticized for not taking seriously issues such as homelessness and violence from the police that disproportionately affect the lives of low-income LGBT people of color (Farrow 2010; Mogul, Ritchie, and Whitlock 2011). Thus, challenges to homophobia that fail to take racism and classism seriously are likely to produce gains for a very narrow segment of LGBT people. Indeed, the way Savage constructs his argument is part of a long history in which LGBT people have been described as if they are all white, and Black people have been described as if they are all straight, effectively marginalizing the experiences of Black queer people. Savage seems aware of this history, since he acknowledges the presence of LGBT people of color, yet he implicitly minimizes their experiences of racism in queer communities.

Describing all LGBT people as white and all Black people as heterosexual not only overlooks the particular challenges confronting LGBT people of color but also pits white queer people and Black heterosexual people against one another. Constructing differently marginalized groups as rivals prevents them from working together toward challenging inequality. Indeed, what keeps marginalized groups from forming coalitions with one another is not necessarily their differences per se, but rather how these differences are used to divide them. Some evidence suggests that media reports exaggerated the degree to which African Americans voted in favor of Proposition 8, thereby encouraging responses such as the one made by Savage. Egan and Sherrill (2009) indicate that the media overestimated Black support for Proposition 8 by at least 10 percentage points and that exit polls from statewide ballot measures have found no statistically significant differences between white voters and Black and Latino voters.[8] Further, publicized e-mails from anti-gay-marriage leaders described efforts to "drive a wedge between gays and Blacks" (Confessore 2012). It seems, then, that certain segments of society benefit from fueling competition among marginalized groups. Those who benefit most are likely powerful white and heterosexual men, but my analysis here suggests that members of marginalized groups can also become caught up in these debates.

The larger problem with constructing homophobia as more severe than other forms of inequality is that this framework can reinforce other systems of oppression. Challenges to homophobia have often attached sexual-orientation-based discrimination to stigmatized ethnic groups, including Black, Latino, and Middle Eastern Americans; these analyses construct heterosexual people of color as "more homophobic" than white heterosexual Americans.[9] Homophobia, however, does not belong to a particular group. Instead, it is institutionalized throughout U.S. society, as it is built into social institutions such as the state and the family. Indeed, homosexuality is not stigmatized in the United States because Black Americans are homophobic. Thus, singling out Black heterosexual people for their homophobia strengthens racism by associating negative characteristics with a racial group that is already marginalized. The costs are high, in other words, of combating homophobia in this way, as this approach reinforces existing racial hierarchies.

Quantitative research that has examined homophobia across racial lines has revealed mixed results, with some studies showing few differences once religion and education are taken into account, while other studies indicate that white Americans tend to have lower rates of homophobia than some other racial groups (G. Lewis 2003). Still, even if sociologists can show through quantitative survey research that white heterosexual Americans generally hold more positive views regarding homosexuality than heterosexual people of color, this line of research distracts from more important inquiries. Examining these racial differences can lead to problematic conclusions, effectively blaming heterosexual people of color for the persistence of homophobia and freeing white heterosexual people of their responsibility for perpetuating anti-LGBT discrimination, even though white heterosexual people have more power than other racial groups to end inequality based on sexuality and gender identity. White heterosexual people frequently engage in practices that maintain the societal privileging of heterosexuality over homosexuality, as evidenced by white heterosexual men perpetrating most of the violence described by the white LGBT people in this study. Thus, homophobia in racial minority communities, while worthy of condemnation, must be viewed as replicating the institutional arrangements of U.S. society, as people across racial lines engage in homophobic practices.

DYNAMICS OF ANTITRANSGENDER VIOLENCE

Privileging homophobia at the expense of race, class, and gender also has the unfortunate effect of marginalizing transgender people. Nevertheless, transgender people's violent experiences are different in many ways from those of lesbians and gay men. Most of the transgender respondents in this study identified as transgender women—people labeled as male at birth who identify as women. Their violent experiences differed from those other female respondents in important ways. In particular, violence against transgender women was more explicitly dehumanizing than antilesbian and antigay violence. Indeed, transgender respondents described many situations in which they were referred to as "it," depriving them of human qualities. For instance, Lakeisha, a thirty-eight-year-old Black transgender woman, described an abusive ex-boyfriend. She said that he was "sweet" at the beginning of their relationship, but became more violent over time, occasionally referring to her as an "it" or a "thing." At the beginning of their relationship, she assumed that he knew of her being transgender, since they had been sexually involved and she had not had breast implants on her upper body. Further, Lakeisha said that they had met in an area "where only trans women [and] prostitutes hang out." As a result, she said that he "must have known" that she was transgender.

The violence began after they had been dating for approximately three months. After having sex, he suggested that they should try to have a baby together—that she should become pregnant. Lakeisha then explained that she could not physically have children, given her transgender identity. His behavior immediately changed, as he began to throw items around the room, yelling, "All this time, you mean to tell me that I was fucking a man?" She insisted that he must have known of her transgender identity, mentioning the area where they met. As they continued to argue, he hit her when she said, "You mean you can't tell the difference between a man's chest and a woman's chest?" After this initial incident, he told her that he was "sorry" and that the violence "would never happen again." Lakeisha said at the time she believed him, but now she viewed him as "controlling" and perceived these statements as emotionally manipulative. She also said "the sweetness left" him after she revealed her transgender identity, and she described a process whereby he became increasingly violent.

In the months after learning of her transgender identity, he began verbally abusing her, referring to her as a "bitch" and threatening to kill her if she left him. On one occasion, she said that he connected his demeaning behavior with her transgender identity, saying, "This is how it is: you're going to play pussy, then you're going to get fucked like pussy." The violence intensified over time, with several extremely violent incidents in which he referred to her as "it," while physically beating her. One incident involved him kicking her in the ribs and punching her face; she suffered a broken jaw and ribs as a result. When she called the police, one of the officers who came to her apartment told her that the violence might end if she "stopped pretending she was something she's not."

In some ways, Lakeisha's experience mirrors a domestic violence situation that many women—heterosexual, lesbian, and transgender—confront. She even said that this experience changed her perception of domestic violence: "When a man says something little to me now, I now take that more seriously . . . Then I know that it might get worse after that and it might not stop." This view of violence as becoming increasingly traumatic was something I heard from lesbian, bisexual, and transgender women who had been in violent relationships with men. Thus, some forms of violence against transgender women resemble many types of misogynistic abuse. At the same time, the violence began after Lakeisha revealed her transgender identity. Her ex-boyfriend's statement "you're going to play pussy, then you're going to get fucked like pussy" indicates that her "play" of a female identity was the reason for his abusive behavior. In this sense, antitransgender violence punishes people for not identifying as the gender they were assigned at birth.

Confronting dehumanizing forms of violence, transgender people face suggestions that anyone who does not match their gender identity with their sex characteristics is not human. This view of transgender people as objects legitimizes a rigid gender binary in which individuals must be either male or female—they cannot be both at the same time, and they cannot switch from one to the other. Indeed, although other societies have had more than two gender identities, the United States does not generally provide the space for people to identify as a gender other than woman or man (Mogul, Ritchie, and Whitlock 2011; Namaste 2000). Consequently, when individuals are perceived as outside of this gender binary, they risk violence and harassment, sometimes becoming viewed as something other than human in the process. Dehumanizing transgender people, then, likely makes it easier for perpetrators to employ violence, as it becomes easier to harm an object rather than a person.

At times, transgender respondents described being blamed for not revealing earlier their transgender identity to romantic partners. Indeed, the police officer essentially suggested that Lakeisha changing her gender identity was grounds for being beaten, as he placed the onus on her to stop "pretending she was something she's not." Rather than placing the responsibility to end the abuse on the man who perpetrated it, the officer focused on her transgender identity as a catalyst. When I asked Lakeisha how she thought the police should have responded, she said, tears welling in her eyes, "That it doesn't matter [whether I was transgender]. . . . He didn't have the right to hit me." Undoubtedly, support and safety are what police officers are supposed to provide.

When being blamed for violence, transgender people faced different comments from those experienced by lesbians and gay men. Lakeisha said that she told an acquaintance at work about this experience; the woman was cisgender—a woman whose gender identity matches the sex she was assigned at birth. When hearing about what happened, the woman responded unsupportively, saying that Lakeisha should have told her romantic partner sooner, otherwise "what did she expect would happen?" The timing of when to tell a romantic or sexual partner was something transgender respondents frequently discussed, and many respondents said that they usually identified as transgender before being romantically involved with someone. At other times, transgender respondents thought the other person knew. Lakeisha insisted that her romantic partner must have known of her transgender identity, repeating "he knew, he knew" throughout the interview. Nevertheless, whether or not Lakeisha had revealed her transgender identity early in the relationship is immaterial as to whether the violence was acceptable. The police, as well as Lakeisha's coworker, unfairly shifted the blame from the abusive man to the woman experiencing the abuse.

Transgender women are certainly not alone in being blamed for their violent experiences, yet only transgender respondents encountered this type of victim blaming, in which individuals are faulted for not immediately revealing their identity. Indeed, when blamed for forms of homophobic violence, lesbians and gay men were typically told that they should have been *less* open about their sexuality. Transgender respondents, of course, also face pressures to conceal their gender identity. Still, choosing when to disclose their transgender identity to romantic or sexual partners—and the blame that can be placed on them for not doing so soon enough—is particular to the transgender experience.

Since lesbians and gay men do not face these same challenges, the "LGBT" umbrella can become problematic to the extent that it collapses the experiences of transgender people with those of lesbians, gay men, and bisexual people. The LGBT umbrella simplifies the differences among LGBT people, as transgender people confront forms of violence that lesbians and gay men do not. Eight out of ten transgender respondents highlighted the idea that transgender people's experiences are different from those of lesbians and gay men. Dominique, a twenty-three-year-old Black transgender woman, emphasized pornographic images that lesbians and gay men do not face: "The gay community and the trans community, it's not the same thing. We are related, but it's not the same thing. We got different issues . . . Like with the media and the pornography industry—the 'shemales' and stuff like that—they don't give us a good name." These representations of transgender women as "shemales," popularized by notions of "chicks with dicks," construct transgender women as sexual "freaks of nature," making their bodies seem abnormal and pathological. Dominique also connected these pornographic images with violence against transgender women: "A straight guy meets a woman of trans experience, and first thing, they're like, 'Oh, a shemale.' They think about freaky and stuff like that. . . . They think that they can hit, they can beat up, and that's fine because they're still beating up a male." These stereotypes of "shemales," unique to the social position of transgender women, suggest that antitransgender violence needs to be considered in its own right, as separate from violence against lesbians and gay men.

THE EFFECTS OF MULTIPLE SYSTEMS OF INEQUALITY

While distinguishing among the violent experiences of lesbians, gay men, and transgender people, analyses of anti-queer violence must also consider the role of race, class, and gender. Certainly, low-income Black and Latina lesbians often viewed these forms of inequality as important. Aisha, a fifty-three-year-old Black lesbian, argued that one of her violent experiences could not be reduced to any individual aspect of her identity: "I'm a Black lesbian woman who works in a job where mostly men work. Change any of those things and [the violence] would not have gone down in the same way." Here, Aisha described an experience working as a security guard, where a former boss of hers—a white man—made derogatory remarks, continually referring to her as his "sweet thing." The workplace harassment continued for several months, culminating in the supervisor cornering her in a room, demanding that she perform oral sex on him or she would be fired. When Aisha refused and told him that she would report the incident, he responded, "You think they'll believe some dumb dyke like you?" She escaped the situation, but upon reporting the abuse to the man's superior the next day, he did not believe her and laughed when she told him about being referred to as a "dumb dyke." Aisha quit shortly thereafter and thought the violence was not taken seriously because all of her superiors were white, presumably heterosexual, men: "They were all white guys or whatever so they were going to look out for themselves. . . . [Further reporting the abuse] was just not worth it."

Multiple aspects of Aisha's identity played a significant role in shaping her experience. As race, class, gender, and sexuality are all germane to the situation—a point that Aisha underscored herself—none of them should be dismissed. Perhaps a white lesbian or a Black heterosexual woman would have found herself in a similar situation, yet Aisha appeared to confront some pressures unique to her social position. A Black heterosexual woman most likely would not have been called a "dumb dyke," while a white lesbian may have felt more comfortable telling a white supervisor about the sexual harassment. It is even possible that the violence would not have occurred if Aisha was white or heterosexual. Further, multiple aspects of her identity intensified the degree to which she felt powerless in the situation. Aisha's identity meant that if she reported the abuse it would be read through the lens of a relatively disadvantaged person, a Black lesbian worker, turning in a comparatively powerful person—a white and male supervisor, in this case. Since her race, class, gender, and sexuality affected the degree to which she felt powerless, her experience must be understood as simultaneously rooted in all of these forms of inequality.

While forms of anti-queer violence are typically rooted in multiple systems of oppression, sexuality norms still play an important role.

Undoubtedly, perpetrators frequently use anti-queer violence to maintain heterosexual privilege, reinforcing inequality based on sexual orientation (Herek 2000). In this respect, homophobic violence can be viewed as an outgrowth of what sexualities scholars refer to as "heterosexism" or "heteronormativity"—the societal privileging of heterosexuality over homosexuality (Bryant and Vidal-Ortiz 2008; Warner 1991). Although these two concepts have slightly different meanings, both of them point to the ways in which heterosexuality is constructed as normal and ideal. In contrast, despite the increasing visibility of lesbians and gay men in U.S. society, homosexuality is not normalized in the same way. As a result, violence against lesbians and gay men can be viewed as a manifestation— albeit an extreme one—of this power arrangement, with individuals perpetrating anti-queer violence to reinforce ideas that homosexuality is wrong or immoral.[10]

Although I am not dismissing the importance of homophobia and heteronormativity, a more satisfactory examination of anti-queer violence must push beyond this narrow understanding. Indeed, missing from analyses that focus solely on homophobia is a systematic examination of power, including the role of gender and sexism in forms of anti-queer violence. As Aisha's experience reveals, male domination, in addition to heteronormativity, plays an important role in structuring forms of antilesbian violence. Conversely, when describing these findings, I have often been surprised by the degree to which my work has been dismissed as having little to do with gendered power dynamics. In particular, I have often been surprised to hear others assume that women, presumably heterosexual women, perpetrated physical violence against the lesbians who participated in this study. Although many respondents did experience verbal harassment from women, and some experienced physical abuse from their mothers during childhood, men perpetrated the vast majority of the physical violence, including physical attacks against lesbian respondents. My results, of course, may not reflect trends throughout the United States, yet macrolevel survey data also suggest that men perpetrate most physical violence against lesbians (Ahmed and Jindasurat 2014; Herek 2009). This trend should not be particularly surprising, given that men perpetrate most violent crime (Britton 2011). Still, the view that women perpetrate most antilesbian violence reveals a misunderstanding of gendered power relations, as women do not typically hit other women in public.[11] Most men, certainly, do not hit women in public either, yet when violence is committed against women, it is usually done by men (Britton 2011; Madriz 1997).

A further problem with viewing anti-queer violence as the product of homophobia is that it reduces LGBT people's violent experiences to the actions of a prejudiced individual. This understanding of anti-queer violence emphasizes homophobic individuals, shifting attention away from how social institutions are set up to benefit some social groups and disadvantage others. Individualizing homophobia makes social inequality appear as an individual problem rather than a societal one. Indeed, my point in describing the forms of violence in this chapter is not that they come from homophobic individuals—although the individuals who perpetrate them are probably homophobic—but that they occur because we live in a society that encourages individuals to think of heterosexuality as superior to homosexuality. That is, anti-queer violence reveals the degree to which heteronormativity persists. Heterosexual people, after all, do not typically experience violence for being perceived as straight.

Living in a heteronormative society, most Americans inevitably internalize some homophobia, yet I find it more productive to focus on changing the social conditions that give rise to homophobia than changing the attitudes of a single homophobic person. These two goals can overlap, of course, but equating homophobia with extreme acts of discrimination potentially shifts focus away from the routine and everyday ways that heterosexuality is privileged and homosexuality is not. Even though violence against minority groups is often associated with organized hate groups such as skinheads and the Ku Klux Klan, considerable evidence suggests that perpetrators of racist and homophobic violence rarely belong to such groups (Levin 2010). Hearing the word "homophobia" or "homophobic" may bring to mind images of a skinhead or a Klansman attacking a LGBT person—most likely, I have argued, images of a white gay man being attacked—but it need not be this way. These stereotypes of victims and perpetrators of homophobic violence not only associate homosexuality with whiteness and middle-class income levels but also link homophobia with extreme acts of violence.

The danger of focusing on extraordinarily violent manifestations of homophobia is that this emphasis obscures the more common ways that LGBT people face discrimination. After all, many LGBT people do not experience hate crime, but nevertheless encounter homophobia in their everyday lives. Since these acts of homophobia, including rejection from family members, are more common than hate crime, it remains important to emphasize routine, rather than extreme, forms of discrimination against lesbians and gay men. Parallel arguments could be made about the widespread focus on antigay bullying; an important topic, to be sure, but this emphasis could potentially conceal the more subtle and insidious ways that anti-LGBT discrimination manifests itself.

Associating homophobia with extreme acts of violence potentially allows heterosexual people to dismiss anti-LGBT prejudice as something that has nothing to do with them.[12] Heterosexual people, however, who do not engage in acts of anti-queer physical violence are certainly capable of perpetuating homophobia. Thus, frameworks that associate homophobia with outward and extreme forms of discrimination might encourage individuals to stop saying homophobic things—after all, they do not want to appear homophobic—but do little in the way of changing their underlying ideas. This dynamic becomes problematic to the extent that it encourages individuals to be less public about their homophobia, while doing little to alter their more fundamental prejudices. In this regard, over the past ten years homophobia has changed more than heteronormativity, as it has become less acceptable to express public disapproval of lesbians and gay men, yet the underlying structures that privilege heterosexuality have remained in place.[13] Starting at a very young age, children in the United States are assumed to be straight and are exposed to countless messages idealizing heterosexuality (Walters 2014). These practices establish heterosexuality as natural and normal and set the stage for "the closet," whereby lesbians and gay men must declare their homosexuality because heterosexuality is assumed, unless evidence exists to the contrary.

Given that many LGBT people in this study described violence that occurred in private settings, a productive strategy for reducing anti-queer violence must not merely encourage heterosexual people to hide their homophobia. As public expressions of homophobia become even more socially unacceptable, it is conceivable that homophobic violence will further shift from public to private arenas. Data from this study and other research projects suggest that this shift would be particularly harmful for marginalized groups of LGBT people, as lesbian and transgender women experience sexual assault at disproportionately high rates, while Black LGBT people encounter police-based violence at higher rates than their white counterparts (Grant et al. 2011; Mogul, Ritchie, and Whitlock 2011;

Spade 2011). These forms of violence most frequently occur outside of public view, suggesting that a shift from public to private displays of homophobia would likely benefit and harm LGBT people in different ways depending on their race, class, and gender identity. Ultimately, of course, the degree to which this shift is taking place remains unclear, but research on anti-queer violence must continue to emphasize that many of its forms are hidden from public view.

The primary problem with viewing LGBT people's violent experiences as rooted solely in homophobia is that many forms of anti-queer violence have as much to do with other types of inequality—namely, race, class, and gender—as with discrimination based on sexual orientation. As a result, by focusing primarily on homophobia, research has inadvertently reinforced the interests of LGBT people who are oppressed predominantly based on their sexuality—most likely, white and middle-class gay men. LGBT people who confront violence based on their race and gender identity remain marginalized under frameworks that focus exclusively on homophobia. Thus, given that race, class, and gender norms, in addition to sexuality-based ones, are implicated in many LGBT people's violent experiences, scholarly and advocacy work on anti-queer violence must move beyond homophobia, taking seriously the experiences of LGBT people who are oppressed in multiple ways.

3 • "I'M MAKING BLACK PEOPLE LOOK BAD"

The Racial Implications of Anti-Queer Violence

Latoya, a fifty-year-old Black lesbian, referred to the racial implications of a Black male stranger punching her arm and telling her to "take that white shit home" and realize that her girlfriend "just needed a dick": "The physical is what gets to me, that's like telling me that I have to stop doing this. . . . Like I have to stop making [my girlfriend] a lesbian. They act like I did this to her. And it's like I'm not supposed to because then I'm making Black people look bad." Black gay men made similar comments when describing the racial implications of their violent experiences. Jayvyn, a thirty-three-year-old Black gay man, described a violent experience in which a group of men called him "nasty" on the street. When Jayvyn said, "The only nasty one I see here is you," one of the men called Jayvyn a "punk faggot" and threw a glass bottle at him, hitting his shoulder. Describing this incident, Jayvyn explained his reasons for believing that some Black heterosexual men have harassed him: "It's like I've let down Black men by being gay or something. That means that I've identified myself with weakness, and I'm not supposed to do that."

Undoubtedly, Jayvyn and Latoya's experiences differed based on their gender identities. Jayvyn viewed the violence as suggesting that he was weak, while Latoya thought that she had been attacked for supposedly "making" her girlfriend a lesbian. Still, despite these gender differences, both Jayvyn and Latoya thought that they were being punished for negatively representing their racial communities—for "making Black people look bad," as Latoya said. Many Black respondents viewed their violent experiences as having these racialized implications; in contrast, white LGBT people typically over-looked the role of race. In this sense, LGBT people of color perceived anti-queer violence as punishing them for "betraying" their racial groups, while white lesbians and gay men did not view their violent experiences in this way. These racial differences occurred in large part because of norms that construct whiteness as an invisible social status, whereby white people are allowed to represent themselves rather than their broader racial community. LGBT people of color, on the other hand, are not granted the privilege of whiteness and, therefore, are made to think about their actions, and the violence to which they are subjected, in relation to their racial and ethnic communities.[1]

THE "MARKING" OF MINORITY GROUPS

The racial differences among LGBT people reflect the ways that individuals in the United States are "marked" based on race. Whiteness is an "unmarked" aspect of an individual's identity, typically viewed as ordinary and unremarkable (McIntosh 2004; Wilkins 2008). Conversely, Black and Latino people are "marked" as representing their racial or ethnic group. An example of this difference occurs when media reports emphasize a person's race only when describing a person of color—referring to the race of a Black person, but not a white person, when reporting similar events. Jayvyn, the thirty-three-year-old Black gay male respondent mentioned above, further illustrated this point. Jayvyn, who worked as a secretary, described an experience at his job where one of his coworkers, a white man, had complained about being hit by a car while he was driving. When describing the event, Jayvyn's coworker emphasized that "this Black guy" had hit him with his car; Jayvyn thought that his coworker would probably not have said "this white guy" had hit him. Jayvyn's analysis, in my view, seems accurate, since individuals in the United States are more likely to mention the race of a Black person than the race of a white person, especially when describing negative behavior. This difference suggests that whiteness remains largely unacknowledged in the United States, whereas Blackness is continually addressed. Thus, part of the privilege that comes with whiteness is that white people can engage in socially disapproved behavior without having their actions attributed to their racial identity.

Of course, statements linking race and negative behavior can just as easily be applied to white people. In reversing the example above, a Black woman could say that "this white guy" had hit her car. Still, these statements—mentioning the race of a white man or the race of a Black man—are not equivalent. They are different because their effects are different. Saying that a Black person has engaged in negative behavior due to their race is likely to cause that person emotional pain because we live in a society where whiteness is constructed as superior to Blackness. Indeed, while institutional racism serves to stigmatize people of color, especially African Americans, as untrustworthy, white privilege grants a considerable amount of trust to white Americans (Alexander 2010; McIntosh 2004). Prejudice and discrimination against white people is not institutionally supported in the same way as it is against people of color.

Homosexuality is also marked in such a way that heterosexuality is not. I noticed this marking of homosexuality at a recent family gathering of mine, where one of my cousins, a straight white man, suggested that gay men only like movies with gay actors and themes. His tone indicated that he meant this statement as a criticism. In response, I asked about his favorite movies and noticed that he seemed to have little awareness of how his social position affected his taste in film. He proudly listed his favorite movies—*Braveheart, Gladiator,* and *The Godfather*—as if his identity had no bearing on his enjoyment of them. To me, these films seemed to reflect the sensibilities of a straight white man, almost to the point that I could not have picked three more perfect examples had I tried. His assertion of impartiality is likely not a coincidence but a product of living in a society where whiteness, maleness, and heterosexuality are unmarked. As decades of feminist scholarship has documented, positions that contend neutrality and objectivity often reflect the views of a particular social group, especially those groups in power (Smith 1987).

While it remains important to address how unmarked aspects of individuals' identities shape their experiences, I find it even more vital to challenge the marking of disadvantaged groups, including women, racial minorities, and LGBT people. The problem with the marking of minority groups is that an individual is made to represent all of the people in that group. As a result, the actions of one person carry different weight depending on one's social position. When a person belonging to a minority group engages in negative behavior, their actions are sometimes viewed as reflecting the larger, implicitly homogenous, community. Conversely, when someone belonging to a privileged group engages in the same behavior, their actions are not viewed as indicative of anything beyond themselves because the larger group is assumed to be heterogeneous. The marking of minority groups, then, becomes problematic to the extent that it constructs disadvantaged groups as homogenous and privileged ones as diverse.

Given this marking of minority groups, individuals are socialized to pay attention to some aspects of their identity—those that are "marked"— because they most frequently experience discrimination based on those aspects. Thus, a person who is "marked" in one way—a straight, middle-class white woman or a middle-class white gay man—usually experiences discrimination based on that aspect. In these examples, the white woman would typically experience discrimination based on her gender, while the white gay man is most likely to experience discrimination based on his sexuality. Similarly, with regard to race, Black people are more likely than white people to experience discrimination based on their racial identity. Consequently, attributing a white person's actions to their race does not have the same effects as for a Black person; after all, existing social arrangements already encourage Black people to think about their racial identity and encourage white people to overlook theirs.

THE ASSOCIATION OF HOMOSEXUALITY WITH WHITENESS

LGBT people of color were more likely than white respondents to empha-size the racial implications of their violent experiences in large part because of the social construction of race, in which white people are not made to think about their racial identities. Still, race alone cannot explain the rea-sons for LGBT people of color believing that their violent experiences had racial implications, as race frequently overlaps with sexuality in important ways. In particular, many LGBT people of color described homosexuality as linked with whiteness. This association is a broad, large-scale cultural phenomenon in the United States, with deep historical roots (Cohen 1999; Collins 2004). While minority communities, including white LGBT com-munities and Black heterosexual ones, may reinforce this association, the linking of homosexuality with whiteness is part of dominant U.S. society.

It may seem odd that a deviant sexual identity such as homosexuality would be linked with an idealized racial identity such as whiteness. Never-theless, racism and homophobia—privileging whiteness and condemning homosexuality—overlap to emphasize white people's homosexuality. That is, this overlap creates negative stereotypes of lesbian and gay people that are raced white, and also frequently male and upper middle class. Indeed, homosexuality has historically been associated with whiteness because it has been viewed as a means of preventing white reproduction and, therefore, as a threat to the white heterosexual family (Collins 2004). This association remains until the present day; even though white people are not any more likely to identify as lesbian or gay than other racial groups, and may be even less likely to identify as LGBT, whiteness is the dominant framework though which homosexuality is understood. The most famous lesbian or gay people in the media have been white; LGBT people of color have more frequently been an afterthought.[2] The reality is significantly different: a 2012 Gallup study of 121,290 U.S. adults found that Black, Latino, and Asian American people were more likely than white people to identify as lesbian, gay, bisexual, or transgender. Of those surveyed, 4.6 percent of Black, 4.0 percent of Latino, and 4.3 percent of Asian people identified as LGBT, while only 3.2 percent of white Americans identified in this way (Gates and Newport 2012).

Although heterosexual communities of color sometimes become implicated in the whitening of homosexuality, white heterosexual people reproduce this association as well. Certainly, a few Black respondents described encounters in which white heterosexual people had responded with confusion to their homosexuality. Cole, a thirty-three-year-old Black gay man who worked as a cook in a restaurant, described a white male coworker who had assumed that he was straight until Cole told him otherwise. Cole said that the man seemed "very surprised" and "very confused" because most of his experiences had been with white gay men. In this situation, Cole thought that his coworker had assumed "all gay men are white," reacting with confusion when confronted with a Black gay man: "It was that 'I've never met one of you [a person who is Black and gay] sort of thing.'" In this regard, homosexuality is broadly associated with whiteness, as the experiences of Black, Latino, and Asian LGBT people have received relatively little mainstream attention.

The whitening of homosexuality is also the product of racist stereotypes that associate people of color with a deviant heterosexuality (Collins 2004; Nagel 2003). In particular, homosexuality has been disassociated from racial minorities because people of color have been constructed as hypersexual throughout U.S. history. Black men, for example, have been stigmatized as excessively masculine and overly sexual. These ideas justified the lynching of Black men after the Civil War and into the twentieth century, as they were often falsely accused of crime, especially rape. Similarly, Black and Latina women's sexuality has been historically devalued, frequently being used to stereotype them as unfit mothers; white women, in contrast, have more often been viewed as pure and chaste. These ideas constructing women of color as hypersexual permitted white men to rape enslaved Black women and justified the forced sterilization of Black women during the twentieth century (Hancock 2004; Roberts 1997).

More recently, Black women have been associated with a deviant heterosexuality through stereotypes regarding motherhood. Ideas of Black women's sexuality as dangerous and out-of-control have led to attempts to limit their reproductive choices, pressuring Black pregnant women to inject Norplant and Depo-Provera, birth control options with harmful side effects that have disproportionately been targeted at low-income women of color (Hancock 2004; Roberts 1997). Further, the modern welfare queen stereotype—a woman, implicitly raced Black, who has children merely to collect welfare money—reproduces ideas of Black women as excessively sexual. Indeed, this stereotype implies that women on welfare are having sex for the purpose of collecting money, an image not so different from a prostitute or sex worker. Despite the unsubstantiated nature of these stereotypes—research indicates that welfare payments do not result in considerably higher pregnancy rates—they persist in media and film, including the Oscar-winning *Precious*.[3]

What all of these stereotypes of Black people's sexuality have in common is that they link people of color with a stigmatized heterosexuality. By depicting people of color as excessively heterosexual, these stereotypes distance them from homosexuality in the popular imagination of many Americans. Racist ideas, then, that sexualize people of color help to produce the whitening of homosexuality; without institutional racism, homosexuality would most likely not be linked with whiteness. At the same time, challenging racism can potentially reinforce the whitening of homosexuality when LGBT people of color are marginalized (Cohen 1999). That is, without taking into consideration LGBT people of color's experiences, Black people are implicitly constructed as heterosexual and LGBT people are implicitly viewed as white, thereby reinforcing the association of homosexuality with whiteness.

THE PARTICULAR CHALLENGES CONFRONTING
LGBT PEOPLE OF COLOR

Black and Latino men described racism in LGBT communities by arguing that queer people of color are often sexualized in such a way that white LGBT people are not. Thomas, a forty-one-year-old Asian gay man, described racial stereotypes in gay male communities: "Like all Black and Hispanic guys are good in bed, and that Asian guys are supposed to be submissive—that Black guys are there to please and Asian men are more than willing to please any white guy. . . . Then white guys are whatever, like the norm." When asked to describe the drawback of these stereotypes, Thomas said, "You're not being looked at as a person. You're just some sexual thing." Obviously, this dynamic is not unique to LGBT communities, as members of racial minority groups have been sexualized throughout U.S. history. Some LGBT people of color, however, argued that sexualized stereotypes seemed heightened in gay communities, with queer people of color being defined largely by their sexual prowess. On the surface, these stereotypes appear complimentary, making LGBT people of color seem more sexually gifted than their white counterparts, yet underneath they frequently reinforce racist ideologies by constructing LGBT people of color as hypersexual. As such, these stereotypes associate queer people of color with their sexual—rather than their intellectual—abilities.

While gay men of color often described sexualized stereotypes, Black lesbians more frequently expressed feelings of invisibility. Butch lesbians of color described sexual representations in the media, in which primarily white and feminine lesbians were presented. Jasmine, a forty-four-year-old Black lesbian, described images of lesbians in pornography: "It's always some white chick. [She is] always hot or whatever. . . . But that's just not reality." As Jasmine noted, lesbians in pornography, who are sometimes even played by heterosexual actresses, do not reflect most lesbians' daily lives.[4] They are exaggerated media representations, depicting lesbians as sexual objects available to serve heterosexual men's fantasies. Further, the race and gender representation of these images—frequently two attractive white women with feminine presentations of self—obscures the experiences of butch lesbians, particularly those of butch lesbians of color.

Mainstream LGBT communities have often perpetuated the marginalization of lesbians of color by associating LGBT people with the experiences of white, upper-middle-class gay men (Moore 2011; Ward 2008). Indeed, even though evidence indicates that gay men make less than their hetero-sexual male counterparts, homosexuality has stereotypically been associ-ated with relatively high income levels (Badgett 2003; Gates and Newport 2012). As a result, these classed stereotypes of LGBT people marginalize the experiences of low-income LGBT people, who are disproportionately women, transgender, and people of color. Even in academic research, the experiences of low-income LGBT people have received relatively little attention. Some scholarship has focused on the experiences of low-income LGBT people of color, including my work here, but even less attention has been paid to the experiences of white, low-income LGBT people.[5]

On the one hand, low-income LGBT people of color have remained largely invisible in mainstream representations of queer people. In another sense, inclusion can be harmful, and many of the representations of low-income LGBT people of color have been less than flattering, associating them with gender deviance. When I asked Frankie, a forty-eight-year-old Latino gay man, if he thought stereotypes of Latino gay men were differ-ent from those of white gay men, he responded: "They're worse. You're lucky if you see them [representations of Latino gay men], but when you do, then they're just really feminine, and not in a good way. . . . They just care about the newest Gucci bag, or some thing." Gay men of color often described stereotypes categorizing them as trivial and superficial; many of these stereotypes were intimately linked with gender. Moreover, they sometimes argued that men's femininity was devalued in gay communi-ties and that Black, Latino, and Asian gay men were marginalized from these communities because of stereotypes associating them with femi-ninity. Daniel, a twenty-six-year-old Black gay man, described gay media as presenting Black gay men as excessively "feminine" or "masculine": "Whenever you see us, we're either really masculine or really feminine, like there's no [in-]between. . . . People don't really like feminine guys in the gay community. It's still looked down on. . . . You're patted on the back if you're masculine, but then if you're not, it's like, 'Oh, you're one of *those* Black [gay] guys—I don't want anything to do with you.'"

Daniel described hierarchies in LGBT communities, suggesting that mas-culine men tend to be more valued than feminine men. He also addressed a relationship between race and gender, arguing that stereotypes of Black gay men incorporate elements of gender deviance, constructing them as "really masculine" or "really feminine." Thus, if feminine gay men are generally the least valued in LGBT communities and if Black gay men are associated with femininity, then gendered hierarchies within these communities are constructed along racial lines: characteristics associated with white gay men are more highly valued than those associated with queer men of color. This intersection of race, gender, and sexuality means that devaluing male femininity may disproportionately harm Black gay men, while improving their position in society is likely to undermine negative attitudes toward men's femininity.

Taking the experiences of LGBT people of color seriously reveals that they confront their own set of challenges, unique to their social position. In particular, LGBT people of color confront racism in white queer communities and homophobia in their race-based communities. Individuals may debate whether racism is "worse" in white LGBT communities or homophobia is "worse" in heterosexual communities of color, but these arguments are largely unproductive because they ignore how racism and homophobia are institutionalized throughout U.S. society. Indeed, just as racism is not restricted to white queer communities, homophobia is not limited to heterosexual communities of color. White LGBT communities and Black heterosexual communities are not exceptional in their racism or homophobia, but reflect mainstream societal values. At the same time, the challenges confronting LGBT people of color are different from those confronting other social groups. While heterosexual people of color confront racism in the larger society, they do not usually encounter it in white queer communities. Similarly, white LGBT people confront homophobia in the larger society, but they do not typically face it in Black heterosexual communities.

Descriptions of homophobia in Black communities can very easily feed into institutional racism by portraying heterosexual people of color as "backwards" and out-of-touch with "mainstream" American values, which are then implicitly associated with white heterosexual people. This understanding of homophobia in Black communities reproduces existing racial hierarchies, ascribing negative characteristics to Black heterosexual people and allowing homophobia in white heterosexual communities to remain unexamined. Still, these concerns, while legitimate, must not prevent an analysis of LGBT people of color's experiences in dealing with homophobia in their race-based communities. During the interviews, LGBT people of color frequently spent a considerable amount of time describing homophobia in their racial groups, possibly viewing me, given my race and social class privilege—a white male academic—as someone who outsiders would listen to and who could bring their concerns to the outside world. For instance, Tamika, a fifty-three-year-old Black lesbian, described one of her violent experiences as reflecting homophobia in Black communities. A man sneered at her while she was shopping at a corner store. She responded by asking, "Is there a problem here?" He then sneered at her again. In response, she said, "I'm sick of this shit," and slammed her hands on the countertop. When she came out of the store, the man called her a "nasty bitch" and laughed. Describing his motivations, Tamika referred to race and sexuality: "It's like I'm not supposed to be gay because I shouldn't give people another reason not to like me. . . . Like I'm already Black, so why would I want people to not like me for another reason?"

This understanding of Tamika's sexuality as "giving people another reason" not to like her relies on ideas that women are born heterosexual and then "choose" to adopt a lesbian identity; this "choice" is then viewed as morally wrong. While white lesbians may also confront these ideas, Black lesbians are more likely to face suggestions that they have given people "another" reason not to like them. In these situations, the assumption is that lesbians of color are already stigmatized based on their racial identity and that lesbianism is an "additional" way of stigmatizing themselves. Tamika also thought the man had justified the verbal violence by viewing her sexuality in this way: "It's like I brought it on myself because I chose it." Indeed, viewing lesbianism as "giving" others another reason not to like her implies that she should not have given them that reason and, therefore, should not identify as a lesbian.

While focusing on homophobia in communities of color remains important, it is also essential to emphasize the role of institutional racism. Given the existence of racial inequality, Black people face pressures that white people do not to present their communities in a positive way. That is, to challenge racism, Black communities sometimes encourage Black people to "put their best foot forward." These ideas become problematic to the extent that they reproduce homophobia, encouraging LGBT people of color to keep their sexualities hidden; these notions become most apparent when queer people of color are viewed as "selling out" or "not genuine" members of their racial communities.[6] Black LGBT people confronted these ideas when their homosexuality was associated with whiteness and thereby distanced from their racial group. Andre, a twenty-four-year-old Black gay man, described several incidents during adolescence in which his family members dismissed his sexuality as a "white thing." On one occasion, Andre's uncle told him to "take that white shit inside" when he had worn makeup and dressed in feminine attire. Andre also described an incident that occurred around the same time when his mother chastised him for watching a gay-themed movie, saying, "We don't do any of that white faggot shit in my house." Conflating homosexuality with whiteness, his mother constructed gay sexuality as an inappropriate expression of Blackness, attempting to make homosexuality seem as if it was only "white faggot shit." These experiences suggest that homosexuality is sometimes viewed as antithetical to ideal or "authentic" expressions of Blackness.

In this sense, some Black lesbians and gay men emphasized the seriousness of homophobia in their racial communities. Jayvyn, introduced at the beginning of this chapter, equated being gay in Black heterosexual communities with a job: "Being gay in the African American community, you're going to come across issues like that. Unfortunately, that's what it is. Doesn't make it right, but it comes with the territory. . . . I know by being an openly gay man and not hiding it, I'm going to have my attacks once in a while. . . . It's like a job, you can complain about it, but you knew it came with the job. I knew by me being openly gay, I was gonna get these verbal attacks, I was gonna get these ridicules." Comparing his sexual identity with an occupation, Jayvyn argued that homophobic violence "comes with the territory" of being an openly gay Black man. Although Black communities should not be viewed as unique in their homophobia, focusing on Black LGBT people's experiences reveals some of the challenges they face in their daily lives and the ways that race and sexuality norms overlap in the United States.

Transgender people of color also pointed to their particular challenges, which sometimes had racial implications. Lakeisha, a thirty-eight-year-old Black transgender woman, described the racial implications of a physical attack that had occurred after she left her abusive ex-boyfriend. To kick him out of her apartment, Lakeisha told her brother to threaten the ex-boyfriend with violence, forcing him to leave. This threat resulted in him leaving the apartment, yet the next morning Lakeisha was attacked by two of his friends. These two men broke one of her fingers, ripped off her clothes, and punched her repeatedly. She said that the men used antitransgender language while punching her, as they said, "You don't have a pussy, you have a fucking dick" and "you're not a woman, you're a mother-fucking man." She described their insults as homophobic as well: "You're a faggot," they said, "who probably has HIV." As Lakeisha explained, "They were calling me every name that you could possibly call a queer."

When I asked Lakeisha if she thought the violence had anything to do with race, she argued that she was being blamed for supposedly "bringing" HIV into Black communities: "They were all saying, 'Oh, [Lakeisha] will be sucking some guy off and giving him HIV before you know it.'" Lakeisha viewed these comments as related to her transgender identity, arguing that they are informed by stereotypes of transgender people as devious: "Because they think of me as tricky, sneaky . . . I'm a freak who brings [HIV in]." Clearly, transgender people confront ideas of them as deceitful in such a way that many other social groups do not; all of the transgender respondents in this study described confronting these ideas. In a society that constructs as "real" or "authentic" women and men whose gender identity matches the sex they were assigned at birth, transgender people are viewed as somehow "false" or "inauthentic." Transgender people are typically viewed as real and authentic in trans communities, yet ideas of them as tricky and false persist in the larger society.[7]

These stereotypes of transgender people as deceitful are likely to be particularly damaging to transgender people of color, who can potentially be blamed for high rates of HIV in minority communities. Men on the "down low"—Black men who identify as heterosexual, but engage in sexual practices with other men—have long been blamed for "spreading" HIV in Black communities (Boykin 2005; Cohen 1999). The problem with these ideas is that they ignore the structural conditions, including poverty, that lead to high rates of HIV transmission. These notions also problematically tie HIV and AIDS to types of people rather than advocating for safe sex practices that drastically reduce the likelihood of transmitting HIV. Lakeisha's experience here suggests that the scapegoating of men on the "down low" extends to Black transgender women, who because of stereotypes of them as deceitful are viewed as "infecting" unsuspecting Black heterosexual people. White transgender people may also confront notions of them as untrustworthy, but are unlikely to be blamed to the same extent for "spreading" HIV in white communities.

THE RACIAL IMPLICATIONS OF LGBT PEOPLE
OF COLOR'S VIOLENT EXPERIENCES

Among butch Black and Latina lesbians, the insinuation that they "change" their girlfriends had racial implications. Judy, a forty-three-year-old Latina lesbian, said that she was usually viewed as a "big dyke"; at the time of the interview she was dating a Black lesbian, Tiara, whom Judy described as more feminine than herself. Judy thought that others sometimes viewed her relationship as one where she had "converted" Tiara into lesbianism. In describing these views, Judy first focused on the gender and sexuality implications: "They think that it's my fault that she's like that. Like, I influenced her. I did this to her. And I'm like, 'Hey, she could have been like that since the day she was born. You don't know that. You don't know her.' I'm not forcing her to be with a woman. That's her choice." Here, Judy highlighted her girlfriend's desire to be sexually involved with a woman to undermine ideas that butch lesbians "change" their girlfriends. At one point, Judy connected these ideas to race, as she described a particular experience where one of her brother's friends, a Black man, was asking Tiara about being "changed" by Judy. When I asked Judy if she thought this experience had anything to do with race, she said, "[He acted] like she doesn't have any control over it. Then I'm bad for doing that to her." As I continued to press Judy on what she thought the racial implications might be, she added, "I'm saying that [the man] wouldn't have cared if [Tiara] was something else." By "something else," Judy meant something other than Black. Judy thought that he would not have cared about Tiara supposedly being converted into lesbianism if Tiara was a different race.

In describing the racial implications of their violent experiences, other lesbians of color were even more explicit than Judy. These overt discussions of race usually occurred because the perpetrator had explicitly addressed race during the violent encounter. Latoya, introduced at the beginning of this chapter, described a male stranger associating homosexuality with whiteness. Reflecting on this experience, Latoya said: "They act like I did this to her. And it's like I'm not supposed to because then I'm making Black people look bad. Like if I left her alone, she wouldn't be gay. . . . They act like she has no control over herself. I didn't do anything to her. They don't know her. She can be who she wants." Although Latoya and Judy overlapped in much of what they said, Latoya went one step beyond Judy, emphasizing the particular pressures faced by butch Black lesbians. While Judy perceived her experience as signifying that she was "bad for doing that to her" girlfriend, Latoya underscored the racial significance of these ideas. That is, Latoya suggested that butch Black lesbians are sometimes viewed as causing harm to their racial communities for supposedly recruiting another Black woman into lesbianism.

Although Judy and Latoya emphasized race to different degrees, they used many similar phrases. Both respondents highlighted their girlfriends' ability to identify according to their own desires: Judy stated, "That's her choice," and Latoya said, "She can be who she wants." In this regard, butch lesbians underscored their girlfriends' autonomy. Sociologists would refer to these statements as attempts to assert one's "agency"—the ability of individuals to make their own choices, despite social structures constraining their behavior.[8] With these statements, Judy and Latoya highlighted their girlfriends' agency in choosing their sexual partner. By doing so, they rejected notions that they had changed their girlfriends; Judy said, "I didn't do anything to her," while Latoya asserted, "I'm not forcing her to be with a woman." Their ability to reject these ideas indicates that individuals have some agency in discarding oppressive notions. At the same time, the structure—the social forces affecting individuals' behavior—is clearly important here, as both of these respondents faced suggestions that they had converted their sexual partner only because they were lesbians with masculine gender presentations of self. The frequency with which butch lesbians confront these suggestions speaks to the pervasiveness of antilesbian prejudice, and although Judy and Latoya rejected notions that they had changed their girlfriends, other lesbians are likely to find these ideas more difficult to overcome (see Mason 2002).

The debate in sociology as to whether social structure or individual agency is more powerful in determining individuals' behavior cannot possibly be resolved here (Gengler 2012; Giddens 1984). Both are obviously important, yet I am arguing that LGBT people confront different pressures depending on their social position. These pressures also establish different avenues for LGBT people to assert their agency. Lesbians and gay men of color both had to deal with notions that they had inappropriately represented their racial communities, but they differed along gender lines in how they went about rejecting such notions. Black and Latina lesbians emphasized their autonomy, while gay men of color focused on how they were strong, both emotionally and physically. These gender differences among LGBT people of color were present among white LGBT people as well, with white lesbians sometimes emphasizing their autonomy and white gay men more frequently highlighting their emotional and physical strength.

Undoubtedly, the different types of violence confronting lesbians and gay men played an important role in their evaluations. Gay men did not encounter violence for "converting" other men into homosexuality; instead, they regularly perceived their violent experiences as a masculinity contest, with heterosexual men trying to impose notions of weakness onto them. Confronting suggestions that they were weak, gay men emphasized their strength. Lesbians, in contrast, rejected notions that they had "converted" another woman into lesbianism by emphasizing their autonomy. These differences between lesbians and gay men reflect not only the development of their violent experiences but also the larger context in which the violence occurred, including U.S. gender norms. Indeed, gendered expectations encourage men to perform masculinity through strength and encourage women to endure hardship in a stoic manner (Asencio 2011; Bridges 2014; Madriz 1997). The word "fag" is frequently used to punish men for showing weakness, and women are routinely told to smile or "cheer up" even when their mood does not reflect a happy disposition (Klein 2012; Pascoe 2007). As a result, the narratives of lesbians, focusing on autonomy, and the narratives of gay men, focusing on strength, must be viewed as the product of social forces that encourage women and men to perform gender in different ways.

Although lesbians and gay men confront different forms of violence, Black LGBT people across gender lines emphasized the racial implications of their experiences. Jayvyn, described at the beginning of this chapter, thought that he had been chastised on several occasions for failing to meet expectations of Black men. When asked to provide an example, he said that it usually occurs in insidious ways: "Like these little looks, a [Black] woman did it on the subway the other day. Like just looking at me like I'm a waste because I'm gay, like that means I'm not portraying Black men very well." Black gay men sometimes felt that they had been marginalized from heterosexual Black communities because of their gender and sexual identities, feeling as if an "authentic" performance of Black masculinity required them to reject homosexuality. In explaining why he thought the woman looked at him as if he was a "waste," Jayvyn noted a relationship between Blackness and homosexuality: "Like if you're gay and Black then you've given up your right to be Black, you're not *really* Black."

Rather than accepting these notions, Black gay men typically argued that identifying as feminine and gay made them no less "authentically Black." In fact, they usually said that homosexuality was a legitimate expression of Black masculinity. Indeed, Jayvyn legitimized his feminine gender performance, while disparaging traditional notions of masculinity: "I don't see what's so great about being all masculine, anyway. It just makes your life closed off and repressed. I'm not that 'strong Black man,' in the sense that most people think of." Here, Jayvyn seemed to contend with stereotypes that have problematically associated the bodies of Black men with hypermasculinity and brute strength (Collins 2004; Garfield 2010). Rejecting these stereotypes, he described himself as feminine, suggesting that other men could potentially benefit from refusing to perform masculinity in traditional ways.[9]

RACIAL DIFFERENCES IN FOCUSING ON AUTONOMY AND STRENGTH

Certainly, LGBT people of color faced ideas and forms of violence that white LGBT people did not. Similar forms of violence, however, were also viewed differently depending on the respondent's racial identity. That is, although respondents across racial lines usually described violence that was intraracial, white respondents and LGBT people of color perceived their violent experiences in different ways. Specifically, gay men of color emphasized strength, and lesbians of color focused on autonomy, more than their white counterparts. Although lesbians confronted some similar forms of abuse across racial lines—violence for "converting" or "recruiting" another woman into lesbianism—their evaluations differed based on race.

Lesbians of color frequently emphasized their autonomy or self-sufficiency to challenge notions that they had not contributed to their racial communities. Jetta, a twenty-eight-year-old Black lesbian, described a violent experience in which a Black man approached her in a public park when she had her arm around her girlfriend, a Black woman whom Jetta described as "feminine and bisexual." The man approached the couple, asking Jetta "what [she] had done" to her girlfriend, and when Jetta suggested that he leave them alone, the man attempted to grab her breasts. When reflecting on this experience, Jetta thought that the man had asked her these questions rather than her girlfriend because "it's obvious I'm a lesbian." Moreover, she referred to her racial identity when addressing the types of violence that bother her most: "It's more about what the person is trying to do. . . . [If] they're telling me that I'm a bad African American or whatever, that pisses me off. I go to church every Sunday. I live my life how I want. A good African American—I live my life how I want. I can take care of myself. I am who I am, that's not gonna change." Rebelling against ideas that she has failed to represent Black people positively, Jetta emphasized her autonomy; she said that she represents Black people well because she lives her life as she wants. In this sense, Jetta argued that she represents her racial community in a positive way.

In contrast to Jetta, white lesbians did not typically have to contend with discourse that they had disappointed their racial groups. As a result, white lesbians placed less emphasis on autonomy than lesbians of color because the former did not confront pressures to emphasize how they had contributed to their racial communities. Martha, a fifty-four-year-old white lesbian, described an experience that was similar in some ways to the one described by Jetta. Martha and her girlfriend, a "femme" white woman, were engaging in public displays of affection on a park bench when a white man approached them, asking Martha why she had "taken" her girlfriend away from straight men. When Martha told the man to "get away from here," he kicked her leg and motioned as if he was going to punch her. In a similar way to Jetta, Martha thought that the man had harassed her rather than her girlfriend because she is "obviously a dyke." When describing the implications of this experience, however, Martha did not make reference to her racial identity: "It'd be nice to know that I can wear all the butch-y stuff I want. That it doesn't matter. I'd just like to be able to do what I want." Jetta and Martha's experiences differed in that Jetta's involved sexual violence, yet their experiences were also similar in several ways: both identified as butch lesbians; both had experienced violence when they were with their "more feminine" girlfriends in a public park. Both respondents also thought that the violence was directed against them, rather than their partners, because they appeared masculine in their gender presentation of self and because they were viewed as a "bad influence," supposedly converting their girlfriends into lesbians.

Despite these similarities, their evaluations placed different emphases on autonomy. Martha said, "I'd just like to be able to do what I want,"
while Jetta declared, "I live my life how I want." Here, Martha wishes she
had more autonomy, while Jetta claims her autonomy. Martha, as a white
person, is perhaps more surprised than Jetta, as a Black person, to face limits on her autonomy; Jetta did not seem surprised that others had tried to
limit her autonomy, while Martha did. Further, their evaluations differed
in other important ways. Jetta focused more on the ways in which she is
self-sufficient, repeatedly underscoring how she lives according to her own
wishes. Twice Jetta said, "I live my life how I want," connecting this autonomy to her being a "good African American." Martha explained her desire
to wear the clothes she wants, but she did not employ the narratives that
were more frequently used by Black and Latina women, in which they suggested that their autonomy makes them valuable members of their racial
communities. These differences between lesbians of color and white lesbians occurred because of the social construction of race. Indeed, Jetta underscored her self-sufficiency to challenge notions that she has negatively
represented African Americans. Martha, on the other hand, speaking from
a position of white privilege, did not have to contend with a discourse that
she had betrayed her racial group, and therefore did not appear compelled
to emphasize her autonomy.

For lesbians of color, these ideas that they had "betrayed" their racial
communities were sometimes related to procreation. Since Jetta's girlfriend
was Black and Martha's girlfriend was white, the meaning of "converting" a
woman into lesbianism took on different forms for these respondents. While
Martha did not struggle with the racialized implications of her supposed
conversion of a white woman into lesbianism, Jetta thought that others
might view this act as causing harm to her racial community. In particular,
Jetta thought that she was being punished for "making" her girlfriend—
another Black woman—a lesbian. In this sense, Black lesbians who identify
as butch may face particularly harsh sanctions, as the act of "converting" a
Black woman into lesbianism may be viewed as preventing a Black woman
from reproducing.[10] As neither white lesbians nor Black gay men are likely to
confront such discourse, Black lesbians with masculine gender presentations
of self face these pressures in such a way that other social groups do not.

While lesbians in this study often focused on their autonomy to challenge
perpetrators' discourse, gay male respondents more frequently highlighted

their emotional and physical strength. Here, the gender dynamic of respondents' violent experiences played an important role, as the majority of respondents described physical violence perpetrated by men. Gay male respondents, viewing their violent experiences as attempts to construct them as weak, frequently underscored the ways in which they were strong. Still, gay men of color placed more emphasis on strength than white gay men because the violence had racial implications for the former but not the latter. Jayvyn, the thirty-three-year-old Black gay man described throughout this chapter, constructed himself as strong to challenge notions that he was performing Blackness inappropriately: "I'm *gay*. Everyone knows it, the second I walk out the door. That doesn't make me a bad African American or whatever. . . . I'm not a weak little thing. . . . I can defend myself. I know how to fight. I can get past things pretty quick. I can handle things emotionally, spiritually. They [people who have attacked me] aren't like that. They'll only go calling me names when their friends are around." Black gay men regularly noted the importance of emotional strength, sometimes even suggesting that other men could benefit from being emotionally or spiritually strong. Here, Jayvyn constructed himself as emotionally stronger than his attackers, who only insult him "when their friends are around." This type of response was one of the ways that LGBT people pointed to their perpetrators' hypocrisy. As heterosexual men used homophobic insults in groups—when their friends could protect them—gay men constructed this behavior as signifying weakness, as indicating that their perpetrators were susceptible to peer pressure and fearful of perpetrating homophobic violence without the protection of their friends. This interpretation, then, inverts the meaning of antigay violence by constructing perpetrators as weak willed, and therefore hypocritical, given that they had tried to construct gay men as weak.

While white gay men also perceived their violent experiences as attempts to construct them as weak, they did not emphasize strength to the same extent as Black and Latino men. George, a forty-five-year-old white gay man who worked as a college instructor, described an incident that occurred after having sex with another man in a parking lot. After the sexual encounter, two white men approached George and asked him what he "had been up to." When George offered to give the men his money, one of the men pushed George, laughed, and called him a "little faggot." Describing the incident, George analyzed his perpetrator's motivations: "He was trying to say that I'm weak, which whatever, I might be.

The whole thing is just kinda stupid. It's easy to be like 'Oh, OK, you're tough, you're macho. Whatever, you can have that.'" Similar to most gay men in this study, George concluded that his perpetrators were trying to construct him as weak. Rather than emphasizing his strength, however, George casually dismissed its importance. Most white gay men did not necessarily reject the value of strength in this way, yet George's offhanded dismissal of meanings of weakness was more consistently expressed by white gay men than Black and Latino men. Indeed, with this statement, George suggested that the posturing of his perpetrator was "easy" to dismiss, which appears to contrast sharply with the more complex evaluations of LGBT people of color. Constructing gay men as weak, then, has different implications based on race. The insinuation that Black gay men were weak frequently caused them emotional pain because they viewed this suggestion as implying that they were weak for "giving in" to homosexuality, which has stereotypically been associated with whiteness; white gay men, in contrast, were able to overlook these racial implications. White gay men did not view suggestions that they were weak as related to their racial identity, and therefore, because of their white privilege, did not appear as compelled to emphasize their strength.

These racial differences indicate that LGBT people interpret their violent experiences in different ways, even when the violence takes on similar forms. Both Black and white lesbians experienced physical violence for "converting" another woman into lesbianism, but this act had different implications for each of these groups. Black lesbians with butch gender presentations of self often thought that their supposed conversion of a feminine woman of color into lesbianism was viewed as harming their racial communities. Since white lesbians did not usually view their violent experiences as having racialized implications, similar forms of abuse were perceived differently based on race. Thus, how LGBT people perceive their violent experiences is not a straightforward process that can be determined simply by examining the type of abuse they have encountered. Indeed, LGBT people view forms of anti-queer violence differently depending on how they are positioned in society.

4 · GENDERED VIEWS OF SEXUAL ASSAULT, PHYSICAL VIOLENCE, AND VERBAL ABUSE

Lesbian and transgender women in this study were more likely than gay men to experience sexual assault. Page, a forty-five-year-old Latina woman who identified as a lesbian but dated men as a teenager, described a date she went on with one of her older brother's friends, a man who raped her. When they were watching a movie, he forced himself on her, after she had told him "no" and tried to push him off. He was drunk at the time, although she was not, and she said that even though she did not want to have sex with him, he made it very clear that he was going to have sex with her "whether she wanted to or not." When she told him, "I don't want to," he told her to "shut up" and forced her arms behind her head. She described the assault in this way: "I wanted to scream, but he kept saying, 'Shut up,' and got more aggressive. . . . I was scared he would hit me, so I didn't say anything." The rapist, whom Page described as "very popular" at her high school, told her after the assault that she better not tell anyone about what happened because "everyone knew" that she liked him and, therefore, they would not believe her. She felt ashamed afterward and did not tell anyone about it, until telling her brother two years prior to the interview, approximately twenty-five years after the sexual assault. She said that her brother was "sympathetic" and "very angry," but questioned why she had not told him sooner. She "sort of regretted" not telling him earlier, but found it impossible to tell him, or others, during high school because she was "scared people wouldn't have [believed her]."

The dominant strain of research on anti-queer violence has focused on homophobia, overlooking the role of sexism and misogyny.[1] Some of these studies have problematically collapsed the violent experiences of lesbians and gay men, attributing both of their experiences to heterosexism and homophobia.[2] As a result, gender has not featured centrally in the literature, and little attention has been paid to the ways that misogyny is deeply implicated in lesbians' violent experiences.[3] One example of the degree to which misogyny has not been adequately explored is the degree to which rape and sexual assault have remained absent from this line of scholarship. Indeed, violence against LGBT people and sexual assault against women have often been studied as if they are separate phenomena. Violence against LGBT people, however, includes sexual assault—disproportionately experienced by lesbian and transgender women. For instance, Carol, a thirty-nine-year-old Latina transgender woman, was sexually assaulted when she was thirty-two. The assault, which occurred in an elevator, began with a male stranger grabbing her breasts. When Carol slapped his hand, he said, "Look at how you're dressed," implying that he had free rein to touch her where he pleased. He then forced himself on her, attempting to rape her. During the assault, he told her that she "liked it" because she was "asking for it." She also thought that he was aware of her transgender identity because he called her a "fucking faggot." When the elevator doors opened, Carol struggled to get out, eventually hitting him in the eye with the tip of her high-heeled shoe. She then ran into the street, where she encountered a stranger, who called the police. After this incident, Carol moved into another building because she "felt afraid to be there," as she was worried that he might come back to the building.

Gay men did not confront experiences such as those described by Page and Carol. While lesbian and transgender women often experienced violence in which a sexual component was introduced into the encounter, gay men described abuse designed to prevent the encounter from becoming sexualized. Andre, a twenty-four-year-old Black gay man who identified as "androgynous," described several violent experiences that occurred during high school, one of which involved several of his classmates taunting him in the locker room during gym class. This incident occurred when Andre was undressing and one of his classmates suggested to his friends that Andre was "checking out" the classmate's penis in the shower. The classmate then came over to Andre and snapped him with a wet towel and said, "Aw, did I just hurt the sissy?" He then threatened Andre by saying, "If I catch you doing that again, I'll beat your ass." Subsequently, Andre said that he always tried to avoid being in the shower at the same time as this boy. Nevertheless, his classmate continued to harass him for the remainder of the semester. A later incident occurred when Andre was taking a shower, and the classmate came into the same area and said, "Don't even think about looking over here." Andre did not move, but then the boy threw a bar of soap at him, hitting him in the back. Reflecting on this experience, Andre said that the harassment made him "really quiet" and made it hard for him to "look at guys." Here, rather than a sexual assault being forced onto him, as more often happened with lesbian and transgender women, the violence was designed to keep the encounter from becoming sexual.

While gay men experienced sexualized forms of violence less frequently than lesbian and transgender women, male respondents occasionally described harassment that was sexual. Andre described other boys in his high school who would "grab [his] ass and smile suggestively." On one occasion, as Andre was walking by a male classmate's desk, the boy grabbed Andre's ass and said, "If you were a girl, I'd fuck you." Andre described this boy as a "complete bully" who would harass him sexually, "push [him], and call [him] 'faggot' as well." Of course, this form of harassment is different from the assaults described by lesbian and transgender women, as the classmate makes a conditional statement, saying that he "would fuck" Andre *if* he was a girl. The violence also involved bullying with an element of sexual aggression, which is different from sexual assault.

Even when women and men confronted violence that was similar in some ways, they viewed their experiences differently because gay men did not think about how sexualized forms of violence might lead to rape. Andre described one occasion in which the same boy who grabbed his buttock also cornered him in the bathroom, grabbed Andre's penis, and said, "You wish I would fuck you, don't you, faggot?" Andre found this experience "very confusing" because he "didn't understand" what the guy was trying to do. Bullying with a sexual component was described by other gay men as well, and they frequently found these experiences painful and confusing. Still, gay men rarely feared that those forms of violence would lead to rape. Andre, rather than focusing on the possibility that this encounter could lead to sexual assault, described the difficulty of hearing "faggot" for the first time: "I didn't understand what the word meant; I had never heard it before. I went home and I told my Aunt, 'What's a faggot?' and she said, 'Why'd you ask that question?'... Instead of explaining to me what it meant or that it was a bad thing—well, from her tone I understood it was a bad thing—she said, 'That's a word we just don't use in this house.' It was never explained to me exactly what it meant and I guess I learned at school that a faggot was a homosexual and it was something bad." Gay men did not necessarily think that rape would occur even in the few cases when the potential for sexual assault was made explicit. Andre described one occasion when the classmate who bullied him was in the hallway with his friends, telling them, "That faggot wishes he got raped." This harassment, part of the homophobic bullying that Andre experienced at the time, was routine and frequent. As a result, Andre "felt intimidated" and "bad" about it, but he did not take this threat of sexual assault seriously: "I didn't think it was serious.... [It was] just the sort of thing he did." Threats of sexual assault against women were viewed much more seriously, as potentially dangerous attacks; gay men, in contrast, viewed such comments as attempts to feminize and intimidate them.

Gay men's violent experiences beyond adolescence also sometimes involved a sexual component, which did not produce fear in the same way as for many women. In the previous chapter, I described a form of violence confronting George, a forty-five-year-old white college instructor, who described two men approaching him in a dark parking lot after he had sex with another man; the men "got in [his] face," threatened, and pushed him. George described their motivations by saying, "The whole thing is just kinda stupid. It's easy to be like 'Oh, OK, you're tough, you're macho. Whatever, you can have that.'" I described George's reaction as reflecting white privilege, since he did not focus on the racial implications of the violence in the same way as gay men of color. His reaction, however, is also an example of male privilege, as the threat to his physical safety, which followed a sexual act, did not produce any concern that the men might rape him. It is difficult to imagine a woman downplaying the seriousness of two male strangers approaching her in a dark parking lot by suggesting that "the whole thing is just kinda stupid." In response to intimidation, the absence of fear on the part of gay men reflects male privilege given that they were not made to think about the possibility of rape to the same extent as women.

Of course, gay men experience fear regarding other types of violence. I found in another research project that lesbians, heterosexual women, and gay men do not differ in their overall fear of crime, but all of these groups experience more fear than heterosexual men (Meyer and Grollman 2013). That study did not distinguish among different forms of violence, and my results here indicate that lesbians are more likely than gay men to experience fear regarding sexual assault. Lesbian and transgender women in this study more frequently experienced sexual assault—four lesbians and four transgender women had been raped —while only one of the men in this study experienced this form of violence. Thus, lesbian and transgender women's greater fear of sexual assault, relative to gay men, may come in part from encountering rape more frequently, yet even lesbian and transgender women who had not experienced sexual assault described more fear than their male counterparts. Indeed, women do not need to have experiences of rape to fear its occurrence, as the threat of sexual assault is present in many contexts. Further, this threat limits women's freedom, including where and when they occupy public space (Collins 1998; Madriz 1997; Miller 2008).

Given these different perceptions of sexual assault, LGBT people viewed the seriousness of physical violence differently depending on their gender identity. Lesbian and transgender women often emphasized the severity of physical abuse, viewing this form of violence as potentially leading to sexual assault. Conversely, gay men more frequently constructed homophobic insults as severe, sometimes even downplaying the seriousness of physical abuse. Gay men were particularly likely to emphasize the severity of homophobic words such as "fag" or "faggot." Frankie, a forty-eight-year-old Puerto Rican gay man, highlighted the long-term effects of homophobic insults to illustrate the pain these words have caused him: "What can hurt as much as anything is the words. The hitting hurts, don't get me wrong, but scars can heal and the words will stay with you." Homophobic words in the United States carry different weight based on gender: words such as "dyke," while certainly insulting, are not used to injure women with the same frequency as words such as "faggot," which signify weakness—a failed performance of masculinity—on the part of men. Most gay male respondents constructed physical and verbal abuse as approximately equal in their severity, yet a few gay men did construct homophobic insults as more severe than a physical attack. Gideon, a twenty-five-year-old Black gay man, downplayed the severity of physical violence in this way: "I can handle some crazy dude putting his hands on me. That's not a big deal to me. The constant comments is what gets [to] me. 'Faggot, faggot, faggot'—that's worse than someone putting their hands on me."

Lesbian respondents did not typically emphasize the severity of words such as "dyke" to the same extent that gay men constructed words such as "faggot" as severe. Instead, lesbian and transgender women more frequently described violent encounters as beginning with them "just being called names," and then escalating with the onset of physical abuse. In this regard, the comments of Carol, the thirty-nine-year-old transgender woman described at the beginning of this chapter, were characteristic: "Like first he was just calling me names, but then it got worse when he grabbed me. . . . People have called me names in the past. That I can get over. But putting your hands on me, that's a whole new thing. That's what I can't stand." Carol's experience described at the beginning of this chapter was a sexual assault in an elevator, yet her comments here about a man first "just calling [her] names" refers to another violent experience. This encounter involved a man approaching her on the street and making sexually harassing comments to her. Then, after questioning whether she was transgender, he began using dehumanizing language ("you're an it") and calling her sexist and homophobic insults (e.g., "bitch," "faggot"), eventually pulling her by the hair. Later during the interview, Carol noted that the man's use of physical violence made her feel as if sexual assault might be imminent: "Putting his hands on me, that made me feel very unsafe. Like he could have tried to rape me." This fear of sexual assault, which was not typically expressed by gay men, led many lesbian and transgender women to emphasize the severity of physical violence. Physical and sexual assault, of course, are not necessarily the same, and lesbian and transgender women often differentiated between them. Still, female respondents frequently viewed these forms of violence as related, constructing sexual assault as more severe than verbal abuse and perceiving physical violence as indicating the possible onset of a sexual assault.

Race also played an important role in respondents' evaluations of physical and verbal violence. In particular, the desire on the part of lesbian women of color to live an autonomous life, free of harassment, frequently led them to condemn physical attacks more harshly than verbal abuse. For instance, Aisha, a fifty-three-year old Black lesbian, described a man on the subway who stepped on her foot after seeing public displays of affection between Aisha and her girlfriend. Comparing physical and verbal violence, Aisha minimized the effects of the latter: "Verbal's not as bad because I can go about my life. When someone says something to me, I can go about my life." Black lesbians regularly underscored the importance of their autonomy and independence, constructing physical violence as a direct attack on their ability to be self-sufficient. As I asked Aisha to elaborate on her perception of physical and verbal abuse, she characterized the difference in this way: "A man says something to me, that gets under my skin, [but] touching me, that's something different... Touching me is gettin' in my space. You're telling me not to be who I am. You're telling me that I should change—change to who you want me to." For Black lesbian respondents, this understanding of physical violence as more severe than verbal abuse seemed to reflect what race, class, and gender theorists have noted about the need for marginalized groups to create a safe space for themselves (Collins 2000). Lesbian and transgender women of color, marginalized from both white LGBT communities and heterosexual communities of color, in addition to the more normative white, heterosexual institutions in society at large, were particularly likely to emphasize this need for a safe space and to highlight how physical violence violated their right to self-determination.

Although lesbian and transgender women did not emphasize the severity of homophobic insults as frequently as gay men, female respondents did sometimes construct verbal threats as severe, particularly when these statements implied that physical or sexual violence might be forthcoming. Jasmine, a forty-four-year-old Black lesbian, described an experience that also occurred in an elevator: a man from her apartment building said that she "needed to be taught a lesson like a good dyke" before touching her face. She perceived the man's actions as a threat to her physical safety, as a suggestion that he could sexually assault her. Later during the interview, she argued that physical violence was worse than verbal abuse, but then immediately said, as if recalling the violent incident in the elevator, "That's only if [the verbal] doesn't intimidate me." I asked her how it might intimidate her: "Like is he going to tell me something that threatens me as a woman. Tell me what he's gonna do." Confronting the possibility of sexual assault, lesbian respondents occasionally emphasized the severity of verbal threats, noting how these statements can invoke sexualized violence.

Only one of the gay men in this study—Andre—described an experience of sexual assault after the age of eighteen; many of the gay men experienced sexual abuse when they were teenagers or younger, but only Andre experienced rape when he was considered a legal adult. Andre's experience of sexual assault occurred at the hands of a white male police officer. The violence took place at a police station, on a day when Andre was being released from a county jail. Andre, twenty-two at the time, spent the night in jail for injuring another man in a group home. Upon being released from jail, Andre went to pick up his belongings; as he waited in line, an officer accused him of spitting on the floor. Andre could not remember if he had spat—his tone indicated to me that he thought he probably had—but he said that even if he had done this act, he "spit on the floor, not on [anyone]." Andre was then taken by two police officers to a holding area, which was in a caged area in the back of the jail.

After about ten minutes, one of the officers came out and accused Andre of trying to escape from the caged area. Andre said that "it made no sense" because it would have been "impossible to get out." The officer continued to accuse him of trying to escape, saying "we have it on tape." Andre then said, "I don't think I need to get arrested or be in any trouble over some bullshit." The officer responded by harshly asking, "What?"—apparently upset that Andre had called this incident "bullshit"—and grabbed him by the wrist. Andre clutched the fence to prevent the cop from "bending [him] up," but then another officer came to the area and "put [Andre] in a choke hold," as he screamed, "Get the fuck off of me! What are you doing?" He then began to gag as he could not breathe, and the officer started to "squeeze tighter," making Andre "get faint a little bit." As Andre recalled, the first officer was white and the second was Black. These officers then took Andre with his hands handcuffed behind his back to an interrogation room, where a third officer questioned him on what had happened and began to search through his possessions.

Andre thought that this third officer, a white man, was of higher rank than the two previous officers because of how deferential the first officers were toward him. Among his belongings, Andre had a tape recorder that he was using for school, which the third officer questioned Andre about. Not believing it was for school, the officer held the recorder up, smashed it, and said, "What are you, some kind of pervert?" The officer continued to ask Andre pointed questions about his sexuality, asking if he "liked to suck dick." At first, Andre said, "You don't have any right to ask me that," but then said that he was "gay and proud of it." At this point, the officer began to insult Andre's sexuality more directly, referring to him as "a faggot" who "likes to suck dick" and "will get AIDS." In response, Andre said that he "just sat there" and "said 'OK.'" The officer continued to badger Andre, asking, "You like to suck dick, nigger?" This question prompted Andre to respond, "Suck *my* dick." The officer then told Andre, "you shouldn't have said that," and that he needed to "learn how to keep his mouth shut." Shortly thereafter, the two previous officers came back into the room, grabbed Andre and slammed his face down onto the table. The head officer then took a nightstick and rammed it into Andre's scrotum, attempting to sodomize him with it. Andre thought that the officer meant to force the nightstick into his anus, but he missed, hitting Andre's scrotum instead. The officers kept Andre in a holding cell for several more hours, but released him later that day.

While homophobia clearly played an important role in this situation, Andre's experience reveals the complexity of many LGBT people's violent experiences. Many queer people of color, particularly Black gay men and Black transgender people, described violence from the police; all of the LGBT people in this study who had experienced physical violence from the police were either Black or Latino. Thus, none of the white respondents described police brutality. Moreover, five of the seven Black gay men and all but one of the Black transgender people described police violence. While LGBT people's violent experiences were typically intraracial—the perpetrator and victim were the same race—police brutality was more frequently interracial: in two-thirds of the cases where respondents identified the police officer's race, the violence involved a white male police officer perpetrating violence against a Black or Latino LGBT person. Even though law-enforcement-related violence is often associated with victims who are Black heterosexual men, data from other studies, while limited, suggest that police brutality against LGBT people of color is also a widespread problem (Mogul, Ritchie, and Whitlock 2011; Moran and Sharpe 2004).

Of course, police violence against Black heterosexual men is a significant social problem; my hope here is not to suggest that it should be ignored. Instead, attention must also be paid to LGBT people of color's experiences of police brutality, as they are likely to encounter violence in some different ways from their heterosexual counterparts. White lesbians and white gay men did not describe experiences of police brutality, indicating that these forms of violence are frequently structured by racism. At the same time, the insults directed against multiple aspects of Andre's identity—exemplified by the officer's question, "You like to suck dick, nigger?"—reveal how violence against LGBT people of color often cannot be classified as entirely racist or exclusively homophobic. We do not know if a Black heterosexual man would have been similarly sodomized—Andre thought not—but the officers' continuous verbal attacks directed against his gay identity surely affected Andre differently than they would have affected a Black heterosexual man. Still, as his experience remains undoubtedly tied to his race, class, and gender identity, homophobia only explains part of the incident.

In a similar way that police violence has been disassociated from LGBT people, homelessness has not been viewed as a traditional LGBT-rights issue. Significant evidence shows that LGBT people, particularly low-income queer youth, are more likely to be homeless than the general population: in New York City, from 30 to 40 percent of homeless people identify as LGBT, percentages that far outnumber the overall percentage of LGBT people in the city (Gibson 2011). Thus, even though homelessness is likely associated with heterosexuality in the mind of many Americans, LGBT people are more likely than their heterosexual counterparts to be homeless (Van Leeuwen et al. 2006; Whitebeck et al. 2004). These differences are the product of LGBT people being kicked out of their homes for identifying as queer, and, when kicked out, having a difficult time finding supportive housing and work environments.

Rates of homelessness obviously differ to a significant extent among LGBT people, with those born into low-income homes being substantially more likely to be homeless than other LGBT people (Cochran et al 2002; De Rosa et al. 1999; Gibson 2011). Other evidence suggests that transgender people are significantly more likely than LGB people to be homeless, in large part because of unsupportive family environments and discrimination facing transgender people in the labor market (Grant et al. 2011; Mottet and Ohle 2006; Spade 2011). Low-income queer people of color are also more likely to become homeless than their white counterparts because of racial discrimination in housing and employment, making it more difficult for them to find steady income and affordable housing (Gibson 2011; Spade 2011). Despite this evidence that LGBT people are disproportionately likely to be homeless—especially the most marginalized queer people—homelessness and LGBT rights have frequently been framed as separate issues. Homeless people have been described as if they are primarily heterosexual, and LGBT people have been framed as if they are rarely homeless.

For example, I once attended a forty-five-minute talk by a well-known academic who was studying homelessness in San Francisco, in which sexuality, gender identity, and LGBT people were not mentioned once. Homelessness also rarely appears in academic work on anti-queer violence.[4] In contrast, low-income LGBT people's experiences reveal that economic marginalization makes possible forms of anti-queer violence, as they are exposed to hardships that their middle-class counterparts are not.

THE ROLE OF MISOGYNY AND HOMOPHOBIA IN LESBIANS' VIOLENT EXPERIENCES

Just as homelessness and police violence have been written out of many narratives of anti-queer violence, the role of sexism and misogyny has frequently been ignored (Perry 2001; von Schulthess 1992). Nevertheless, misogyny shaped much of the violence confronting lesbians. Diamond, a fifty-one-year-old Black lesbian, described two violent misogynistic incidents. The first occurred when she engaged in public displays of affection with her girlfriend, Jane, a forty-four-year-old Black bisexual woman. At the time, Diamond was unemployed and spent a lot of time at her girlfriend's apartment, where she was "practically living." On one occasion, they had gone out to eat at a local restaurant. On the way back to their apartment building, they held hands, and then made out on the steps in front of the building. As they were kissing, a man came next to them, and asked Jane, "What's [Diamond] got?" The women ignored the man's question, but he continued with his line of inquiry, asking Jane, "What could she do that I can't do?" Diamond then motioned to Jane, saying "Let's go," indicating that they should go inside. The man then said, "Damn, that vibrator must be working," and grabbed Diamond's arm. Diamond said that she "completely flipped out," yelling at him, "Keep your fucking hands off of me!" The man then pushed her and called her a "stupid bitch." As a result, Diamond ran inside, trying to escape the situation as fast as she could.

Descriptions of anti-queer violence have often focused on kissing, yet most LGBT people described experiences of making out that preceded violence (Haritaworn 2010). This difference is important, since "the gay kiss" narrative can be used to privilege normative practices of homosexuality—such as a kiss on the lips between same-sex partners—and marginalize less normative, more in-your-face, practices such as making out in public. While these less normative practices precede violence more frequently, descriptions of homophobic violence have usually focused on the normative behavior (Haritaworn 2010). The problem with focusing on "the gay kiss" is that these narratives reinforce ideas that same-sex partners making out in public is wrong—somehow "deserving" of violence—while more normative practices such as kissing briefly or holding hands deserve protection.

Although representations of anti-queer violence have focused on normative practices of homosexuality, an equally pressing problem is the degree to which sexism has been overlooked, particularly with forms of antilesbian violence. Similar to Diamond, many of the lesbians in this study described experiences where the perpetrator used misogynistic language: ten of the fifteen lesbians described being called a "bitch" during an experience of physical violence. These misogynistic insults were often paired with antilesbian comments, but sometimes they were not. Indeed, more of the lesbians in this study described situations in which they were called "bitch" than encounters in which they were called a homophobic slur such as "dyke," as seven lesbian respondents were called the latter. Diamond's other violent experience, a sexual assault, involved many misogynistic insults. Diamond described herself as "100 percent gay," but said that she once would have identified as bisexual, as she had dated men in the past. One of the men she had dated sexually assaulted her on their third date, when she was twenty-two. The assault occurred in his car, after they had gone to a movie. They kissed for a moment, but when he began to feel her breast, she told him, "no," and tried to remove his hand. She said that he "didn't take no for an answer" and "just continued to do what he [wanted to do]." She tried to get out of the car, but he hit her and said, "stay still bitch," as he continued to assault her. He raped her with his hands alternately around her throat and wrists. Subsequently, Diamond heard rumors from her friends that the rapist was telling others that she was a lesbian and that they broke up because she would not have sex with him. She thought these rumors were meant to make her more fearful of telling others about the rape, shifting the blame onto her and making it seem, if she did tell others, that her accusations were mere revenge, bitterness for being "outed" as a lesbian.

The absence of misogyny from analyses of antilesbian violence seems absurd when many forms are so clearly woman-hating. Exclusive emphasis on homophobia inevitably ignores the role of misogyny, yet in response to the privileging of sexuality, some feminist scholars have gone too far in the other direction, effectively downplaying the role of homophobia and heteronormativity. An early and influential study of antilesbian hate crime conceptualized "lesbianism as an extension of gender and conceptualize[d] anti-lesbian violence as an extension of misogynistic violence" (von Schulthess 1992, 71).[5] These attempts to privilege gender over sexuality provide for an inaccurate understanding of antilesbian violence, which is typically rooted in both gender and sexuality norms. Von Schulthess (1992, 71) has suggested that lesbians' violent experiences should be categorized "along a continuum ranging from exclusively antiwoman at one end to exclusively anti-lesbian at the other." Determining whether an experience is "antiwoman" or "antilesbian" assumes that misogyny and homophobia can be separated from one another. Obviously, forms of antilesbian violence will differ in the degree to which they relate to misogyny or homophobia; one form may occur largely because of homophobia, while another may extend primarily from sexism. Diamond's experience of rape might be characterized as largely misogynistic, while her experience with her girlfriend could be viewed as having more to do with homophobia. Still, making these determinations rarely aids in our understanding of LGBT people's violent experiences. It is often difficult, if not impossible, to determine whether an experience is primarily sexist or homophobic when it is clearly both; lesbians themselves often had no idea whether one of their violent experiences was primarily rooted in misogyny or homophobia because it seemed to have occurred for both of these reasons. Further, determining whether an incident is antilesbian or antiwoman keeps attention away from more important questions, including how gender and sexuality overlap.

Accepting that lesbians' violent experiences are typically rooted in both gender and sexuality norms can potentially lead to a better understanding of their intersection. Homophobia frequently reinforces the subordination of women and femininity; Pharr (1998) has referred to homophobia as a "weapon of sexism." Gendered power relations also reproduce negative attitudes toward lesbians and gay men, as lesbians are denounced for finding sexual pleasure with other women and gay men are stigmatized for their association with femininity. At the same time, homophobia does not merely amplify sexist violence, but it makes certain forms of misogynistic violence possible; without homophobia, some forms of violence against women would not occur. Take the experiences of Latoya, a fifty-year-old Black lesbian, who described a violent encounter in which a man approached her on the street, told her that she was "beautiful," and then asked for her phone number. She repeatedly expressed disinterest, indicating that she was in a hurry. After several minutes, she told him, "Listen, I'm going to pick up my girlfriend from work, I really don't have time." Confused, he then asked if she was a lesbian, which she confirmed. His demeanor suddenly changed as he began insulting her, screaming "you pussy-eating bitch" and "you nasty, disgusting bitch." Fearing for her safety, Latoya ran away from him. He eventually caught up with her, grabbing her by the hair and pulling her to the ground. As she screamed for help, another man intervened, which allowed her to run away.

Scholars focusing on homophobia would likely highlight how the physical violence began after Latoya revealed her lesbian identity. This sudden shift in the encounter indicates that Latoya's declaration of her homosexuality led him to become violent, most likely because of his negative attitudes toward lesbians. Nevertheless, analyzing this experience solely through the lens of homophobia glosses over important aspects of what occurred. Latoya's gender identity determined how the incident developed, as the man's assumption that a woman would want to be approached on the street was the basis of the entire encounter. His repeated sexual advances indicate not only his assumption that she was heterosexual but also his assumption that a woman would be interested in this kind of overture, even when explaining that she was not. Thus, Latoya's experience cannot be divorced from either her gender or her sexuality, as both of these aspects of her identity played an important role in what she faced.

Unlike the gay men in this study, Latoya expressed fear that this incident would lead to a sexual assault. When I asked if it hurt when the man grabbed her hair, she responded, "Yes, it hurt!," but then added shortly thereafter that she just wanted to make sure "it didn't get worse." Latoya had experienced an incident of date rape when she was eighteen, which she said she did not want to discuss during our interview because it "brought back too many bad memories." This incident of street violence invoked memories of the date rape, making her fearful that she might be sexually assaulted again. She declared that she "didn't care what [he] was calling me," but thought that the physical violence made sexual assault possible, bringing back "all sorts of memories" and making her realize that she "just had to get the hell out of there." Gay men who have experienced rape are also likely to express fear over it occurring again, yet women face the threat of sexual assault to a greater extent, as misogynistic violence frequently involves a sexual component, perpetrated against the woman's will.

TRANSGENDER WOMEN'S EXPERIENCES OF VICTIM BLAMING AND SEXUAL ASSAULT

Transgender women, while similar to lesbians in expressing fear that physical violence might lead to sexual assault, confronted some forms of abuse unique to their own social position. These challenges were most apparent as transgender people faced ideas of themselves as objects—notions that cisgender lesbian, gay, and bisexual people do not confront. Transgender people's experiences also differed from those of LGB people with regard to negative reactions from service providers, particularly the police. Eva, a forty-six-year-old Black transgender woman, described a sexual assault that occurred in a back alley near a church, where a man pushed her to the ground and she twisted her foot. She described the sudden attack in this way:

> I screamed very loudly because I've got really tender ankles. . . . And one of the workers heard the scream, and it must have sounded very feminine because I head someone scream, "Someone's beating up on a lady," and about five of the biggest, burliest guys with hard hats and with work belts came screaming into the alley. There was a gate up and whoever the person was ran out the other end. . . . [The man] hadn't got to below the waist, but [he] had torn my bra and my blouse up and copped a feel. It happened so quick, it was just so shocking and so invasive that I didn't respond. I just didn't know what to do. I just lay back thinking the guy was going to stab me or shoot me or something. I thought I was dying.

Eva described the men who helped her as the sort of guys "you'd think would be macho types," but she said that they were "completely nice" in helping her. Although she described medical personnel who came to the scene as very nice and helpful, she said that the cops "refused to take [her] seriously," telling her that she "couldn't be raped" because she "wasn't a real woman."

Transgender respondents described many incidents of secondary victimization—unsupportive acts that occur after the initial violent experience that can be as traumatic as the physical attack (Campbell and Raja 1999). Against transgender people, these acts often had a dehumanizing quality, related to standards of "realness" and "authenticity." The suggestion that Eva "couldn't be raped" reveals how connecting sexual assault with the bodies of cisgender women can potentially lead to the problematic conclusion that men and transgender women cannot be raped. We do not know whether the police officer believed that men "couldn't be raped," or if this statement was simply a reflection of his prejudice toward transgender people. Regardless of his motivations, notions of "realness" were deeply implicated in many of the negative reactions that transgender people confronted, and it remains important to remember that cisgender LGB people do not face these ideas. Indeed, transgender respondents described occasions in which service providers who were supposed to provide support had referred to them as an "it" or a "thing."

In Eva's experience with the police, she said that one of the officers used the words "he" and "she" interchangeably as a way of mocking and undermining her identity: "[The police officer] went back and forth. . . . Once I was a 'she,' then he would be like, 'he.' Like I can't make up my mind." While lesbians and gay men, and especially bisexual people, may confront ideas of themselves as "confused," transgender respondents described these reactions to an even greater extent. As the mainstream gay rights movement has advocated for notions of sexual orientation as fixed and biological, ideas that lesbians and gay men "choose" their homosexuality are likely becoming increasingly outdated (Bernstein 1997; Green 2007; Walters 2014). Lesbians confronted suggestions that they had "chosen" their sexual identity more frequently than gay men. Still, the mainstream gay rights movement has overlooked many transgender people's concerns, challenging notions that sexual orientation is something one "chooses"—a strategy that many queer theorists have argued against—while not disputing that transgender people are somehow "confused" about their identity (Seidman 2002; Walters 2014; Warner 1999). In contrast, transgender respondents argued that they were quite certain of their gender identity—that they were not confused at all. Nevertheless, ideas of transgender people as confused remain pervasive, stemming from notions that one's gender identity should remain fixed throughout one's life. In this sense, transgender people challenge notions that one's sex characteristics determine one's gender, revealing the complexities in the relationship between sex and gender.

Eva's experience reflects mainstream representations of rape, in which a stranger suddenly and randomly attacks a woman. These common representations have problematically overemphasized "back alley," stranger-based assaults (Maier 2012; Mardorossian 2014). Unfortunately, these descriptions reinforce rape myths whereby sexual assault perpetrators are viewed as mentally disturbed individuals; considerable research suggests, in contrast, that rapists do not typically suffer from psychological disorders but are rather ordinary men (Scully 1994; Maier 2012). The myth of stranger rape also obscures the more common forms of violence that women confront, including sexual assault on a date. Built into these descriptions of stranger rape is the assumption that any reasonable person would agree that the assault was wrong or immoral. These types of violence, in which the victim has not "done anything wrong," are then either implicitly or explicitly contrasted with other types of violence, in which the victim "should have known better." These ideas not only refuse to acknowledge that all rape is wrong but also place the responsibility to end sexual assault on women rather than on men. As a result, the assumption that some rape victims "should have known better" justifies and normalizes much of the violence against women, establishing their behavior as somehow "deserving" of rape (Hlavka 2014; Mardorossian 2014).

In focusing on the conditions in which sexual assault occurs, scholarship can dispel notions that rape is most frequently perpetrated by strangers who suddenly and randomly attack victims in public. For instance, transgender respondents described experiences of date rape that contrast with stereotypical representations. Dominique, a twenty-three-year-old transgender woman, described two experiences of sexual assault, the first of which occurred when she met a man at a bar. On their first date, she had a few drinks with him and then went back to his apartment, where he started to kiss her. She felt that it was "fun" at first, but then he became "very aggressive" when he touched her breast and she told him, "No, I don't want to." He then pushed her down onto the bed, holding her arms, as he raped her. She characterized the assault as her "sleeping with [him] because I was afraid that if I didn't, he would beat me up or worse." Dominique feared that he might kill her if she resisted. Regrettably, these experiences are often viewed through the lens of personal responsibility, in which women are told to

avoid situations that potentially put them at risk of sexual assault. In analyzing this situation, many people in the United States would focus on Dominique's drinking rather than on his drinking, even though research shows
that men who are drunk are more likely to rape than men who are not
(Abbey et al. 2006). In these situations, the emphasis is placed on women
to prevent rape rather than on men to avoid raping. Conversely, if we start
from an understanding that rape is never acceptable, then the question
becomes less about what women can do to avoid it and more about what
can be done to prevent it from happening. This approach shifts the focus
from the actions of the woman experiencing the rape to the social conditions, including dominant constructions of masculinity, which encourage
violence against women.

In other cases, social structures that increase the likelihood of sexual
assault include economic conditions. Dominique had been a sex worker for
three years, starting when she was eighteen. She described the experience as
something she "did not regret," but felt that it was "sometimes dangerous."
On one occasion, a man approached her on the street and told her that he
would pay for oral sex. As Dominique was performing fellatio on the man,
he took out a gun, put it to her head, and said that he was going to "fuck"
her "like a faggot." Dominique said that she "asked him to put a condom
on because I got no shame." He did use a condom, but sexually assaulted
her with a gun pointed at her head. Dominique did not know whether the
gun was loaded, but said that she was "very, very afraid" that she might "not
make it out alive." After the assault, Dominique went back to the street
where she was previously and found a police car in the area. She told the
police officers what happened and said that they ignored it: "I told them
which way the [guy's] car went and [the officers] went the [opposite] way."

Taking seriously the experiences of transgender women involved in sex
work requires challenging notions that some women are more deserving
of protection from sexual assault than others. Demands that women must
be "protected" frequently imply that some women are worthy of this protection, while others are not. Transgender women involved in sex work are
likely to be disproportionately viewed as unworthy of protection, which
makes it necessary to challenge the separation of "worthy" and "unworthy"
victims of rape. Transgender sex workers described occasions in which the
police failed to take seriously their reports of sexual assault, believing that
the police viewed them as unworthy of police protection; as a result, sex

worker advocates have often called for decriminalizing sex work to decrease police surveillance and improve safety conditions (Mogul, Ritchie, and Whitlock 2011; Weitzer 2012). Of course, not all transgender people are sex workers: of the ten transgender people in this study, three did not have any experience with sex work and only two respondents were currently involved in this work. Several of the transgender people also described the pain it causes them when others assume they are sex workers. Thus, while sex work is an issue that disproportionately affects transgender women in comparison to the general population, it must not be generalized to all transgender people.

In contrast to transgender respondents, lesbians and gay men rarely described violence during involvement with sex work. At the same time, Dominique's experience reveals that transgender respondents confronted homophobic insults, rather than comments directly mentioning their transgender identity; the man called Dominique a "faggot," but did not refer to her as transgender. This trend reflects societal patterns in which transgenderism is more frequently collapsed into homosexuality than the other way around (Halberstam 2005). The media and the mainstream gay rights movement have also focused considerably more attention on homosexuality than transgenderism (Feinberg 1999; Namaste 2000). More emphasis on transgender people's violent experiences would reveal how their particular needs and concerns cannot be collapsed with those of LGB people. Since considerable evidence suggests that transgender people have a more difficult time finding employment than lesbians and gay men, and therefore engage in sex work to support themselves, the context of anti-transgender violence often differs from homophobic abuse (Grant et al. 2011; Spade 2011). Still, even though transgender people's violent experiences must be viewed as different from those of lesbians and gay men, transgender people identify as both heterosexual and homosexual. Gender identity—whether one is transgender or cisgender—is distinct from sexual orientation. Thus, transgender women may identify as lesbian or heterosexual, just as transgender men may identify as gay or straight.

Although arguments that one group has "worse" experiences than another are generally problematic, transgender respondents were more likely than lesbians and gay men to describe multiple experiences of physical and sexual assault. Transgender respondents described the most experiences of abuse, with all but one of these respondents experiencing physical or sexual violence on multiple occasions; they also described some of the most shockingly brutal experiences. Data from advocacy groups reveal widespread discrimination facing transgender people: 90 percent have reported experiencing harassment, mistreatment, or discrimination in the workplace, while 41 percent have attempted suicide, 57 percent have experienced significant family rejection, and 19 percent have experienced homelessness, with 55 percent of those trying to access a homeless shelter being harassed by staff or residents (Grant et al. 2011). While I am not diminishing the prejudice confronting lesbians and gay men, survey results also generally show that transgender people report higher rates of violence and discrimination than their LGB counterparts, with particularly high rates among transgender women of color (Ahmed and Jindasurat 2014; Namaste 2000; Stotzer 2009). All of these trends make it even more troubling that media and scholarship have focused little attention on transgender people's violent experiences, suggesting that these forms of violence must be given more serious consideration and must be viewed as separate from antilesbian and antigay violence.

5 • RACE, GENDER, AND PERCEPTIONS OF VIOLENCE AS HOMOPHOBIC

One of the ways lesbians and gay men determined that violence was based on their sexuality was by examining what their perpetrators had said about gender. Dorothy, a forty-nine-year-old white lesbian, addressed this dynamic when arguing that violence directed against her gender identity was also rooted in homophobia. The violence occurred during the late 1980s in a suburban town of southern New Jersey, in a place where Dorothy said the presence of the Ku Klux Klan was well known. At the age of twenty-seven, she was attacked by three men on the street, one of whom punched her. Dorothy was walking down the street, when a man came from behind and grabbed her purse. At first, Dorothy held on to the purse, but when the man motioned as if he was going to hit her, she let go. The man then hit Dorothy on her arm, running off with her purse. Dorothy noticed that the man ran toward two other men, who were laughing. Dorothy thought she heard one of them call her a "bitch," and another one yelled that she had "no business being on the street." Describing the violence, she believed that her gender nonconformity marked her as visibly "out," as she was dressed "very aggressively—suit and tie." Dorothy, a thin woman with very short blonde hair, similar to a buzz cut, said that people typically read her as a lesbian; her hair was also short and blonde at the time of the attack. In this situation, although the men never mentioned homosexuality, she perceived the violence as homophobic: "I wasn't doing anything, but it was obvious that I was a lesbian. That's why they attacked me. They hated gay people."

Similar to Dorothy, most respondents saw a relationship between how they performed gender and how their sexuality was perceived, arguing that gender nonconformity signaled their queerness to others. When describing this relationship, LGBT people argued that appearing as gender nonconforming increased their chances of experiencing violence. This relationship was particularly true when they were young. Frankie, a forty-eight-year-old Latino gay man, described his "coming out" process as one in which he appropriated a feminine appearance, wearing eyeliner and occasionally coming to school in drag. As he explained, the amount of violence he experienced during this time increased: "When I came out completely—when it was obvious to a blind man—that's when I got more of the violence and the comments and stuff like that. . . . It intensified." Performing femininity resulted in more violence and harassment coming in his direction. This relationship undoubtedly encourages gender conformity, as many people remain aware on some level, even if they are not conscious of it, that violating gender norms could potentially lead to negative attention. Indeed, Frankie thought if he had performed gender in a more traditional way, he would not have experienced violence: "If they couldn't tell that you were gay, you won't experience violence; you might get away with being gay." Although Frankie's statement arguably oversimplifies— LGBT people may still experience violence when conforming to gender norms—his argument is nevertheless consistent with what other respondents described: anti-queer violence often occurs when LGBT people violate dominant gender norms.

Given the association of gender nonconformity with homosexuality, lesbians and gay men often perceived violence as related to their sexuality even when the perpetrator did not explicitly mention their sexual orientation. In such cases, they viewed violence directed against their gender identity as based on homophobia. Paul, a fifty-seven-year-old white gay man, perceived violence in which he was told "you're not a woman" as an attempt to punish him for publicly identifying as gay. The violence involved three men, one of whom Paul knew prior to the attack. This man and Paul had been in a fistfight previously, when the man was dating Paul's sister. On the previous occasion, Paul and his sister argued with the man when learning that he had cheated on her. During the argument, Paul called the man a "liar," which prompted him to say, "You stay out of it, faggot." The two men then fought physically. About a year later, Paul ran into this man on the street with two of his friends. His sister's ex-boyfriend said to his two friends, "that's him, that's him," and Paul characterized the men as making "a lot of little comments" to themselves. One of the friends then came over to Paul and said that he "walks like a girl." Paul laughed and responded, "I noticed the same thing about you," and then the man pushed Paul, telling him, "You're not a woman." When I asked Paul why he thought the man had approached him, he said that the man "wanted to impress his friend . . . [but I also] think it happened because I'm gay. They didn't like that I'm feminine because it showed that I'm gay." Paul's homosexuality was not mentioned, but the reference to his feminine gender performance led him to believe that the violence was based on his sexuality.

Women made similar judgments: Lisa, a thirty-six-year-old Latina heterosexual woman, perceived violence directed against her gender identity, which she had experienced from her mother, as related to homophobia. Throughout her adolescence, Lisa wore combat boots and had purple-colored hair. During this time, she was physically beaten by her mother. When beating Lisa, her mother exclaimed, "You're a fucking girl, what the fuck is wrong with you?" Lisa said that the beatings were "the worst" during her early adolescence, around the age of thirteen or fourteen, before she "could fight back," yet her gender performance continued to be a source of conflict with her mother until she moved out of the house to attend college. Although her mother never mentioned homosexuality during the beatings, Lisa understood the violence as an attempt to control her sexuality as well as her gender performance: "She never said, 'Don't be a lesbian,' but [she said] 'Don't you dare look like that' . . . She wanted to make sure I didn't grow up [to be a lesbian]." Lisa thought that her mother's violent behavior was not only a way of insisting on gender conformity but also an attempt to prevent her daughter from identifying as a lesbian. In this regard, Lisa viewed violence directed against her gender performance as partially based on homophobia. Further, given that Lisa was heterosexual, her experience indicates that anti-queer violence is not only directed against people who identify as lesbian or gay. Instead, homophobic violence is frequently used to ensure that people conform to dominant gender norms—that men properly perform masculinity and women appropriately perform femininity.[1]

PERCEPTIONS OF RACE, GENDER, AND SEXUALITY

Although some respondents highlighted the importance of gender and sexuality in structuring their violent experiences, others argued that anti-queer violence could not be reduced to these two aspects of their identity. These arguments were especially common among LGBT people of color. Black and Latino LGBT people highlighted the role of racism, as well as homophobia and sexism, in structuring their experiences. Kevin, a sixty-two-year-old Black gay man, maintained that his violent experiences could not be separated from his racial identity: "I've experienced violence because I'm Black *and* gay. When the police beat me up, they called me a fag. . . . I would be surprised if they had done the same thing to a white gay guy, though." Here, Kevin argued that violence directed against his sexual identity was also rooted in racism. He highlighted the significance of race in structuring forms of anti-queer violence and suggested that if he were white and queer, he might not experience homophobic violence to the same degree or in the same way.

Kevin's experience involved two white male police officers searching him for stolen merchandise because they had a report of someone who "matched his description" stealing something from the store. Kevin had not stolen anything from the store, but he had some crack cocaine on him at the time, which resulted in him being arrested. At the police station, Kevin described one of the police officers as "going completely nuts," calling him homophobic names, and slamming his head into a table. It is certainly possible that this officer would have reacted in a similar way to a white gay man; after all, the officer focused most explicitly on Kevin's homosexuality rather than his racial identity. Still, a white gay man most likely would not have been accused of shoplifting in the same way as Kevin. The suggestion that Kevin "matched [a] description" indicates that the police officers singled him out because of his race. If he was a white gay men, he likely never would have been profiled, taken to the police station or, consequently, experienced the violence.

In this sense, Kevin's interpretation of the officers' behavior seems accurate, as he would have been "surprised if they had done the same thing to a white gay guy." Thus, although LGBT people across racial lines experience forms of anti-queer violence, Black LGBT people face forms of police violence that white LGBT people would be at relatively little risk of confronting. Indeed, racism makes possible certain forms of anti-queer violence. Among the respondents in this study, fifteen of twenty-one Black LGBT people and five of eight Latino respondents described negative experiences with the police, while only four of the sixteen white LGBT people did. Although these results may not reflect larger societal patterns, macrolevel data also indicate that LGBT people of color face police brutality more than their white counterparts (Comstock 1991; Dunbar 2006; Mogul, Ritchie, and Whitlock 2011).

Of course, gender is also important here, given that Black men generally experience higher rates of police violence than other groups (Alexander 2010; Moran 2000). Black gay men and Black transgender women in this study described more experiences of police violence than Black lesbians, especially with regard to physical violence from the police. Undoubtedly, Black lesbians, as well as white gay men, experience police brutality, but this social problem likely confronts Black gay men with greater frequency. At the same time, Black transgender women also experience police brutality at high rates (Grant et al. 2011; Mottet and Ohle 2006; Namaste 2006); all but one of the Black transgender women in this study described violence from the police.

Several transgender women thought that police officers did not view them as "real" women, worthy of respect. Dominique, a twenty-three-year-old Black transgender woman, referred to this idea throughout the interview: "If they think I'm a [cisgender] woman, they'll be like, 'OK, she's just trying to make a living.' . . . It changes to them being very nasty if they think I'm trans because then suddenly I'm a man that they don't think of as ladylike. And that's not so bad because they're being nasty to [someone] they see as a guy." Gender norms that encourage men to perform chivalrous, respectable behavior toward cisgender women in public, while masking the violence that cisgender women confront in private, do not operate in the same way for many transgender women; as a result, police officers likely perpetrate physical violence more frequently against transgender women than their cisgender counterparts (Grant et al. 2011; Stotzer 2009). Transgender women also confronted higher rates of police violence than lesbian and bisexual women because the former were more likely to be involved in sex work. Nevertheless, Dominique said that when she was perceived as a cisgender sex worker she was more likely to be "treated with respect" by police officers than when she was perceived as transgender.

If many forms of police brutality are shaped by racism and prejudice against transgender people, then homophobia provides an incomplete picture of these experiences. Just as forms of sexual assault against lesbian and transgender women are clearly shaped by misogyny, police brutality against LGBT people often cannot be fully understood through the lens of homophobia. Indeed, LGBT people of color frequently viewed their experiences as shaped by racism even when their race was not explicitly addressed. Kevin, for example, argued that racism played a role in the police violence, even though the officer did not directly mention his racial identity.

Many lesbian and gay men of color also determined that violence directed against their racial identities was at least partially rooted in homophobia. Andre, a twenty-four-year-old Black gay man, perceived racist police violence, in which an officer called him the n-word, as directed not only against his racial identity but also against his sexuality. While racism clearly played a significant role in the violence, Andre thought that he would not have been victimized had he been heterosexual: "[The police officer] would not have done that if I was straight. He called me that because I'm a *gay* Black man." Andre believed that the violence either would not have occurred or would not have occurred in the same way had he been a Black heterosexual person. We do not know, of course, whether Andre's perception is accurate, but some forms of racist violence are caused by homophobia. Although the police officer perpetrating the violence was white, another officer, who knew of the violence and aided in its occurrence, was Black. This officer may have also encouraged violence against Black heterosexual men, but it is possible that homophobia largely fueled his actions toward Andre. The relative degree to which racism and homophobia shaped Andre's experience is impossible to know, yet these findings reveal that Black gay men often view their violent experiences as related to their race and their sexuality. Andre and Kevin argued that both racism and homophobia shaped their experiences of police brutality.

Focusing on multiple dimensions of inequality, rather than only one, more accurately captures many LGBT people's violent experiences. Queer people of color usually thought that violence was based on more than one aspect of their identity. For lesbians of color, this perception involved focusing on the role of misogyny, among other dimensions of inequality. Page, a forty-five-year-old Latina lesbian, argued that her experiences cannot be reduced to any one factor: "It's much more complicated politically than 'I'm a woman so this happened.' Things are just not necessarily about any one category, misogyny or homophobia or whatever." In assessing the cause of their violent experiences, lesbians of color emphasized more than homophobia. At the same time, their experiences cannot be explained entirely by gender. Thus, examining Black and Latina lesbians' violent experiences through the lens of only one form of inequality—whether that form is race, gender, or sexuality—inevitably leaves out much of what is happening.

EXPRESSING UNCERTAINTY: DIFFERENCES ALONG RACIAL LINES

Although in many situations lesbians and gay men determined that violence was at least partially rooted in homophobia, in other contexts LGBT people found it impossible to determine whether violence was based on their sexuality or gender identity. Indeed, LGBT people frequently responded to questions concerning why they thought the violence had occurred with phrases such as "I don't know" or "I'm not sure." In these situations, they expressed uncertainty as to whether violence was based on their sexuality or gender identity. LGBT people usually responded with a sense of uncertainty for two reasons: (1) perpetrators had insulted many aspects of the victim's identity; or (2) the violence had occurred in situations in which the perpetrator said very little about the victim's sexuality or gender identity. These two situations are, in some sense, opposites. The latter occurred when perpetrators said very little; the former occurred when they said a lot. In both of these situations, respondents struggled to make sense of their violent experiences because they could not be certain of the cause. When perpetrators insulted many aspects of the respondent's identity, LGBT people thought that the violence may have been based on something other than their sexuality or gender identity. Similarly, when perpetrators did not mention the respondent's homosexuality or transgenderism, LGBT people frequently expressed uncertainty as to the cause of the violence.

The degree to which respondents expressed uncertainty differed along racial lines, with queer people of color being more likely than white gay men to express uncertainty. This difference occurred because of the reasons outlined above: LGBT people of color often faced situations in which many aspects of their identity had been attacked and they frequently encountered situations in which perpetrators did not mention homosexuality or transgenderism. For these reasons, queer people of color found it more difficult than white gay men to determine whether violence was based on their sexuality or gender identity.

When LGBT people of color experienced violence in which perpetrators did not mention homosexuality or transgenderism, the violence was usually intraracial—the victim and the perpetrator were the same race. Black LGBT people described some forms of violence in which their sexuality or gender identity was not mentioned; in these situations, the violence was generally perpetrated by a Black heterosexual person. Conversely, when queer people of color felt as if many aspects of their identity had been attacked, the violence was typically interracial. In this sense, when Black LGBT people experienced violence in which multiple aspects of their identity had been attacked, a white heterosexual person usually perpetrated the violence. Thus, patterns of activity reveal that these two situations differed regarding the racial makeup of the victim and the perpetrator.

Queer people of color had the most difficulty determining whether violence was based on their sexuality, their gender identity, or their race when their perpetrators were white. In such situations, they often felt as if multiple aspects of their identity had been attacked. Dominique, a twenty-three-year-old Black transgender woman, described this dynamic rather succinctly: "When I'm called a fag or a freak by a white person, I have a hard time telling if they hate me because I'm trans or because I'm Black." White perpetrators often mixed racist insults with homophobic or antitransgender ones. This blurring of racist and homophobic language then made it difficult for queer people of color to determine whether violence was based on their sexuality or gender identity. In these situations, they could not be certain whether violence was rooted in homophobia because racism may have played an equal or even more significant role. Gideon, a twenty-five-year-old Black gay man, confronted a wide range of racist and homophobic language when he was attacked in a group home as a teenager: "They called me so many names that I'm not even sure if it happened because of my sexuality. It could have been because I was Black or how I behaved or any number of things. There's just no way of saying." Confronting homophobic and racist insults made it difficult for Gideon to determine the reasons he had experienced violence. He felt as if many aspects of his identity had been attacked, which then made any single explanation seem simplistic.

Lesbians of color made similar arguments as they encountered violence that was simultaneously racist, sexist, and homophobic. Tina, a twenty-one-year-old Latina lesbian, described an incident in which a white man approached her on the subway to ask her out on a date. When she told him she was not interested, he asked "Why not?," to which she responded, "Because I don't date white men." She said that he then "made a face" and went back to talking with his two friends. At this point, the men were laughing and making it seem as if they were going to engage in a prank. Tina looked the other way, and when she turned around, one of the guy's friends was there. He began to move his crotch closer toward her. She told him to "back off" and saw another one of the men motioning as if he was performing oral sex on a woman, moving his lips between his fingers. The man who was closest to her said that she thought she was "hot shit" because she was "Little Miss Latin," but she was really only a "fat bitch." When the subway stopped at the next station, Tina got off and moved to the next subway car. The men then followed her, coming through the subway doors. Tina said they did not do anything else, but she felt as if they were stalking her. In analyzing the situation, she emphasized how it was difficult to determine whether the harassment had to do with homophobia: "Did it occur because I'm a lesbian? Who knows. They called me so many names. . . . So, it's really hard to tell [why it happened]. I wonder if they weren't just calling me any name they thought might hurt me."

Tina's experience illustrates the importance of racism and misogyny in shaping violence against Latina lesbians. Her gender was mentioned repeatedly, as she was referred to as a "fat bitch" who thought she was "hot shit." Similar to many lesbians in this study, Tina experienced a man approaching her in a public space, where he sexualized the encounter against her will. Tina's ethnicity was also drawn attention to, with the man referring to her as "Little Miss Latin." Further, she struggled with what she had said to the man, as she thought that it was a mistake for her to have said that she "doesn't date white men"; she thought this comment may have been part of what infuriated him. Tina identified as a lesbian and said that she does not date men regardless of their race. At the time of the incident, however, she chose to say that she does not date "white men" to make her rejecting the man seem less personal, and therefore less harsh. Conversely, in looking back on the incident now, Tina believed that saying she "doesn't date white men" may have infuriated him in such a way that saying she "doesn't date men" would not have. This man may have responded violently to being rejected regardless of what Tina had said; individuals committing abuse, after all, may justify their behavior by pointing to just about any reason. Thus, despite Tina second-guessing herself, blame for the incident must be placed on his shoulders, not hers.

At the same time, Tina's experience, as well as those of other lesbians of color, reveals the simplicity of examining forms of anti-queer violence solely through the lens of homophobia. When Tina said that she "doesn't date white men," this statement was a way of not publicly identifying as a lesbian; if she had said that she "doesn't date men," then she would have "outed" herself. In this situation, Tina's "closeting" herself did not protect her from violence. In fact, her statement that she "doesn't date white men," which conceals her lesbianism but emphasizes her race and ethnicity, may have been what angered the man. In contrast to traditional understandings of homophobic violence, Tina "outing" herself may have been less likely to result in violence than saying that she doesn't date white men. "Staying in the closet" did not keep the man from perpetrating violence because he had prejudices other than homophobia, including racism and misogyny. Feeling attacked in multiple ways, Black and Latina lesbians found it difficult to determine whether violence was based on their sexuality because racism and misogyny had also clearly played a role.

While queer people of color sometimes expressed difficulty in determining whether interracial violence was based on their sexuality or gender identity, white gay men almost always argued that their violent experiences were rooted in homophobia. Responses such as "it happened because I'm gay" or "it happened because of my sexuality" were common among white gay men. Even when perpetrators mentioned race, these respondents determined that interracial violence was based on their sexuality. Greg, a forty-three-year-old white gay man, believed that two Latino men had harassed him because the men were homophobic. The violence occurred on the subway, when Greg accidentally stepped on a man's foot. After Greg apologized, one of the men turned to his friend and muttered what Greg thought he heard was "stupid faggot." Greg then asked the man, "What did you say?," to which the man declared, "You heard me." Greg responded, "No, I didn't." The man's friend then said, "he called you a fag," and both of the men laughed. In response, Greg called the men "idiots"; the first man responded by swinging his backpack, hitting Greg in the chest. The second man told Greg that he should "take that white shit somewhere else." This comment, referring to homosexuality as "white shit," is similar to what LGBT people of color described in their experiences of violence. Still, despite this similarity, Greg focused on the homophobic rather than the racial implications of the violence, describing his perpetrators' motivations in a rather matter-of-fact way: "Oh, I think it happened because I'm gay. What else could be the reason?"

In stark contrast to the uncertainty expressed by some queer people of color, white gay men almost always determined that violence was based on their sexuality. Greg's response was representative of how white gay men reacted, even though he more explicitly dismissed the possibility that factors other than homophobia had played a role. White gay men's emphasis on homophobia was usually more restrained. Jacob, a forty-year-old white gay man, described an incident where he was shoved to the ground for making out with his boyfriend on the streets of Manhattan. The violence occurred inside of a subway station, several minutes after the couple had been kissing, when Jacob was attempting to buy a subway pass. As he stood at the ticket machine, Jacob was hit on his side with an object; he did not know what the object was, but he felt a sharp pain in his bicep. The man then pushed Jacob to the ground as he was grabbing his arm in pain. Jacob did not see the stranger nor did he hear anything that was said. He described the object he had been hit with as "something hard." Similar to the other white gay men in this study, Jacob perceived the violence as homophobic. When I asked him to describe why he thought the violence had occurred, he shrugged, looked at me as if I had not been listening to him, and said, as if he was making a very obvious point, "Because I'm gay."

This difference between how queer people of color and white gay men responded to violence can be explained largely by white privilege (McIntosh 2004). White gay men could perceive their violent experiences as rooted entirely in homophobia because social norms encourage them to overlook their racial identity. In this sense, white gay men do not have to think about the role of race and they can view their sexuality as the most salient factor in structuring their violent experiences. Thus, being able to view forms of anti-queer violence as primarily rooted in homophobia is part of the privilege that comes with being a white gay man in comparison to other LGBT people. In contrast, Black and Latino LGBT people more frequently have to think about the role of race and ethnicity in structuring their experiences, leading them to view violence, particularly when perpetrated by a white man, as having as much to do with racism as with homophobia.

LGBT people of color were the most likely to express uncertainty in situations in which a white man perpetrated the violence, yet they sometimes expressed uncertainty when being attacked by a heterosexual person of the same race or ethnicity. In such situations, LGBT people of color usually expressed uncertainty because perpetrators had not explicitly addressed homosexuality or transgenderism. Frankie, a forty-eight-year-old Latino gay man, found it difficult to determine why three Latino men had mugged him at knifepoint: "I don't know. It could have been because I was gay or because they just needed money. . . . I really want to know why they chose me, but they didn't say anything. I really have no way of knowing." When perpetrators did not mention the victim's sexuality or gender identity, respondents had to speculate as to whether the violence was based on those aspects of their identity. In such situations, they often expressed uncertainty because they were forced to rely on contextual cues.[2] Frankie thought that his violent experience may have been rooted in homophobia because his perpetrators went out of their way to degrade him; they slapped him during the mugging and then spit on him after it. Nevertheless, because they did not mention homosexuality, he could only hypothesize that homophobia was one of many possible reasons for the attack.

Queer people of color were more likely than white gay men to describe violence in which their sexuality or gender identity was not explicitly addressed. Some gay and lesbian people of color focused on race when addressing why their perpetrators had not mentioned homosexuality. Cole, a thirty-three-year-old Black gay man, referred to race when explaining his reasons for believing that his perpetrators had not used homophobic insults. When I asked, "So, they didn't use any homophobic slurs?," Cole responded: "Slurs? Well, you see, in the Black community, it's a little different. They don't always say 'faggot.' They'll say 'too sweet motherfucker' or they'll just call you a sissy. . . . It's more about you being weak than being gay. . . . For them to call me a 'faggot' would have meant that homosexuality exists, so they'd rather just beat me and not say anything." Many of the Black gay men in this study described being called homophobic words such as "faggot," yet they were also more likely than white LGBT people to make arguments similar to the one made by Cole. Here, the intersection of race, gender, and sexuality seems particularly stark, with Cole suggesting that Black gay men frequently encounter violence in which perpetrators focus on gender nonconformity rather than homosexuality. Transgender respondents also said that perpetrators had not directly addressed their transgender identity; most of these respondents were Black or Latino as well. Thus, LGBT people of color confront some forms of intraracial violence in which perpetrators do not mention homosexuality or transgenderism, leading queer people of color to express uncertainty as to the cause of their violent experiences.

DIFFERENCES BETWEEN LESBIANS OF COLOR AND GAY MEN OF COLOR

Black and Latina lesbians were more likely than their male counterparts to encounter violence in which perpetrators did not explicitly address homosexuality. Gay men of color described violence in which perpetrators used homophobic insults such as "homo" or "faggot," while lesbians of color more frequently described violent encounters in which perpetrators did not use explicitly homophobic words. In some of these situations, lesbians' perpetrators used misogynistic insults rather than homophobic ones. Jasmine, a forty-four-year-old Black lesbian, found it difficult to determine whether her experience of being spat on when holding hands with her girlfriend was based on her sexuality, since it also seemed to be rooted in sexism: "I don't know if it happened because I'm lesbian. . . . It could have happened just because I'm a woman, but it seems like it happened because I'm gay, too. I don't know why they chose me and not [my girlfriend], though." When perpetrators did not mention homosexuality, respondents examined the context to determine if their violent experiences were rooted in homophobia. Lesbians were more likely to encounter these situations; the experiences of Judy, a forty-three-year-old Latina lesbian, are also an example of this trend. Her experience involved a man attempting to rape her, in which he called her a "bitch" and a "whore." The assault did not involve explicitly homophobic insults—he did not refer to her as a "dyke," for example. Consequently, Judy expressed uncertainty about whether the violence was rooted in homophobia, as she could not "be sure if it occurred because of [her] sexuality or just because [she's] a woman."

When reflecting on the violence, lesbians of color found it difficult to distinguish between misogyny and homophobia. Latoya, a fifty-year-old Black lesbian, described a violent encounter in which a man approached her on the street, asked for her phone number, and then became physically violent when she said that she was on her way to pick up her girlfriend from work. He grabbed her by the hair and called her a "nasty, disgusting bitch" upon learning that she was a lesbian. While the man used homophobic insults, calling her a "pussy-eating bitch," his use of these terms did not spur the same certainty for Latoya as for many white gay men. Latoya explained her difficulty in distinguishing between misogyny and homophobia in this way: "I thought it was mostly about my sexuality, but he kept calling me a 'bitch' and doing this sexual stuff, so I really don't know. . . . I thought that he was mad because I was a woman who didn't want anything to do with him. But then he just seemed mad because I was a lesbian. So, I guess both [misogyny and homophobia] had something to do with it."

The differences between lesbians of color and Black and Latino gay men can be explained in part by patterns of victimization: heterosexual men perpetrated most of the violence. As a result, one would expect straight male perpetrators to use homophobic insults more frequently against gay men than against lesbians, as perpetrators may have wanted to emphasize how they were "more masculine" than gay men. Using homophobic insults, heterosexual men could distance themselves from homosexuality. In this sense, homophobic insults allow heterosexual men to construct themselves in opposition to the supposedly deviant men—the "fags" or "homos"—they have attacked (Kimmel 2001; Pascoe 2007). Thus, as heterosexual men perpetrate most forms of anti-queer violence, lesbians may encounter fewer homophobic insults than gay men. This difference is due largely to gender: lesbians across racial lines encountered violence in which their sexuality was not mentioned and, consequently, found it difficult to determine if the experience was rooted in homophobia.

As only five white lesbians and two white transgender people participated in this study, I can speak with greater certainty regarding gender differences among queer people of color than among white LGBT people. Still, race and gender shaped what respondents confronted and how they viewed their violent experiences. In particular, while white gay men generally expressed certainty and encountered violence in which perpetrators mentioned their homosexuality, gay men of color more frequently expressed uncertainty, feeling as if multiple aspects of their identity had been attacked. Further, Black and Latina lesbians often expressed uncertainty because perpetrators had not used explicitly homophobic language, leaving lesbians of color to question whether racism and sexism had also played a role.

SOCIAL CLASS AND HATE CRIME LEGISLATION

Social class also shaped how queer people assessed whether that violence was based on their sexuality or gender identity. Middle-class respondents usually expressed more willingness than low-income LGBT people to examine their perpetrators' motivations. Eva, a forty-six-year-old Black transgender woman, described herself as middle class and worked as a receptionist at a nonprofit organization. However, she said that she had very little money when she had experienced antitransgender violence several years prior to the interview. When describing her struggle with poverty, she argued that being poor made it more difficult to determine whether violence was based on her gender identity: "I didn't want to think if it was a hate crime. I didn't have heat. I didn't have heat! . . . How was I supposed to sit around and spend time thinking about whether I had been bashed?" Eva's experience suggests that low-income LGBT people have more pressing concerns than determining whether their violent experiences are rooted in bias. Indeed, living without heat is likely to cause one considerable stress. Other troubles, including managing to make ends meet without a steady income, are obviously experienced by poor people more than other social class groups. The stress of barely being able to pay one's bills—or not being able to—frequently affects one's emotional and physical health, including being able to think about the causes of one's experiences. Here, Eva indicates that poverty hinders the ability of LGBT people to determine whether violence is based on their sexuality or gender identity, as they must concern themselves with basic needs such as finding enough money to pay for heat or food.

At times, low-income respondents began to wonder over the course of the interview whether more of their violent experiences were rooted in prejudice than they had previously thought. Nevada, a thirty-six-year-old white person who identified as intersex and lived in a homeless shelter at the time of the interview, conveyed this feeling: "I had never thought about all of this as related to my sexuality [or gender identity]. Maybe it was now that I think about it." Nevada's response was fairly common among low-income respondents. They often began the interview by describing a violent incident that they thought was rooted in homophobia or prejudice against transgender people, and then, as the interview progressed, began to perceive more of their violent experiences as related to their sexuality or gender identity. Conversely, middle-class respondents usually said that they had spent a considerable amount of time thinking about the cause of their violent experiences, responding with phrases such as "I've thought about this before" or "I've thought about this a lot" when analyzing their perpetrators' motivations. Thus, having money and access to work granted privilege to middle-class LGBT people, allowing them to think about whether their violent experiences were rooted in prejudice.

Eva and Nevada's statements indicate that poor LGBT people may spend less time than their middle-class counterparts thinking about whether their experiences are bias-related. Social class, then, may affect the likelihood of pursuing hate crime charges, since individuals must first view their violent experiences as rooted in bias if they are going to pursue prosecution. Hate crime statutes increase criminal penalties against perpetrators who commit violence based on protected categories of the victim's identity such as race, religion, or sexual orientation. If someone attacks another person because they are Black, Muslim, or gay, then that form of violence would be considered a hate crime. In contrast, if someone mugs someone on the street simply for money, then that attack would not be viewed as hate-motivated. The rationale behind hate crime laws is that some forms of violence, including those directed against someone's race, religion, or sexual orientation, are more severe than other forms of violence, such as being mugged on the street. As a result, this line of thinking understands hate crimes as worthy of greater punishment from the state because these laws signal that intolerance will not be tolerated.

Despite the arguably worthy goals of hate crime laws, LGBT people benefit from these statutes in different ways depending on their race, class, and gender identity. White gay men in this study benefited from hate crime statutes more than other groups because they found it easiest to determine that violence was based on their sexuality. Hate crime laws benefit victims who are willing to define violence as bias-motivated; victims who cannot classify violence as motivated by bias are less likely to report it as a hate crime and, consequently, less likely to have it prosecuted as one. Given that white gay men were more likely than LGBT people of color to express certainty as to the cause of their violent experiences, hate crime statutes based on sexual orientation serve the interests of white gay men more than queer people of color.[3] Of course, the relationship between determining that violence is rooted in bias and pursuing hate crime charges is not a direct one; the latter does not necessarily follow the former. White gay men, for example, may determine that violence is based on their sexuality but choose not to report the incident to the police.

Still, white LGBT people in this study had the most involvement with pursuing hate crime charges. Overall, respondents' experiences with hate crime laws were minimal, yet none of the LGBT people of color had any involvement with the statues, while a few white respondents did. Five middle-class white respondents—two lesbians and three gay men—had discussed potential hate crime charges with the police. These racial differences are particularly surprising given that low-income people of color described more experiences of anti-queer physical violence than middle-class white respondents. These differences are due in large part to institutional racism in police departments, which made LGBT people of color less trusting of the police to provide help. At the same time, white gay men's certainty in viewing their violent experience as homophobic also played a role. Being able to view violence as definitively rooted in homophobia—part of the privilege that comes with being a white gay man in comparison to other LGBT people—helps one in pursuing hate crime charges.

While white gay men perceived some incidents as rooted in bias or hate, their experiences in reporting violence to the police were generally negative. Jacob, the forty-year-old white gay man shoved to the ground inside of a subway station, reported this incident to the police. He told the officers that it was "practically a hate crime," but said that the police did not appear to take it seriously, as the officers "looked at [him] like, 'What do you want us to do?'" Since Jacob did not get a good look at the man who had hit him, the police officers told him that they would see if they could find a security tape of the incident. The officers took down Jacob's phone number, but never called him. Reflecting on the incident, Jacob thought that they did not even look for security footage because their tone indicated that it "didn't really matter."

My sense is that part of the reason the police did not take Jacob's experience seriously is because the perpetrator did not use any homophobic language. In contrast, Greg, the white gay man who encountered violence on the subway in which a Latino man slammed his backpack against Greg's chest, described how two police officers responded very differently once they discovered that the perpetrator had used homophobic language. According to Greg, at first the police officers recorded the incident, responded "respectfully," but did not seem to think much of the violence until he told them that the man had called him a "faggot." Ironically, Greg said that the police officers did not seem to care that he had been bruised from being hit with the backpack, yet their interest in the violence immediately changed upon hearing that the man had used a homophobic slur. Learning this information, the officers brought up the possibility that the violence could be charged as a hate crime. Greg said that the police kept asking him if his attacker "had called him anything else," noting that it was "almost like they wanted me to [say that the men had said other homophobic things]." Nothing ever came of his reporting the incident, and Greg found the experience "incredibly frustrating" because the police seemed to care more about apprehending and punishing the perpetrator than about Greg's well-being.

Although Greg's experience with the police and the possibility of pursuing hate crime charges did not lead anywhere, his certainly in believing that the violence was rooted in homophobia played an important role in his approaching the police. If his experience had matched a more traditional hate crime incident, his certainty would have also helped him to pursue hate crime charges. Greg, who emphatically believed that his violent experience had occurred because he was gay, benefited from hate crime laws in comparison to the LGBT people of color who had a more difficult time classifying violence as homophobic or transphobic. Indeed, LGBT people of color had more opportunities to report incidents of hate crime, since they had encountered anti-queer physical violence with greater frequency, yet they did so less often than white respondents. This difference can be attributed in part to what I have highlighted here: white gay male respondents expressed greater certainty than LGBT people of color in viewing violence as based on their sexuality or gender identity.

Of course, LGBT people of color may pursue hate crime charges based on race. Nevertheless, none of the LGBT people of color in this study pursued these charges, even though LGBT people of color experienced racist violence. This trend is due in part to what Kimberlé Crenshaw (1989) has noted about antidiscrimination laws. Such laws often require Black women to assert either race-based or gender-based discrimination, which effectively excludes their experiences at the intersection of race and gender. Similarly, requiring Black LGBT people to classify their violent experiences as either racist or homophobic hate crimes is likely to prove particularly challenging for LGBT people of color, whose experiences are simultaneously racist and homophobic, and therefore cannot easily be classified as race-only or sexuality-only attacks.

While white gay men are privileged in comparison to other LGBT people in being able to view their violent experiences as rooted in homophobia, this idea can unfortunately be used to dismiss white gay men's discriminatory experiences. As a white gay man who focuses on homophobia and heteronormativity in his teaching, I encounter this response from some of my heterosexual students, who see me first and foremost as a gay man, and therefore often distrust my emphasis on homophobia. In these situations, my claims of homophobia are viewed as pure self-interest, something merely "in my head." These narratives are problematic to the extent that they dismiss homophobia and heteronormativity, constructing white gay men as "biased" and heterosexual people as somehow "objective" with regard to sexuality. At the same time, we must acknowledge that white gay men, in comparison to other LGBT people, are more likely to emphasize the effects of homophobia, as racism, sexism, and classism play an equally important role in the lives of many other LGBT people. In this sense, white and middle-class gay men, who do not typically experience racist, sexist, or classist forms of violence, remain privileged in comparison to other LGBT people, including low-income lesbians, transgender people of color, and Black and Latino gay men. Indeed, while white gay men certainly experience homophobia, we are undoubtedly privileged based on our race and gender identities, and, depending on our wealth and income levels, perhaps our social class position as well.

6 • "NOT THAT BIG OF A DEAL"

Social Class Differences in Viewing Violence as Severe

White middle-class respondents were more likely than low-income LGBT people of color to perceive their violent experiences as severe, even though the latter experienced more physical violence than the former. This difference was due largely to the various groups with which LGBT people compared themselves. Middle-class white respondents compared themselves with individuals who had experienced relatively little violence, while low-income LGBT people of color contrasted their experiences with people who had experienced a substantial amount of abuse. When doing so, middle-class white respondents emphasized the severity of their experiences; low-income people of color downplayed the severity of theirs. Diamond, an unemployed fifty-one-year-old Black lesbian, characterized being pushed and called a "stupid bitch" as something that was "not that big of a deal." Similarly, Daniel, a twenty-six-year-old Black gay man who worked as a receptionist, described his violent experience, in which a white police officer pushed his face against the side of a building as something that "could have been worse." As Diamond and Daniel described their violent experiences, they compared themselves with individuals who had experienced a lot of violence. Diamond contrasted herself with a Black gay man who had been hospitalized due to a homophobic attack, and Daniel compared himself with someone who died from being stabbed in gang-related violence.

In contrast to Diamond and Daniel, middle-class white respondents did not usually know anyone who had experienced physical violence. In general, these respondents were also the most likely to emphasize, rather than downplay, the severity of their violent experiences. Bob, a fifty-four-year-old white gay man who worked as a high school teacher, described his violent experience as "really bad"; he was called a "fag" by a male stranger on the street. Along the same lines, Julia, a twenty-eight-year-old white woman who worked as a pediatrician, described her experience of receiving a homophobic letter from her girlfriend's mother as "a really bad thing." Both of these respondents did not know anyone who had experienced homophobic violence, and they compared themselves with others who had not encountered abuse. Bob characterized the violence he confronted as "really bad" when comparing himself with a gay male friend. Of his friend, Bob said, "He made it seem like I should be like, 'Oh, whatever, no big deal.' But he hasn't had that happen to him, so it's easy for him to say that when he hasn't had something really bad happen to him like that."

Some of the contrasts among respondents seemed fairly stark, both in terms of the groups with which they compared themselves and the severity with which they perceived their violent experiences. I first noticed these differences on a day when conducting two interviews—one with Julia, the white woman described above, and another with Frankie, an unemployed forty-eight-year-old Latino man who had his face cut with a knife during a homophobic attack. Of these two respondents, I interviewed Frankie first and noticed that he continually downplayed the severity of his experiences, saying things such as "it could have been worse" and "it didn't end up being so bad." In contrast, Julia repeatedly emphasized the severity of receiving a homophobic letter. Most observers would probably view Frankie's experience of being cut on the face as "more severe" than Julia's experience of receiving a homophobic letter, and yet the former downplayed the severity while the latter emphasized it. These differences occurred along social class lines, as respondents' reference groups—the groups with which they compared themselves—shaped their perception of severity (England 2010; Merton 1957).

By comparing these respondents, I have arguably implied that the violent experiences of Julia and Bob were less severe than those of Daniel, Diamond, and Frankie. The point is not to dismiss or belittle Julia and Bob's violent experiences, as they were undoubtedly painful, but to suggest that the severity with which LGBT people perceive violence does not automatically spring from its form. Instead, LGBT people's perceptions are shaped as much by their social class position as by the type of violence they confront. Looking only at the form of the violence, one would expect low-income LGBT people of color to perceive their experiences as the most severe; after all, they had encountered the most physical violence. Yet, because of the effects of social class, low-income LGBT people were the least likely to view their violent experiences as severe.

While it remains important not to dismiss the pain caused by experiences such as receiving a homophobic letter, differences certainly exist in the severity of violence. Much of the quantitative work on this research topic has shown that lesbians and gay men experience the most psychological trauma from physical violence related to their sexuality (D'Augelli and Grossman 2001; Herek, Gillis, and Cogan 1999; Rose and Mechanic 2002). This finding has been repeatedly shown in quantitative survey research, and it is not my goal to disprove it. Indeed, it makes intuitive sense: a lesbian or gay person is likely to experience more pain from being attacked because of their sexuality than from many other forms of violence. Lesbians would likely experience more pain for being attacked based on their lesbian identity than for another, less personal, reason such as being mugged on the street. At the same time, distinguishing between homophobic physical violence and other forms of abuse simplifies a considerable amount. An extremely broad category such as "homophobic physical violence" ignores the frequency of the abuse, as well as the relationship between perpetrator and victim. During adolescence, a lesbian or gay teen might experience abuse every day from a parent, which is very different from an adult who encounters violence once, at the hands of a stranger. It is, then, an arbitrary decision to categorize forms of violence based on some criteria—such as physical or verbal—and not based on other criteria, such as whether the abuse was perpetrated by a stranger or a family member. Thus, as individual forms of violence all differ in some way, attempts to categorize them inevitably group together dissimilar events.

Although forms of violence certainly differ in terms of their brutality and severity, it is difficult, if not impossible, to determine the seriousness of violence objectively. Respondents frequently disagreed about the severity of certain types of violence, with some LGBT people constructing physical violence as more severe than verbal abuse, while others made the opposite argument. In this sense, the seriousness of individual forms of violence is largely in the eye of the beholder. LGBT people in this study would have differed in determining where a form of violence fits along a scale, sometimes used in quantitative survey research, from "1" (not very serious) to "10" (very serious). Moreover, the same form of violence—for instance, a father slapping his teenage son—will be perceived in different ways depending on the context of the abuse, which includes the prior history between father and son as well as the events immediately preceding the violence.

In exploring the effects of social class, I have used the categories of "downplaying" and "emphasizing" as heuristic devices rather than labels that apply to a particular person. Indeed, respondents moved back and forth from downplaying and emphasizing the severity of their experiences. Bob, described above, emphasized throughout the interview the severity of being called a "faggot" by a male stranger, yet he also asked me whether being called a "homo" by his father "counted" as violence. At the same time, even though Bob downplayed the severity of this incident by asking whether it "counted" as violence, he also underscored the pain it had caused him, saying that it "hurt a lot" and "really fucked with [his] mind at the time." These apparent contradictions were fairly common among respondents, as they seemed to fluctuate in and out of these categories—downplaying the severity of a violent experience at one moment and then emphasizing its significance at a later time. Despite these variations within a particular interview, respondents differed along the lines of social class.

The people who participated in this study were somewhat bifurcated along race and social class lines: most LGBT people of color were unemployed or worked in low-income occupations, while white respondents most frequently worked in professional, upper-middle-class jobs. Moreover, of the nineteen participants who did not attend college, eighteen were Black or Latino. Conversely, all but three of the white respondents had a college degree. Thus, with regard to the intersection of race and class, most middle-class participants were white and most low-income respondents were Black or Latino.[1]

Given these demographic characteristics, I compare middle-class white respondents and low-income LGBT people of color to highlight differences in how respondents perceived their experiences. Collapsing race and social class in this way can be problematic in leading to the assumption that all people of color are poor and all white people are middle class. Obviously, this assumption would not reflect larger dynamics of U.S. society, in which the growth of a sizeable Black middle class has drawn attention to class divisions among Black Americans (Lacy 2007; Pattillo-McCoy 2000). Certainly, race and social class are separate categories, even if they overlap in important ways. People still judge someone's social class position based on their racial identity; I have heard from colleagues—Black and Latino college instructors with my same educational level, working in the same job—that they have a harder time being viewed as intelligent and professional because of their race and ethnicity. In this regard, individuals' racial identities are used to judge their social class position, with Black and Latino people sometimes being assumed to have a lower educational level than they do. While not hoping to reinforce these prejudices, I can speak only of the people I interviewed, and the most salient differences in terms of how respondents evaluated the severity of their violent experiences were between middle-class white respondents and low-income LGBT people of color.

THE ROLE OF FRIENDS AND FAMILY MEMBERS

Low-income LGBT people of color were often encouraged by their friends and family members to compare themselves with individuals who had encountered a lot of violence. Jayvyn, a thirty-three-year-old Black gay man who worked as a secretary, felt that he was consistently compared with people who had experienced more violence than himself: "For the longest time, I didn't see it as a big deal. Everyone kept telling me, 'Well, you weren't hurt, you weren't killed, like so and so.' But I *was* hurt. I mean, I had the scars to prove it." When Jayvyn expressed the severity of his violent experience, in which he had a glass bottle thrown at his shoulder, others diminished its importance by classifying it as commonplace. Indeed, by suggesting that Jayvyn could have been murdered, the assumption here is that his experience was not all that bad. In comparison to murder, what he encountered could be viewed as comparatively insignificant. Jayvyn, however, dismissed these assumptions by pointing to the negative consequences of the violence. He rejected ideas that it was not a bad experience because the violence hurt him: as he says, he has the scars to prove that he was hurt. I found these statements sad and difficult to listen to during the interviews—who wants to have their pain dismissed by others?—but I was also impressed by Jayvyn's ability to reject others' unsympathetic views.

While Jayvyn discarded ideas that his experience should be viewed as insignificant, other low-income LGBT people of color were more accepting of these notions. Jasmine, a forty-four-year-old Black lesbian who worked as a security guard, described her brother's response when she told him about being spat on when holding hands with her girlfriend: "He told me that I was fortunate not to end up in the hospital like his friend [who was stabbed in gang-related violence]. . . . It made sense, what he said. It could have been worse. I could have ended up in the hospital. I guess I should feel lucky that I didn't." Jasmine's brother downplayed the severity of her violent experience by suggesting that she could have been hospitalized. By doing so, he minimized her experience, comparing it with a violent incident that he perceived to result in "more serious" injuries. Low-income LGBT people described this type of response more frequently than their middle-class counterparts, when the former were encouraged to view their violent experiences as less severe than those of someone else. As a result, low-income respondents' reference groups did not simply arise out of thin air, but they were asked to compare themselves with certain groups of people, particularly individuals who had experienced a lot of violence. Low-income LGBT people sometimes perceived their violent experiences as insignificant because they had been encouraged to think of the abuse in this way.

White, middle-class LGBT people were rarely told to compare themselves with individuals who had experienced a lot of violence. Nevertheless, they were occasionally encouraged to downplay the severity of their violent experiences. In these situations, they were asked to compare themselves with individuals who had encountered relatively little violence. Ted, a thirty-three-year-old white gay man who worked as a lawyer, described his mother's comparison of him with one of her friends: "Right after I told her about [being mugged and called a "faggot"], she told me this story about her [gay] friend who was *almost* mugged. . . . It had nothing to do with him being gay and he wasn't even mugged. . . . I just thought, 'What does this have to do with me?'" Ted felt that his mother had diminished the severity of his violent experience by comparing him with someone who had not encountered violence. This comparison, which seemed unfair to Ted, equated his experience with an incident that he perceived as trivial. Similar to most middle-class white respondents, Ted was compared with someone who had encountered less violence than himself. Low-income people of color, in contrast, were usually compared with individuals who had experienced considerable amounts of violence.

Although both middle-class white respondents and low-income people of color sometimes felt as if others had downplayed the severity of their violent experiences, the former were also more frequently encouraged to perceive their violent experiences as severe. George, a forty-five-year-old white gay man who worked as a college instructor, described the reaction of his friends to him being pushed by a man who called him a "little faggot": "Everyone said that I should go to the doctor's. . . . [One friend] told me that I should report it as a hate crime. . . . Another friend set me up with a therapist. He was a big help." White, middle-class LGBT people encountered this type of response—in which others emphasized the severity of the violence—more often than low-income LGBT people of color. Indeed, middle-class white respondents described how their friends or family members had encouraged them to seek out service providers and sometimes even took them to the hospital or the police station. These respondents were encouraged to seek help in dealing with the effects of the violence. Indeed, the personal support that George received was essential in motivating him to find institutional support: after receiving encouragement from others, he met with a therapist, reported the incident to the police, and went to the hospital to get a bruise on his chest examined. Low-income LGBT people, in contrast, were less frequently encouraged to seek out service providers and were sometimes not even able to afford their hospital bills, much less a therapist.

The friends and family members of white middle-class LGBT people frequently served as a support network, assisting these respondents in navigating institutional settings. In these situations, service providers may have unwittingly underscored the severity of anti-queer violence as they tried to alleviate the suffering of white, middle-class LGBT people. Certainly, through their involvement in institutional settings, these respondents had others listening and responding to their demands. They were often in these settings—such as a doctor's office, a police station, or a therapy session—where individuals were serving them and, therefore, emphasizing the severity of the violence. To be sure, the role of service providers is to assist people in need of help.

Of course, low-income LGBT people of color also received support from their friends and family members. Even so, this assistance rarely connected them with institutional support; it seldom involved helping them find a doctor, lawyer, therapist, or police officer. Instead, it usually focused on providing emotional support. Consequently, low-income LGBT people of color did not interact with service providers as frequently as middle-class white respondents and, therefore, did not have as many encounters in which others were underscoring the severity of their violent experiences. Low-income LGBT people of color often could not afford to visit a doctor or a therapist, and distrust of the criminal justice system kept many Black and Latino respondents from contacting the police.

SOCIAL CLASS DIFFERENCES IN EXPECTATIONS, REFERENCE GROUPS, AND CONSTRUCTIONS OF VIOLENCE AS SEVERE

LGBT people's expectations concerning the likelihood of experiencing violence differed based on social class. Most low-income people of color thought that anti-queer violence could conceivably happen to them because they knew others who had experienced it. Tamika, an unemployed fifty-three-year-old Black lesbian who lived in a homeless shelter, expressed little surprise at being assaulted for revealing her sexuality: "I wasn't surprised; I almost expected it to happen. Most of us have to go through something like this, I think. . . . Most of my friends have had similar experiences." Tamika's response was common among low-income people of color, many of whom expected to encounter anti-queer violence because their friends had experienced it. Tamika described two physically violent experiences, one of which involved a man she had dated at a homeless shelter hitting her after she broke up with him and "came out" as a lesbian. When reflecting on this incident, she related it to the context in which she found herself: "You see, [in a homeless shelter] all kind of crazy stuff goes on, so I knew that in breaking up with him and telling others that I roll with women, I was putting my life in his hands. . . . Like I said, 'expected it.'"

While low-income LGBT people of color's expectations were certainly related to their social class position, their racial and sexual identities also played a role. Diamond, a fifty-one-year-old Black lesbian who was unemployed, explained the various types of violence she could confront: "[Being attacked by someone] might happen again, I have no way of knowing. . . . It's a tough world out there. Someone could beat me because I'm Black or gay or a woman or some other thing that I have no control over. I mean, I look at my friends and see that most of them have been harassed for at least one of these things." Similar to Tamika, Diamond compared herself with her friends, many of whom had experienced violence at some point in their lives. Moreover, low-income LGBT people of color often anticipated experiencing violence in the future, given that their race, class, gender, and sexual identities had been attacked in the past.

In contrast to low-income people of color, most middle-class white respondents said that they did not know anyone who had encountered anti-queer violence. Frank, a fifty-one-year-old white gay man who said that he was viewed as gay "wherever [he] goes," described a violent experience in which he was called a "homo" and had a glass bottle thrown at him on the street. In describing his surprise over the incident, he explained the effects of not knowing others with experiences of homophobic violence: "It seems like it doesn't happen to most people because I don't know anyone who it's happened to. So, yeah, it was surprising." Frank perceived homophobic violence as relatively rare because he did not know anyone who had experienced it. This understanding of homophobic violence then structured his expectations—he expected that it would not happen to him.

Frank had a working-class job, but he identified as middle class; he worked as a part-time auxiliary police officer and lived in a low-income neighborhood in Brooklyn. He was raised in a middle-class, two-parent home, where his mother was a teacher and his father was a family physician. He also had a college degree and described his friends as "all middle class." Thus, even though Frank had a working-class occupation, he compared himself with largely middle- and upper-middle-class people, most of whom had not experienced violence. In this sense, the social class position of LGBT people's friends and family members structured their expectations. LGBT people who had working-class jobs, but were raised in low-income homes and were friends with other working-class people, did not express similar surprise at experiencing violence because they compared themselves with other low-income people. Much of the sociological research on reference groups has drawn similar conclusions, as individuals' expectations depend on the groups they use as a standard of comparison (Anderson 2002; Runciman 1966). Middle-class white respondents, comparing themselves with their friends, often did not expect to experience anti-queer violence because they did not know others who had encountered it. Low-income LGBT people of color, in contrast, usually knew others who had experienced violence, which led them to perceive it as something they could conceivably encounter in the future.

LGBT people's expectations and reference groups led them to evaluate violence differently based on social class. In particular, low-income people of color sometimes downplayed the severity of anti-queer violence because their experiences had turned out better than expected. In such cases, they compared themselves with individuals who had experienced a lot of violence. Daniel, a twenty-six-year-old Black gay man who worked as a receptionist, diminished the severity of his experience of police brutality by comparing himself with a gay male friend who was also the victim of homophobic police violence: "The cops beat [my friend] much worse. He got it really bad, so I sorta see myself as lucky, in some respects." Many people would probably not refer to Daniel—who had his face bruised by a police officer—as "lucky." In comparison with his friend, though, Daniel could perceive himself as relatively fortunate—as his friend was supposedly beaten "much worse," in a comparable situation. Latoya, a fifty-year-old Black lesbian, also compared herself with a friend who had encountered homophobic violence, downplaying the severity of a man who had pulled her hair when she told him that she had a girlfriend: "It was never too violent. . . . Yeah, I had some scrapes, but it's not like I had to go to the hospital or anything, like [my friend]. . . . I know that it could have been worse." Gender is relevant here as well, since Latoya's suggestion that it "could have been worse" was her way of being thankful that the man did not rape her; she said that she "didn't care what [he] was calling me," but expressed fear that the violence would lead to sexual assault, which brought back "all sorts of memories" of when she was sexually assaulted as a teenager. Men did not typically emphasize the severity of sexual assault in this way, yet social class structured these sorts of evaluations: low-income LGBT people downplayed the severity of their violent experiences when comparing themselves with their friends and family members.

In contrast to low-income people of color, middle-class white respondents almost always constructed their violent experiences as severe. White, middle-class LGBT people often responded to questions concerning the severity of violence with phrases such as "it's a big deal" or "it's a really bad thing to have happened to me"; low-income LGBT people rarely used these phrases. This difference occurred because respondents compared themselves with different groups of people. White, middle-class LGBT people frequently emphasized the severity of their violent experiences by suggesting that other queer people did not have similar experiences. Mark, a forty-six-year-old white gay man who worked as a paralegal, described a violent experience that occurred in the late 1980s, at the height of the AIDS crisis when gay men were stigmatized as sexual deviants. The violence occurred after Mark had been at a gay bar. After leaving the bar, Mark noticed two men behind him, one of whom called him a "faggot." The men did not do anything physical to him, but they stalked him on the street, following him for approximately ten minutes and disappearing only when Mark got on the subway. Mark described the stalking as an attempt to "intimidate" him, saying that "it worked," since he did not go to a gay bar for several years after the incident. In contrast to low-income respondents, Mark underscored the severity of this experience by comparing himself with other gay men: "I wanted to kill someone after it happened. . . . It just seems like this sort of thing doesn't happen to most gay men. So, I guess maybe that's why it pissed me off so much." Constructing his experience as relatively rare—as something that "most gay men" do not encounter—led Mark to view it as extraordinarily awful.

Other white middle-class respondents highlighted the severity of their violent experiences by comparing themselves with specific people they knew, usually their friends. Julia, the twenty-eight-year-old pediatrician described earlier in this chapter, compared herself with people she knew to emphasize the severity of receiving a homophobic letter from her girl-friend's mother: "It seems like a really bad thing, looking back on it now. I mean, I felt like, 'Why would this happen to me?' . . . Sure, I wasn't killed or anything, but how many people have to go through this? . . . It's just not something anyone I know has to deal with." Julie later explained that she did not know other lesbians or gay men who had experienced violence. These comparisons with the people she knew led Julia to perceive herself as rela-tively deprived, viewing her experience as infrequent ("how many people have to go through this?") and severe ("it seems like a really bad thing"). Along the same lines, Jacob, a forty-year-old white gay man who worked as a surgeon, emphasized the severity of his violent experience, in which he was hit after making out with his boyfriend, by comparing himself with one of his gay male friends: "It felt like such bullshit. . . . My friend Ben, he's always making out with his boyfriend in public, and *this* has never happened to him. . . . So, I thought, 'Why does this have to happen to me, and not him?'" Jacob expressed a sense of unfairness by comparing himself with someone who had engaged in similar behavior, which then made his own experience seem atypical and extreme.[2] This comparison was very different from those made by low-income respondents, who more frequently compared them-selves with people who had encountered violence.

Although low-income LGBT people were more likely than their middle-class counterparts to downplay the severity of their violent experiences, the former did sometimes construct their experiences as severe. Jayvyn, the thirty-three-year-old Black gay man quoted earlier, is a prime example, when he said: "Everyone kept telling me, 'Well, you weren't hurt, you weren't killed, like so and so.' But I *was* hurt. I mean, I had the scars to prove it." Here, Jayvyn dismissed the implications of what others were saying to him—that his violent experience was relatively minor, since he was not murdered. His response suggests that LGBT people have some agency in being able to discard notions that their violent experiences are not severe. Further, when sharing these results, I have often been surprised to hear others describe the perceptions of Black LGBT people as evidence that violence is an "accepted way of life" for low-income people of color. These ideas are problematic to the extent that they associate violence with marginalized groups rather than the structural conditions, such as poverty and unemployment, which make violence possible. The results presented here, in which low-income LGBT people of color sometimes downplayed the severity of their violent experiences, are not inevitable but are the product of social conditions that cause low-income people of color to experience violence at higher rates than other social groups.

Low-income LGBT people of color are also not a monolithic group, and Black and Latino respondents did sometimes emphasize the seriousness of anti-queer violence, constructing this abuse as widespread. Lela, a forty-eight-year-old Black transgender woman, described her friends' violent experiences to emphasize the severity of anti-LGBT discrimination: "It's a big problem. All of my friends have experienced something negative because they're trans or gay. Every single one of them. . . . We're not going away anytime soon, either. The violence just has to stop." Lela mentioned other LGBT people's violent experiences not to construct her own as more severe—as some white middle-class respondents did—but to construct anti-queer violence as a serious social problem that "just has to stop." Similarly, Jetta, a twenty-eight-year-old Black lesbian, perceived anti-queer violence as ubiquitous: "It hurts because you can't escape it. It's everywhere. I know for a fact that I'm not the only one who has experiences like this. I'm not alone. If everyone could just come together to put a stop to it, then the world would be a lot better off." Low-income LGBT people of color, knowing others who had experienced anti-queer violence, perceived prejudice and discrimination as affecting large numbers of people. Further, these respondents thought that multiple forms of inequality were worth changing, as they knew others who had experienced violence related to their race and social class position. In contrast, middle-class white respondents, who did not typically know others who had experienced anti-queer physical violence, constructed their violent experiences as atypical rather than widespread. Of course, some white, middle-class LGBT people viewed anti-queer violence as a pervasive problem, particularly those involved in activist work, but this response was less common than among low-income queer people of color.

Some sociologists would respond to these differences as entirely the product of social class. Low-income LGBT people were more likely than middle-class respondents to downplay the severity of their violent experiences—that trend could be viewed as a consequence of social class. Nevertheless, race and social class remain deeply intertwined, as people make assumptions about others' social class positions based on their racial identities, and race profoundly affects a wide range of one's experiences related to social class, ranging from the likelihood that one will be arrested to the likelihood that one will be hired for a job (Alexander 2010; Pager 2007). Thus, although social class plays a significant role in how LGBT people evaluate the severity of their violent experiences, race is still important. Indeed, the few Black middle-class respondents who participated in this study emphasized the severity of their violent experiences, yet they did not do so to the same extent as the white, middle-class LGBT people.[3] I am not arguing for an analysis that attempts to figure out whether race or social class is more important, but arguing that both of them must be taken seriously. While examining the perceptions of Black, middle-class LGBT people and white, low-income LGBT people is outside the scope of this study, their evaluations undoubtedly differ from those of the LGBT people I have described here. In this sense, neither race nor social class should be overlooked.

The few Black, middle-class LGBT people who participated in this study differed from white middle-class respondents in important ways, as the former emphasized their distrust of the criminal justice system in ways similar to low-income Black respondents. Kevin, a sixty-two-year-old Black middle-class gay man, was the only Black gay male respondent with a college degree; he also worked as a coordinator for a nonprofit organization and reported an annual salary of around $40,000. Kevin had several experiences of police brutality, yet he had also encountered homophobic violence when a teenage boy had rammed his knee into Kevin's back, pushing him to the ground. When I asked Kevin about his reasons for not reporting this incident to the police, he emphasized his distrust of the criminal justice system: "That's not something I would do. I don't talk 'improper'—'we be talking.' But it doesn't matter, [the police] will still look at me as a violent person." Black men across social class lines expressed this suspicion that the police would not provide justice for racially marginalized groups. Of course, low-income Black men and their middle-class counterparts face police surveillance and abuse to different degrees, but Kevin's experience of police harassment indicates that Black, middle-class men are not immune from its effects.

At the same time, although Black men across social class lines share some similar experiences, their different social locations regarding social class have important consequences. Similar to how the experiences of low-income Black lesbians differ from those of their middle-class counterparts, social class remains an important marker regarding one's life chances. Indeed, many privileges and advantages are given to those lucky enough to be born into a wealthy home, as individuals from rich families are considerably more likely than those from poor families to attend good schools, live in relatively safe neighborhoods, and avoid hunger and malnutrition (Lareau 2003). These privileges are not simply small conveniences but profoundly affect one's likelihood of being financially successful, as those born into wealthy families are substantially more likely than their poor counterparts to be rich later in life. Being born into a family with social class privilege enables future economic success.

AVOIDING HIERARCHIES OF VIOLENCE

Feminist scholarship has frequently emphasized that forms of inequality must not be ranked from "most oppressive" to "least oppressive" (Crenshaw 1991; Hancock 2007; King 1988). Similarly, if we accept that systems of oppression cannot be ranked—that sexism cannot be privileged over racism, for example—then we should also accept that individuals' experiences of oppression cannot be categorized in hierarchical ways. While accepting that LGBT people may rank forms of violence on their own, constructing hierarchies of violence is generally problematic. As Patricia Hill Collins (1998, 923) has argued, "Within dichotomous thinking that juxtaposes actions to words, speech can never be violent. It can only provoke violence." Hierarchies privileging physical violence as more severe than verbal abuse reinforce the sentiments that many LGBT people encounter—that some of their violent experiences are not severe. LGBT people's verbally violent experiences are diminished by the argument that physical violence "hurts more" than verbal abuse (Iganski 2001, 626). Given that many respondents spoke of the pain they felt when others had disparaged their experiences, hierarchies of violence should be rejected to avoid making some forms of abuse appear as if they do not "count" as legitimately severe. Indeed, many racist, sexist, and homophobic insults are likely to cause marginalized groups considerable pain. By privileging physical violence over verbal abuse, scholarship risks overlooking situations in which individuals view verbal abuse as being as traumatic as physical attacks and risks reinforcing attitudes that some forms of violence are insignificant.

In this regard, low-income LGBT people of color confronted arguments that diminished the severity of their violent experiences, which they were told "could have been worse." Of course, almost any violent experience "could have been worse"; thus, this phrase can be employed at almost any moment in time, in response to almost any violent experience. Still, when this phrase is used depends on power relations. Respondents spoke of heterosexual people using phrases such as "it could have been worse" as a way of ending the discussion, preventing a further exploration of prejudice and discrimination. Although LGBT people of color most frequently described these reactions from heterosexual people of color, a few Black respondents described this response when interacting with white people. Daniel, the twenty-six-year-old Black gay man introduced at the beginning of this chapter, described a second experience of racism, which was verbal. This experience involved a white man at his job saying that even though he "had no problem with Black people," he "didn't understand why so many of them had to be on welfare."

Although Daniel found this comment frustrating, he also expressed anger at the unsupportive reaction of one of his white friends to this racist comment: "[My friend] just looked at me like 'what's the big deal?' . . . I don't remember what he said, but it was basically like 'So? So what? Who cares? You got off easy.'" Daniel interpreted his friend's reaction as the equivalent of "what do you expect," implying that he should "get over" the experience. Recall that Daniel is the respondent who said that he was "lucky" when describing the police officer who bruised his face, and yet here he underscores the severity of this statement concerning race. This difference indicates not only that LGBT people shift from downplaying to emphasizing the seriousness of their experiences but also that they do not always view physical violence as more severe than insulting statements.

Constructing physical attacks as more traumatic than verbal abuse can potentially lead to the sort of reaction that Daniel confronted. Power relations are frequently reinforced by focusing only on extreme acts of violence, as such emphases potentially imply that individuals face discrimination only if they have been brutally beaten. According to this view, racism involves only an explicitly racist insult or an act of physical violence; anything short of physical violence or explicitly hateful language becomes understood as nonracist. Although physical violence against minority groups continues to occur, and is therefore important to recognize, prejudice and discrimination typically operate in more subtle ways. Moreover, while individuals occasionally make explicitly racist or homophobic remarks, such comments have become increasingly stigmatized. As a result, individuals tend to express racism and homophobia less overtly, for example, by negatively characterizing social policies such as welfare, as Daniel's coworker did, and then associating Black people with the stigmatized item or behavior. Research indicates that many individuals remain unaware of their prejudices, distancing themselves from racism and homophobia at the same time that they harbor prejudicial thoughts or engage in discriminatory acts (Ziegert and Hanges 2005). That is, people in the United States may think of themselves as unprejudiced, while simultaneously favoring some people based on attributes such as race, gender, and sexuality (Bonilla-Silva 2006; Pager 2007).

While avoiding hierarchies of violence and viewing all of its forms as harmful remains important, differences also exist with regard to who confronts violence. Low-income LGBT people of color in this study had more experiences of physical violence than middle-class white respondents. The significance of this trend is not that middle-class white respondents had harmless experiences, but that they confronted physical violence less frequently than LGBT people of color. Still, this emphasis on the differences among LGBT people must be balanced with sensitivity to the traumatic experiences of all queer people. Such a balance entails avoiding endless debates over whose painful experiences are the worst, while also emphasizing how social groups confront prejudice and discrimination in different ways.

Various forms of violence, including physical and verbal abuse, often overlap with one another as well. Indeed, respondents' comparisons of physical and verbal violence revealed the difficulty of distinguishing between them, as their violent experiences did not fit neatly into one category or another. For instance, Judy, a forty-three-year-old Puerto Rican lesbian, described an attempted rape in which a man used a mix of sexist and homophobic insults while forcibly trying to remove her clothes. When asked to compare physical and verbal violence, Judy problematized the politics of making such distinctions: "It's hard to tell which is which. It goes back and forth. So, sometimes you don't know. . . . It can't be said that what happened is one or the other, because when both are happening, then I have to sit there and be like, 'OK, what was bothering me about it?' That would drive me crazy." Emphasizing how physical and verbal violence occur alternately and simultaneously, Judy underscored the futility of distinguishing between these two types of abuse, arguing that such attempts require people who have experienced violence to engage in the psychologically taxing process of differentiating between concurrent events.

Although I have not entirely discarded distinctions between physical and verbal violence, the meaning that LGBT people ascribe to a violent experience is more important than the type of violence itself. LGBT people's perceptions do not depend solely on the form of the violence: even though middle-class white respondents described fewer experiences of physical violence than low-income LGBT people of color, the former were more likely than the latter to perceive their violent experiences as severe. Consequently, social class structures LGBT people's perceptions of their violent experiences.

Ironically, while studies of anti-queer violence have often constructed homophobic physical violence as the most traumatic, this line of research has also generally overlooked the experiences of low-income LGBT people—a social group that likely experiences comparatively high rates of physical violence.[4] In contrast, my work here contributes to scholarship arguing that more attention must be given to issues affecting the most marginalized queer people (Moore 2011; Spade 2013). Low-income LGBT youth disproportionately confront homelessness, as this group remains more likely than the general population to be kicked out of their home by family members (Gibson 2011). Of course, middle-class LGBT people experience rejection from family members as well, yet because low-income LGBT people typically have fewer resources, homelessness becomes considerably more likely for this group. Important differences also exist among low-income LGBT people based on race and gender, as police brutality affects low-income LGBT people of color more than their white counterparts, and low-income lesbians confront sexualized forms of violence that their male counterparts do not. These differences among LGBT people, which vary based on race, class, and gender, become exceedingly complex, yet because many aspects of social class—poverty, homelessness, and disadvantaged neighborhoods—shape the likelihood that LGBT people will even encounter abuse, social class remains a particularly important power structure to consider when examining anti-queer violence.

7 • THE HOME AND THE STREET

Violence from Strangers and Family Members

Tamika, a homeless, unemployed Black lesbian, expressed considerable sadness when explaining how her mother had disowned her: "She cut me off, forever," Tamika said sorrowfully. This "cutting off" was swift, sharp, and everlasting. Tamika, fifty-three at the time of the interview, "came out" to her mother when she was thirty-three, in the late 1980s. At the age of thirty-three, she had already moved out of her mother's home and begun to live with her girlfriend; the couple had lived together for two years when Tamika revealed her sexuality to her mother. Tamika thought her mother would react negatively, but she did not expect her to "turn her back [on me]." She disclosed her sexuality when they were talking in the kitchen of her mother's house. Tamika described herself as being very nervous— "the butterflies were a flying"—but she thought that her mother needed "to know who [she] was." Reflecting on this experience, she "just sort of told her," letting it "spill out." She told her mother that she was "living with a woman" and "always knew" she was a lesbian. Her mother then "exploded," yelling "I didn't raise you this way," slamming several doors in the process. Her mother also invoked Tamika's father, who died when she was young: "He would be ashamed." When I asked Tamika if they were on speaking terms now, she said, "funerals," and then added that her mother would not even look at her girlfriend when they dated. She described her mother as "very religious" and thought she always knew about her daughter's homosexuality, but did not want it publicly acknowledged.

Although the rejection Tamika experienced from her mother did not lead to her homelessness, other LGBT people did experience rejection that resulted in their becoming homeless. These experiences were particularly

121

common among transgender respondents. Ebony, a twenty-year-old transgender woman, was kicked out of her home at the age of sixteen. During her teenage years, Ebony said that her parents constantly "went through [her] things" and kept questioning her gender identity. Raised as a boy, she began at the age of fourteen to go to school in clothing traditionally reserved for women, wearing earrings and, occasionally, a dress. Ebony said that the kids at school were "really bad," but felt that her parents were "even worse." She described being hit by classmates at school and then coming home, where her father would "beat [her] for getting beat up." These beatings from her father occurred on an almost daily basis for two years, culminating in a conversation where her mother said that if Ebony did not change, it was "best" for her to move out. The next day, in early 2005, Ebony left home, moving in with one of her friends, an older transgender woman, whom she had met at a transgender support group. At this time, she also dropped out of high school, in eleventh grade. Since this incident, she had only spoken to her parents once, on the telephone, when she said that her mother acted as if it was Ebony's "choice" to move out, for she had supposedly turned her back on them. Ebony, with an immediacy that sounded as if she was describing the death of her parents, said that she doubted "she would ever talk to [them] again."

Much of media and scholarly attention on anti-queer violence has overlooked these familial forms of abuse (Horn, Kosciw, and Russell 2009; Kenagy and Bostwick 2005). Instead, considerable attention has focused on public violence, perpetrated by strangers; emphasis on hate crime reflects this trend. Although public forms of anti-queer violence certainly occur, LGBT people experience even higher rates in the home (Barton 2012; Kenagy and Bostwick 2005; Munoz-Plaza, Quinn, and Rounds 2002). Indeed, verbal abuse from family members, described by all of the people in this study, is marginalized under frameworks that focus on public, stranger-based forms of violence. Homophobic abuse frequently operates in families, as heterosexual people may have little problem with strangers who are gay or lesbian, but then become distressed when their son or daughter publicly identifies in this way. Tamika said that her mother worked with a gay man, and yet she never spoke negatively of him. Accepting an immediate family member as LGBT is different from accepting a stranger's queer identity.

Emphasizing only extreme manifestations of violence overlooks LGBT people's less overt, but still painful, violent experiences. Tamika's mother was not physically abusive toward her daughter, but her rejection of Tamika profoundly affected her life. As a result, attempts to challenge homophobia and heteronormativity must not only emphasize public forms of violence but also address abuse in the home. Such a focus challenges stereotypes of homophobic violence. Certainly, when Americans hear the phrase "violence against lesbians and gay men" particular ideas are likely to arise, especially hate crime and bullying in schools. These forms of violence, while part of the landscape of LGBT people's violent experiences, obscure many other forms, including those that occur in the home. Respondents sometimes even asked me if their familial experiences "counted" as abuse, which suggests that stereotypes of antigay attacks affect individuals' perceptions of "real" or legitimate forms of violence.

Associating LGBT people's violent experiences with public, stranger-based forms of violence reproduces the interests of some LGBT people more than others. Victims receiving the most media attention, from Matthew Shepard to Tyler Clementi, have been largely white and middle-class gay men. With regard to social class, both Shepard and Clementi were college students, and media representations have generally marginalized the experiences of low-income LGBT people, whose challenges differ from their middle-class counterparts. Ignoring these differences effectively collapses low-income LGBT people's experiences with the middle-class representations, since media have typically used the latter's experiences to represent all queer people (Ward 2008). Rather than using middle-class LGBT people's experiences as the standard by which others are compared, social class differences need to be acknowledged, as low-income queer people face challenges that their middle-class counterparts do not.

The challenges confronting low-income LGBT people also differ based on gender, as social class constraints affect lesbians, gay men, and transgender people in different ways. Low-income lesbian and bisexual women described experiences of domestic violence in which social class played an important role in limiting their ability to leave abusive relationships. Gay men, while occasionally describing abuse in relationships with other gay men, did not encounter domestic violence at the hands of heterosexual men. In contrast, lesbians' coming out experiences sometimes involved violence from male partners, including ex-boyfriends and ex-husbands. Tamika's experience of domestic violence is one such example; this abuse occurred at the age of twenty-nine, several years prior to being disowned by her mother. While living in a homeless shelter, Tamika dated a man for several months; this man lived in a different shelter within walking distance. At this time, although she had been sexually involved with women and felt she always knew she was a lesbian, she had not publicly identified as queer. She described this particular homeless shelter as having "lesbians all over" and became close friends with an out lesbian there. Her friend knew Tamika was a lesbian, but it was "just not talked about much." At the same time, this friend told Tamika that she had to break up with her boyfriend immediately because the longer she drew it out, the more likely he was to react negatively.

When Tamika broke up with him, she said that he did not "have much of a reaction," but he refused to leave her alone. He continued to come to her room, where he invaded her space, asked if they could talk, and refused to leave. She described these encounters as him being "in my business," but she did not take them very seriously, until one day he approached her, grabbed her by the arm, and demanded to know, "Why didn't you tell me you were a dyke?" This incident occurred a few weeks after she had broken up with him. Tamika assumed that someone had told him she was sleeping with her lesbian friend, even though their relationship was strictly platonic. As he yelled at her, demanding that she answer him, she tried to escape the situation by finding a staff member. When she briefly got away from him, he caught up to her and hit her across the face. After this incident, Tamika went to the staff members, who assured her that she would be transferred to another shelter as soon as possible. Nevertheless, Tamika worried that the process would take too long, since forty-eight hours later she was still there and the man was continuing to stalk her. She said that he did not perpetrate physical violence against her again, but he would follow her around, looming as close as possible.

Tamika's experience reveals that low-income women face significant financial constraints in leaving intimate violence, which middle-class women often do not face to the same extent. Indeed, her options—living on the streets or waiting until she was transferred to another shelter—made it difficult for her to escape the violence. While Tamika chose to live on the streets, other women would likely stay in the shelter, waiting to be transferred and continuing to deal with the harassment and stalking. In contrast, after living on the streets, Tamika moved from one friend's apartment to the next, until she was eventually placed in a domestic violence shelter months later. Two years after this experience, she moved in with her ex-girlfriend and four years later she came out to her mother.

Other lesbian and bisexual women experienced domestic violence over more prolonged periods. For lesbians, the violence typically occurred after revealing their lesbianism, while for bisexual women the male partner was more likely to know of their bisexual identity from the beginning of the relationship. Compare the experiences of Dorothy, a forty-three-year-old lesbian woman who worked as a security guard, and Leslie, a fifty-year-old bisexual woman who was unemployed. Dorothy, who came out as a lesbian at the age of twenty-four, married her high-school boyfriend when she was nineteen. She knew she was bisexual at a young age, but she did not always feel that she was a lesbian. She began dating her boyfriend in high school and married him after they had been together for two years. When they married, Dorothy worked as a cashier at a fast food restaurant, while her husband was a mechanic. Dorothy felt happy in the marriage initially, but said that it quickly turned unpleasant, as they spent a lot of time fighting. The disagreements usually centered on him staying out late at night and her not wanting to have children. She began to suspect that he was cheating on her, since he started to spend less time at home and she thought that she smelled perfume on him several times. Eventually, the arguments subsided and the couple led "separate lives," according to Dorothy, sleeping in separate beds and rarely seeing one another. This aspect of their relationship lasted for about a year, when Dorothy met a bisexual woman, another cashier, at her workplace. Dorothy said that she "fell completely in love" with this woman and that her husband began to suspect "something was up" because she was happier at home. Her husband's suspicions were confirmed when he listened in on one of Dorothy's phone calls with her lover.

After this incident, he became physically abusive. Dorothy said that the possibility of her being a lesbian was only mentioned once, immediately following the phone conversation, and even then it was not explicitly addressed. When she hung up the phone, he came into her room, demanding to know whom she had been talking to. His veiled reference to lesbianism included the question, "What are you?" After that night, he began to come home more often, leaving their apartment only for work and returning home during his lunch breaks. He also demanded that she quit her job and refused to let her leave the house at night. The first incident of physical violence occurred on a day when she tried to leave home: when explaining that she had to go to work, he hit her and told her that she was not going anywhere. The next day, he threatened her, saying that if she left him, he would kill her; Dorothy said that she "believed him." The violence continued for several months. Sometimes it occurred when he learned that she had left the house, while at other times it occurred when the phone rang.

She described the fear she felt at the time in this way: "He would degrade me, degrade my spirit. . . . 'I will kill you if you leave.' . . . I had no money, no place to go. No anything. I thought I would die from him." Financial constraints clearly limited Dorothy's options in being able to leave the relationship. Even though she eventually began dating this woman from work and moved in with her, at the time of her husband's abuse Dorothy felt as if she had "no place to go." Nevertheless, she left him approximately two months after the abuse had begun. She moved in with her lover from work, and began to file for divorce. Luckily, her ex-husband did not ever initiate contact with her again. Still, his threats continued to affect her subsequent relationship: she and her girlfriend began to quarrel over whether both of them should find another job. Since they both worked at the same fast food restaurant, Dorothy feared that her ex-husband would come to the workplace and put their lives at risk; her lover, in contrast, did not want to quit her job. The couple broke up after several months of being together, which led Dorothy to move in with her sister.

Although it remains important to emphasize the pressures confronting victims and survivors of abuse, scholarship has pointed to the continuous and problematic emphasis on women's "choice" to end abusive relationships, whereby this discourse obscures men's role in perpetrating the violence and places the burden of responsibility on women to end the abuse (Anderson and Umberson 2001; Berns 2001). Similarly, feminist research has challenged frameworks that separate domestic violence from gendered power relations by making it seem as if women and men perpetrate domestic violence to the same extent, with equally brutal consequences (Jakobsen 2014; M. Johnson 2006; Kimmel 2002). Thus, as gender remains deeply implicated in lesbians' violent experiences, homophobia alone cannot explain much of what they encounter. Indeed, although Dorothy's husband became violent because of her involvement with a woman, the abuse is considerably more complicated than simply reflecting homophobia. His hypocritical double standard whereby his cheating was normalized, while hers became problematic, reflects dominant gender and sexuality norms, whereby adultery from men is excused or justified—merely part of "who men are"—while women's adultery is viewed as violating fundamental social norms.

It is impossible to know whether Dorothy's husband would have reacted the same way had she had an affair with a man. At the same time, her lesbianism affected her decision to leave. In domestic violence relationships with men, lesbians, not yet "out," face their own set of pressures when trying to leave their abusers, especially to become involved with a woman for the first time. Dorothy's decision to leave her husband and move in with her girlfriend involved not only deciding to end her marriage but also choosing to enter into her first lesbian relationship. This decision did not necessarily make it "harder" for her to leave, yet the pressures are different from those faced by heterosexual women, who do not typically have to worry about "outing" themselves when leaving their abusive partners.

While lesbians usually experienced domestic violence when men learned of their lesbianism, one of the bisexual women in this study—Leslie, a fifty-year-old unemployed woman—did not experience a "turning point" in terms of when the violence began, as her bisexual identity was known from the beginning of the relationship. She met her ex-husband through a mutual friend; they began dating about five years prior to the interview, when Leslie was in her midforties. The relationship lasted for approximately three years, and they had one child together. Leslie told him on their first date that she was bisexual. She described him as "very nice" at the beginning of their relationship, but said that "things changed" once they got married. When he first became abusive, he did not mention her bisexuality, but Leslie now thought that the abuse was related to her sexuality from the very beginning. A few months into their marriage, he became what Leslie characterized as "controlling." He began to check up on her at all times and accused her of flirting with other men and women. Leslie characterized his accusations in this way: "I wouldn't be doing anything, like talking with the clerk at the checkout lane at the supermarket. 'Here's your fifteen cents, ma'am.' And he'd get mad. . . . [He would] hit me for that." These beatings at first did not directly address her bisexuality, yet Leslie thought that he viewed her as hypersexual because of her sexual identity; he also increasingly addressed her bisexuality over time.

Although her ex-husband usually accused her of flirting and cheating with men, Leslie thought that he became "most angry" when he viewed her as interested in another woman. At first, his accusations involved only men, but then he began to alternate between women and men. Leslie recalled one incident where he referred to her bisexuality, on the night of their two-year anniversary, when she was pregnant and he accused her during dinner of wanting to sleep with their waitress. When they arrived home, he insisted that she "would leave him for that" and asked her "how do you know what you want?" This question addresses her bisexuality, as "how do you know what you want?" is the type of question bisexual people confront in a society where heterosexuality and homosexuality are viewed as "stable" and unchanging identities, whereas bisexuality is more commonly viewed as elastic and variable. Even though bisexual people frequently view their identities as valid—perhaps stable in their fluidity—individuals who harbor negative attitudes toward bisexuality are troubled by its rejection of dichotomous sexual orientation (McLean 2007; Rust 2000). Prejudice confronting bisexual women is different from that confronting lesbians, and some evidence suggests that bisexual women experience violence from an intimate partner at higher rates than lesbian and heterosexual women; a 2010 survey from the Centers for Disease Control and Prevention found that bisexual women were the most likely to experience rape, physical violence, or stalking from an intimate partner (Walters, Chen, and Breiding 2013). The survey results showed that 35.0 percent of heterosexual women and 43.8 percent of lesbians had experienced violence from an intimate partner, while 61.1 percent of bisexual women had experienced this abuse. Among bisexual women, the vast majority—89.5 percent—reported having only male perpetrators of intimate partner violence; a smaller percent—67.4 percent—of lesbians reported having only female perpetrators (Walters, Chen, and Breiding 2013).

Similar to other bisexual women, Leslie certainly faced some challenges that lesbians would not face, and yet her experiences are not entirely rooted in prejudice against bisexual people. In particular, Leslie's status as a mother informed her experiences; while Dorothy did not have children, Leslie was pregnant during much of the abuse. Mothers in abusive relationships find themselves in particularly precarious positions, as they often remain in the relationship out of fear that their partner will murder the child if they were to leave (DeKeseredy and Schwartz 2009; Semaan, Jasinski, and Bubriski-McKenzie 2013). Indeed, on the night of their anniversary, Leslie's husband beat her with a belt and held a gun to her temple, telling her that if she left him, he would kill their "unborn baby," in addition to her. Narratives of domestic violence that focus on the role of mothers in providing a loving environment for their children frequently have problematic implications—effectively blaming the abused woman for not providing a safe home for her children, when the abusive man has created the unsafe living conditions for the children and the mother.

Assumptions about staying and leaving abusive relationships often associate separation with agency, yet women who stay in these relationships have agency as well (Mahoney 1994). Further, separation from an abusive relationship is often not a static, one-time event but a process that occurs over a considerable amount of time.[1] Given that violence sometimes does not end when women exit abusive relationships, the options of staying or leaving are both frequently dangerous acts (Elizabeth, Gavey, and Tolmie 2012; Mahoney 1994). At the same time, the risk posed to children's safety prompts some mothers to leave the home, as Leslie indicated when she described her husband threatening their child: "[That's when] I got all kinds of scared . . . [But also] knew that I should get out." This fear for her child's safety is what she now viewed as part of the reason for her leaving the relationship, although at the time she was also concerned about raising her child in a domestic violence shelter. Of course, not all victims would respond in the same way as Leslie: mothers often stay in abusive relationships because the lives of their children have been threatened, citing their children's safety as their primary concern and expressing fear that their children would be in greater danger if they were to leave (M. Johnson 2006; Stark 2007). Moreover, perpetrators of domestic violence frequently use the children to keep the mother from leaving (DeKeseredy and Schwartz 2009; Semaan, Jasinski, and Bubriski-McKenzie 2013). Thus, mothers in abusive relationships face these concerns in such a way that childless women do not, as only the former manage their children's well-being.

Although Dorothy and Leslie faced different concerns, neither of their experiences fit neatly into traditional understandings of anti-LGBT violence. Their experiences, however, are exactly the sort of incidents that lesbian, bisexual, and transgender women in this study described repeatedly. The experiences of transgender women in domestic violence relationships differ from those of lesbian and bisexual women, yet none of their experiences have figured prominently in discussions of anti-queer violence. Domestic violence in LGBT relationships has typically been examined as something that occurs among gay and lesbian couples, and occasionally, among transgender people and their cisgender partners (Kenagy and Bostwick 2005; Renzetti 1992; Ristock 2002). I am not dismissing the importance of domestic violence in LGBT relationships, but questioning the reasons that little attention has focused on abuse perpetrated by heterosexual, cisgender men against lesbian, bisexual, and transgender women.

Part of the explanation for this gap is due to male-centeredness, whereby most attention has focused on the violent experiences of gay men. This emphasis has erased many forms of anti-queer violence from the public imagination. Although transgender women are likely to experience violence at the hands of heterosexual, cisgender men at rates far outweighing public, stranger-based hate crimes against gay men, the latter forms of violence have received greater attention in the mainstream press (Grant et al. 2011; Halberstam 2005; Spade and Willse 2000). Of course, many experiences of antigay violence that I have emphasized have also not featured centrally in public conceptions of homophobic abuse. Certainly, homeless and low-income gay men have been largely ignored. Thus, it is not that the experiences of all gay men have been emphasized equally, but that the experiences of gay men with a particular race and social class position—largely white and middle class—have been given the most weight.

By focusing on middle-class gay men, lesbian and transgender women's experiences of domestic violence at the hands of heterosexual men are rendered invisible. Although several gay male respondents experienced violence from heterosexual men they had been sexually involved with, gay men did not experience domestic violence in relationships with these men. Erasing transgender women's experiences also contributes to the separation of domestic violence from traditional understandings of anti-LGBT abuse. A few lesbians experienced domestic violence from men after becoming sexually involved with women, yet these experiences were even more common among transgender women, many of whom described situations in which romantic or sexual partners became increasingly violent. Kayla, a thirty-six-year-old Black transgender woman, went on a date with a man she met at a bar. At the time of the interview, Kayla was unemployed, and two years prior to the interview she was living in a homeless shelter when she began dating this man. After dating for a month, the couple moved in together. She told him when they met that she was a "woman of trans experience." They dated for several months, and Kayla described his behavior as growing more violent over time.

Reflecting on his behavior, Kayla now viewed him as "one of those guys [who dates] trans women because he thinks he can get away with treating us [like] shit." She said that many people viewed him as a charming "people person" and that he generally treated her "like a princess." While he frequently complimented her and gave her gifts, over time he would mix these compliments with insults. Increasingly, he made derogatory comments about her body, referring to it as "gross" and "disgusting." She said that usually during sex he would not look at her and that he routinely implied she was "lucky" to be with him. The last time she saw him, he "exploded" when he felt her breasts, saying that he could no longer be with anyone "so disgusting." When Kayla told him their relationship was over and attempted to leave his apartment, he took out a knife and cut her face.

Transgender women have too frequently been written out of narratives about anti-queer violence, as their needs and concerns have become secondary to those of cisgender lesbians and gay men. Even in cases where antitransgender violence has been emphasized, mainstream attention has collapsed it with homophobic attacks. The film *Boys Don't Cry*, while revolutionary in some sense in its depiction of antitransgender violence, has even been accused of presenting the life of Brandon Teena, a transgender man brutally raped and murdered in 1993, as a lesbian love story (Cvetkovich 2003; Halberstam 2005). The experiences of transgender women should not be ignored or collapsed with those of lesbians, and yet in traditional analyses of anti-queer violence lesbians have often been written out of these narratives as well, as the victims generating the most media attention have typically been white gay men.

FAMILIAL REJECTION AND HOMELESSNESS

Low-income gay men's violent experiences have also been excluded from dominant discussions of anti-queer violence. Jayvyn's experiences—those of a thirty-three-year-old low-income Black gay man—differ from stereotypes of antigay attacks: he experienced routine violence while living in a group home throughout his twenties. Several men in the group home referred to him as "the faggot" and would constantly threaten his safety. The men would take crushed up glass and sprinkle it in his bed while he was sleeping. When Jayvyn woke up, he would have pieces of glass stuck in his skin. He described the violence and harassment in this way:

Let's say you've been in a place for like four or five years and it's the same thing every day. . . . And I never fought back. For the first two, three, four years, I never fought back. I would just take it. They would hit me with shit, throw shit at me. I would be the pit of all the jokes. I would just feel so low. There were points I was sitting there, I was just thinking, "I want to die." Because I'm like, "What do I do?" . . . Nobody did anything, so I was like, "You know what? Fuck it. I am just going to go the fuck off, and I am just gonna kill these motherfuckers."

In response, Jayvyn did the same thing to the men as they did to him: "I used to take lights like that and crush them up into a fine glass and sprinkle it in their bed while they slept. And they'd wake up and scratch the glass into their arms. . . . I don't know if they died or not, but that's kind of dangerous. But I used to do that because it came to a point where I would go to the staff—the staff wouldn't do anything about it."

The idea that home is not a safe space for many LGBT people assumes they have a home in which to live. For Jayvyn and other low-income LGBT people, their home was frequently a homeless shelter, group home, or even the streets. At other times, they lived with friends or romantic partners. Their experiences reveal that one's home is not always a fixed, stable location, but can be considerably more fluid. Jayvyn, similar to several other low-income LGBT people, ran away from home during his late teenage years, when he was eighteen and had graduated from high school. His biological parents died when he was young, and he was raised by an aunt, who served as his adoptive parent. He described his aunt sorrowfully and said she knew he was gay, but "never approved." She beat him almost every day when he was a teenager; some of these beatings occurred when she criticized Jayvyn's feminine gender performance. He described her as "hating gay people," but he did not run away solely because of her homophobia, as he described her as a "very abusive" person, perpetrating violence arbitrarily and routinely in ways that could not necessarily be connected to her homophobia.

Although media and scholarly attention have occasionally focused on homophobic violence in the home, homelessness and abandonment have not typically been part of these narratives. Indeed, the arc of Hollywood movies and TV shows typically focuses on the "coming out" narrative, followed by others' triumphant acceptance. These narratives, however, conceal the rejection that many LGBT people face, especially familial abandonment. For low-income LGBT people, the consequences of familial rejection are particularly harsh, as they have fewer resources—little or no money to fall back on, fewer friends and family members who can help financially—than their middle-class counterparts. My students—and, I imagine, much of the public at large—tend to love narratives that Americans should just learn to be nice, tolerant people and accept others' differences.[2] Although tolerance can be a worthy goal, I doubt that these ideas do much to challenge the societal privileging of heterosexuality over homosexuality.[3] Hollywood movie narratives that suggest that everyone should simply overcome their prejudices imply that they are easy to overcome. That idea is far from accurate: privileged people hold on to their privileges and have a hard time seeing how others might be disadvantaged. Moreover, as substantial sociological research shows, individuals discriminate and hold prejudicial views, even when insisting that they do not (Bonilla-Silva 2006; Ziegert and Hanges 2005). As a result, while discrimination frequently occurs behind closed doors—when others are not looking—it nevertheless happens in these contexts because individuals have many prejudices of which they are not aware and feel most comfortable engaging in discriminatory acts when others cannot judge them as intolerant people.

Acknowledging that many of us hold unconscious prejudices can potentially lead to questions about how to change them, yet inequality is a social rather than an individual phenomenon. Dominant U.S. narratives construct prejudice as something that one person should change rather than something that should be changed societally. Prejudice is thus seen as a personality trait rather than a structural feature of society. These ideas are comforting to believe because as long as we are not hateful or highly prejudiced—and not many people will admit that they are—then we do not have to worry much about how we contribute to these institutionalized systems that privilege some people and disadvantage others. Still, systems of oppression such as racism, sexism, and heteronormativity exist beyond what any one person does, as they are institutionalized throughout our society—the attributes associated with some privileged groups of people are held in higher esteem than the attributes associated with other marginalized groups. Our society distributes privileges unequally based on many characteristics, including race, class, gender, and sexuality, and it does little good to ignore this reality. Men, white people, and heterosexual people continue to enjoy many advantages that their female, Black, and queer counterparts do not. LGBT people being kicked out of their home may be a consequence of an individual prejudiced person's actions—their parent or legal guardian rejecting them—but these actions are made possible by a social structure that encourages individuals to view homosexuality, but not heterosexuality, as something that brings shame onto one's family. Discrimination, after all, may appear as an individual act, yet it stems from social conditions.

Although low-income LGBT people experience particularly severe consequences from familial rejection, including homelessness, middle-class LGBT people experience violence and rejection from family members as well. Thomas, a forty-one-year-old Asian gay man who worked at a marketing consulting firm and described his salary as "six figures," said that his father disowned him when he "came out." Thomas grew up in a middle-class family, where his mother was a school teacher and his father was in the military. At the age of thirty-two, he told his father that he was gay while home for vacation; his father threw him out of the house, saying, "I don't want to see you anymore." They had not spoken to each other since this incident, nine years before the interview. His father's abusive behavior started when Thomas was young, however. Thomas recalled several occasions in which his father would beat him for crying, telling him to "stop acting like such a sissy [and] be more of a man." Thomas gave very long, drawn-out answers during much of the interview, but his answers to questions concerning his father were curt. Abrupt responses to familial violence were common, as respondents frequently found these experiences the most difficult to discuss.

Thomas was active now in the Log Cabin Republicans, a conservative gay rights group, and criticized gay men for not "taking responsibility" in dealing with familial violence: "Yes, gay people get discriminated against, but at the same time people have to take responsibility for their own perception of how they present themselves in the world and stop complaining and do something about the discrimination." These ideas were tied in part to strength, as Thomas described people "complaining" and associating with "victim culture" as an example of "people identifying themselves from their weakness instead of from their strength." Ideas of "personal responsibility" remain problematic to the extent that they leave social structures unchanged. If anti-LGBT discrimination arises out of social conditions, then collective attempts to change these conditions would be the most effective. Reducing violence against LGBT people is a societal and collective responsibility, not an individual one.

Most gay men did not address personal responsibility as directly as Thomas, yet his emphasis on strength was commonly expressed among gay men. Thomas described his strengths by picking up the tape recorder and placing it near his mouth, listing off his many attributes:

> I am much more than my biology, my history, my experience. I am an individualized, unrepeatable, creative, whole, perfect, complete, ageless, timeless, limitless, boundless, infinite, bold, self-actualized, open, receptive, teachable, reachable, unbeatable, unstoppable, multidimensional, faithful, loving, strong, wise, powerful, imaginative, understanding, willing, willful, orderly, enthusiastic, pure, spiritual, outlaw, powerhouse person who is made in the image and likeness of all infinite possibility, and I refuse to stand there and sit around in this whole victim culture with two stiff buns so tight that they're bouncing off the wall.

Thomas spent much of the interview focusing on his strengths. This speech, which he told me he had memorized, reveals his desire to reject notions of himself as weak. Hegemonic forms of masculinity—the ideal set of masculine practices— prescribe that men should reject behavior associated with femininity; as weakness remains associated with devalued masculinities, gay men regularly went out of their way to emphasize their strength (Anderson 2002; Asencio 2011; Connell 1995).

Similar to Thomas, most gay men were kicked out of their homes only when "coming out" as gay, but the violence typically began at a young age, when they had performed gender inappropriately. Gideon, a twenty-five-year-old Black gay man, described times during his childhood when his mother physically abused him for playing with dolls and reading books with female characters: "She would hit me and say, 'Do you want to be a faggot? Do you want to be a sissy?'" During this time, he was also beaten by classmates and called homophobic names. When he told his mother about the violence he had experienced at school, she was dismissive, attributing it to his feminine behavior: "That's why they call you a faggot," she told him, pointing at a book he was reading that had a female protagonist. Gideon's mother, like Thomas's father, told him that she "never wanted to see [him] again" when he disclosed his sexuality at the age of seventeen. Gideon did not have a steady job at the time and moved in with his older sister after being kicked out of his home. He had remained unemployed since moving in with her. In contrast, Thomas revealed his sexuality to his father much later, at the age of thirty-two, when he had a college degree and full-time job. Although Thomas undoubtedly experienced considerable pain from his father's rejection, it did not have the same economic consequences as the rejection Gideon faced, in which he no longer had a parent providing emotional and financial support for him when he was a teenager.

In this sense, familial rejection affected LGBT people's social class standing. A few LGBT people grew up in middle-class homes, but now scraped by on little economic resources. This downward mobility was particularly common among transgender respondents, who sometimes experienced familial rejection that led to their becoming poor. Nevada, an intersex thirty-six-year-old white person, grew up in a middle-class home with a stepfather, also white, who worked as a sales representative and a biological mother who worked in a beauty salon; Nevada was now unemployed, living in a homeless shelter. Raised as a boy, Nevada regularly experienced anti-queer violence from her family members, particularly her stepfather who would tell her to "toughen up."[4] At the age of five, she told her parents that she might be a girl. After this conversation, Nevada said that she was beaten "almost every day," primarily by her stepfather but sometimes by her mother as well. She described her stepfather as beating her and telling her things such as "I'll kill you if I think you're gonna be a fag." During high school, she began to view herself as intersex, perceiving her sex characteristics as both female and male and viewing the "corrective" surgery on her ambiguous genitalia as a form of "butchery." At this time, Nevada's parents became even more violent, forcing her to adopt a masculine image: "The normalization process was them forcing me to be a boy. Even though they knew it was hurting me, they didn't care. They just forced me to present a male image, so they could have the functional family."

When the violence became "too much," and Nevada realized they would "never accept" her, she ran away from home at the age of eighteen. Nevada was not speaking to her parents, and at the time of the interview, she had recently decided never to speak to her brother again: "He calls me 'brother it.' Like the last time I called him, he called me 'brother it,' and called me by the name that I grew up by. I told him, 'You can't give me respect?' . . . He was like, 'No.' I was like, 'All right, bye.' I'll never phone his fucking stupid ass again. I'm tired of being hurt." Nevada fought back tears when describing this incident, as her brother's casual way of dehumanizing her—referring to her as "brother it"—caused her considerable pain. While lesbian and gay male respondents, regardless of social class position, usually described at least one family member who had provided emotional or financial support, intersex and transgender people were more likely to describe rejection from all of their immediate family members.

This rejection from the entire family was often coupled with transgender people having a difficult time finding work because of prejudice in the formal employment sector. Employment discrimination was particularly common when transgender people were in the process of transitioning from one gender to another. Lela, a forty-eight-year-old Black transgender woman, described a former boss telling her that she was not allowed to work in front of customers at a fast food restaurant because she "might make them sick."[5] Similar to many transgender respondents, Lela experienced familial rejection and could not find work as she began the transitioning process—that is, as she began to change her gender identity from the sex she had been assigned at birth to the gender she felt aligned with her sense of self. As transgender respondents went through this process of transitioning, they often, but not always, underwent sex reassignment surgery and hormonal replacement therapy. Transgender people regularly described this process as a fluid one that took place over their entire life, without a clear starting and ending point. Nevertheless, when undergoing hormonal replacement therapy, the violence directed against transgender people frequently increased, as it became more apparent that they were transitioning their gender. Lela, who left home at the age of sixteen when her mother would not accept her transgender identity, said that her siblings "seemed OK" with her being transgender at first, but then "turned [their] backs" on her after she underwent sex reassignment surgery and began to live her life as a woman; strangers more frequently harassed her during this time as well. At this point, Lela also had difficulty finding work. She initially took the job at the fast food restaurant, under the assumption that she would be working as a cook, but then quit when her boss told her that she could not work at the cash register because she "might make [the customers] sick."

These dual occurrences of being kicked out of home and having difficulty finding work led Lela, at the urging of her transgender friends, to become involved in sex work. Lela, unlike a few of the other transgender women in this study, never experienced sexual assault or physical violence during her time as a sex worker. She described the experience as "good overall" because it let her "pay the bills." At the same time, the potential for violence and harassment undoubtedly increased as a result of her involvement in sex work, which resulted in large part from being kicked out of her home and having difficulty finding work in the formal economy. Familial rejection potentially sets in motion a series of events in which transgender people must support themselves through means such as sex work and, therefore, subject themselves to the potential hardships that accompany it in the United States.

For transgender people, familial rejection has particularly harsh consequences, given the widespread discrimination they confront in the formal economy (Grant et al. 2011; Spade 2011). After all, while Lela found a job at a fast food restaurant, many other transgender people cannot find any work, especially during their transitioning process when employers are particularly likely to discriminate (Grant et al. 2011; Lombardi et al. 2002). Even when transgender respondents did find work, they were more likely than gay and lesbian respondents to describe workplace harassment that drove them from their jobs. Helping transgender people to find safe, accepting workplace environments and helping parents accept their transgender children are strategies likely to aid transgender people considerably more than increasing police surveillance of sex workers. The former strategies address the problems that lead to a whole series of other challenges, while the latter strategy simply encourages greater policing of transgender people—a problematic solution given that many transgender respondents experienced violence from the police. Increasing police involvement in transgender communities potentially heightens the prospect of abuse; helping transgender people, in contrast, find constructive home and workplace environments inevitably reduces their likelihood of confronting violence.

Finding safe living environments for homeless transgender people is difficult in a context where most homeless shelters are segregated based on birth sex rather than gender identity (Mottet and Ohle 2006; Spade 2013). Indeed, Lela, after working at the fast food restaurant, lived in a homeless shelter for a period of six months, but described it as "so bad" that she could not stay. She was the only woman living among hundreds of men. At night, when she was sleeping, Lela said that the men did "all sorts of horrible things," which included occasions in which two men would hold her hands and feet while other men would hit her with hard objects—typically socks with rocks or marbles in them. In describing the violence, Lela became particularly angry at the response she received from the staff members, one of whom was a gay man that Lela went to for help, only to be told, "There's nothing that can be done, no." Other transgender respondents also shared their frustrations at unsupportive LGB people, revealing that lesbians and gay men are not exempt from transgender prejudice. Even more important than the actions of the staff members is that many homeless shelters are set up in such a way that transgender people are placed in harm's way. Certainly, the housing of transgender women with cisgender men makes antitransgender violence possible—likely, even. In leaving the homeless shelter, Lela effectively viewed the streets as a safer alternative: "I couldn't escape [the violence]. . . . They'd just tell me how I had to be with the men. . . . It got so bad that I just had to leave [and become homeless]." Lela's experience, and that of other transgender people like her, reveals the limits of attributing homelessness to personality characteristics, as Lela viewed the streets as her safest option when confronting formal isolation in the employment sector and institutionalized violence in the homeless shelter.

EXPRESSIONS OF RACISM, CLASSISM, AND MISOGYNY

Some of the statements made by LGBT people reveal that attempts to undermine homophobia can reproduce racism, classism, and sexism. Respondents engaged in this process of challenging anti-queer prejudice by expressing racist and classist statements: Page, a forty-five-year-old Latina lesbian, told me, "I do not like Black people," and Ted, a thirty-three-year-old white male respondent, said that he expected violence from "someone like that" in response to being attacked by a Black man. Further, Mary, a forty-seven-year-old white transgender woman, described one of her perpetrators as "a wise ass," before pausing as if she was going to use a racial slur, and then said "ethnic person" instead, in a disgusted tone. Mary's response was also shaped by social class. She responded to a question concerning her perpetrators' motivations by saying, "These people, it's just like they're lazy and don't have anything better to do." Her inflection when saying "these people" suggested Black people—one of the men who called her a derogatory slur was Black—or perhaps people of color more generally. Pejorative characteristics such as "lazy" people who "don't have anything better to do" have been attached to low-income Black and Latino people throughout U.S. history (Provine 2007; Roberts 1997). As a result, low-income Black and Latino people confront classism more frequently than their white counterparts, even though low-income white people certainly experience it as well. While overtly classist, Mary's comment masks blatant racism; at times, classist statements are less stigmatized than overtly racist ones, leading some individuals to make classist comments while harboring racist thoughts. Knowing that public expressions of racism may be challenged, individuals sometimes condemn low-income people of color based on their social class position.

Mary's statement illustrates that in response to violence white LGBT people may express racism or classism as a way of condemning their perpetrators. In dealing with the pain of their violent experiences, LGBT people may blame other marginalized groups for causing them anguish. As other scholars have demonstrated, members of marginalized groups sometimes deal with oppression by reproducing dominant social norms (Espiritu 2005; Garcia 2012; Wilkins 2008). The LGBT people in this study confronted suggestions that their lesbian, gay, or transgender identity was morally wrong; respondents also faced insinuations that they were inferior to their attackers. One way of attempting to overturn these suggestions, as Mary did, is by drawing on existing power relations to point out the inferiority of poor heterosexual people of color. What this strategy does, however, is produce gains for white LGBT people on the backs of poor, heterosexual people of color; it also reinforces dominant power structures—institutional racism and social class inequality—that many LGBT people confront.

A few LGBT people of color described other, usually white, queer people enacting racism. Daniel, a twenty-six-year-old Black gay man, when asked if he had experienced racism from gay men, gestured "a little bit" with his hands and then described a time when two white men—one of whom was gay—had joked about how he had gotten into college just "because of affirmative action." This idea is the logic by which institutional racism obscures itself, as if society is somehow set up to benefit Black people. These discourses are particularly popular in white supremacist groups, whereby white people are constructed as the victims of racial prejudice (Blee 2002; Ferber 1998). Conservative media have also advanced these narratives in which white, presumably straight, men are supposedly the last social group it is safe to attack. Nevertheless, insults directed toward women are far more acceptable than those toward straight white men: women in the public eye are more likely to be ridiculed and disparaged. Institutionalized norms in our society, then, actually shield white heterosexual men from ridicule, and pointing out their privilege is a quick way to have one's ideas or work dismissed as "political."

My work here does not focus on white and affluent heterosexual men, although it remains important to note their relative privilege in comparison to most LGBT people. At the same time, sexism and misogyny in LGBT communities remains underexamined, in need of more serious consideration. The phrase "misogynistic gay man" is certainly not an oxymoron. Most gay men in this study did not use openly misogynistic language, yet a few distanced themselves from femininity, arguably to the point of expressing misogyny. Walter, a twenty-four-year-old Black gay man, rejected notions of himself as feminine when he said, "I ain't no bitch, I'm just a man." When asked what he meant by the term "bitch," he responded with the following: "I don't date a person who considers themselves a homosexual or a girl or this kind of stuff. He considers himself a man or he considers himself a young adult. [The guy I'm sexually involved with] considers himself a grown ass man. He's a grown ass man. That's all I hang out with: people who consider themselves a man. I don't hang out with people who consider themselves a homo or a fag or some girly thing. I just don't like how they carry themselves. They carry themselves in a very disrespectful way." Throughout the interview, Walter equated women with feminine gay men, using the same terms—"bitch," "girl," "weak"—to describe both of them. He seemed to have internalized homophobia, linking femininity with many of the things that are wrong with the world.

At one point, he overtly expressed misogyny, saying that he "hates females with a passion." This response came when describing an ex-girlfriend who had threatened to tell others that he was gay. Walter indicated that he had served jail time for an "altercation" between the two of them. I interpreted his statement as an indication that he had been arrested for domestic violence—for hitting her after she had threatened to tell others of his sexuality. Moreover, one of his violent experiences involved a man calling him a "bitch," which prompted Walter to threaten the man with a knife. The male stranger then hit Walter in the face and ran away. Several weeks later, when Walter ran into the same man at a deli, he cut the male stranger on his face. Describing his motivations, Walter seemed most upset that he had been called a bitch: "I do not like someone calling me a bitch. I do not like females at all. That's my opinion about them. And for somebody to call me that, that gets under my nerves even more. So, that's why I react to that word." Walter seemed to retaliate against challenges to his masculinity, disassociating himself from femininity and directing his rage at women and feminine gay men.

Since gay and especially Black men have historically been stereotyped as misogynistic, we must be cautious about making too much of Walter's response. Indeed, most Black gay men did not respond in this way; instead, they typically valued femininity. Thus, it would be a mistake to view Walter as representative of LGBT people of color in general or Black gay men in particular. Nevertheless, to challenge unequal power relations, we must pay attention to marginalized groups advancing their own position by reinforcing other inequalities. If the goal is to overcome all relations of domination, then these strategies must be challenged and ultimately abandoned. Attempts to undermine racism by reproducing sexism and homophobia reinforce discrimination against lesbians, gay men, and heterosexual women, just as attempts to undermine homophobia by bolstering racism and classism further the oppression of middle-class people of color and low-income people across racial lines.

8 • CONCLUSION

Anti-Queer Violence and Multiple Systems of Oppression

Many LGBT people's violent experiences are considerably more complex than simply reflecting homophobia. Lesbians encountered forms of violence that were simultaneously sexist and homophobic, facing suggestions that butch lesbians had "converted" feminine women into homosexuality. Black gay men confronted violence simultaneously directed against their race and sexuality, often from the police; Black lesbians shared some similarities with their male counterparts in that both of these groups confronted ideas that they should represent their racial groups in a positive way—ideas that white LGBT people did not face. Still, Black lesbians' experiences differed from those of gay men of color in that the former more frequently faced sexual assault and sometimes even confronted domestic violence perpetrated by heterosexual men. Social class played an important role in these experiences: low-income lesbians found it difficult to leave domestic violence relationships because they had few resources and feared that their partners would harm their children, while low-income Black gay men experienced violence in group homes and homeless shelters. Familial rejection also had particularly harsh consequences for low-income LGBT people, as they had few resources to rely on for help. When low-income queer people were kicked out of their home, they usually experienced homelessness; middle-class LGBT people, in contrast, did not typically become homeless because they had resources—wealth and formal education—they could use to find work and avoid homelessness.

Antitransgender violence must be viewed as separate from prejudice and discrimination based on sexual orientation given that transgender people, in contrast to their cisgender LGB counterparts, encountered dehumanizing forms of violence in which they were constructed as objects. Facing widespread job discrimination, transgender women were sometimes involved in sex work, where they confronted sexual assault and abuse through their involvement with clients and the police. They also faced widespread violence in institutionalized settings such as prisons and homeless shelters, both of which are often segregated based on birth sex rather than gender identity. Such policies house transgender women with cisgender men; as a result, the former are exposed to considerable abuse, at times making them the only transgender woman housed with hundreds of men. A few transgender respondents even "chose" to remain homeless because the streets were safer than the conditions they faced in homeless shelters, and these respondents especially experienced little help from law enforcement, with one respondent being told by a police officer that she "couldn't be raped" because she "wasn't a real woman."

All of these findings point to significant differences among LGBT people—differences profoundly shaped by race, class, and gender. My analysis could be expanded upon to include other dimensions of inequality, such as age, religion, or immigration status, yet the larger point is that the mainstream gay rights movement needs to move beyond single-issue advocacy that focuses solely on sexuality. To challenge homophobia, scholarly and activist work has too frequently made it seem as if LGBT people experience violence uniformly. Under the rubric of "hate crime," scholarship on anti-queer violence has emphasized the broad, negative effects of this form of abuse (D'Augelli and Grossman 2001; McDevitt et al. 2001). Politics is built into this work, as homophobic hate crime has been made to seem extraordinarily awful in its consequences, and as broadly affecting LGBT people. What this strategy has done, however, is to gloss over the many differences among sexual minorities. Consequently, this scholarly and advocacy approach has made anti-queer violence into something it is not—a similar experience among LGBT people. Overlooking these differences serves some LGBT people's interests more than others—primarily those who do not need to concern themselves with anything but reducing homophobia. Queer people affected by racism, sexism, and social class inequality benefit considerably less from political strategies that focus only on homophobia; in some cases, they are actually harmed by such approaches.

New ways of speaking about anti-queer violence are necessary, as it has frequently been linked with notions of "stranger danger." Hate crime brings to mind images of a stranger brutally attacking a gay or lesbian person. These notions reinforce problematic race and social class politics, constructing the perpetrators of anti-queer violence as irrationally and extraordinarily violent. The hate crime against Matthew Shepard, the most well-known antigay attack, is a prototypical example: perpetrators who brutally murdered a gay man simply because of his sexuality. Unfortunately, "stranger danger" narratives rely on notions of violence as involving an "unstable," and implicitly low-income, person of color attacking an innocent, and implicitly middle-class, person. Indeed, given that low-income people of color, particularly Black men, have historically been stereotyped as "unruly" and out of control, narratives that focus on random attacks from strangers inevitably reinforce these stereotypes, implying that low-income people of color are in need of being controlled (Collins 2000; Hanhardt 2013; Roberts 1997). Individuals across race and social class lines commit acts of anti-queer violence, but the language of hate crime implies a white gay male victim and a low-income perpetrator of color. As victims are frequently associated with privileged LGBT subjects, and perpetrators are implicitly linked with marginalized race and social class groups, the idea of homophobic hate crime challenges homophobia by strengthening inequality based on race and social class.

These concerns are particularly important given that the U.S. prison population has expanded rapidly over the past three decades (Alexander 2010; Wacquant 2009). Although this expansion is due largely to the war on drugs, hate crime laws are also part of this history of expanding criminalization, in which punishment has increasingly been valued over rehabilitation (Garland 2001; McCorkel 2013; Rios 2011). Indeed, stranger-based forms of violence that suddenly and randomly occur are quite rare, yet media and conservative movements have exaggerated their frequency, calling for more punitive laws, which inevitably increase the prison population (Beckett and Sasson 2004; Soss, Fording, and Schram 2011). Hate crime laws, quite simply, do not protect LGBT people from violence, as perpetrators do not avoid committing this abuse because they will serve additional jail time.[1] Advocates of hate crime laws often respond to this argument by suggesting that the laws have symbolic effects, encouraging greater tolerance and acceptance of LGBT people and thereby decreasing the likelihood of anti-queer violence in the future (Lawrence 1999). Still, progressive approaches must question for which LGBT people hate crime laws supposedly facilitate safety. The statutes expand the scope of police and prosecutorial power by funding bias crime units, encouraging police officers to apprehend offenders, and allowing prosecutors to charge defendants with extraordinarily harsh sentences. Given that the police frequently administer rather than prevent anti-queer violence, many LGBT people should be suspicious of these efforts to increase police and prosecutorial power, as such attempts are likely to harm queer people vulnerable to police violence—disproportionately low-income LGBT people of color.[2]

Sexual-orientation-based hate crime laws also benefit LGBT people in different ways based on race. Inevitably, the laws benefit individuals who find it easiest to determine that violence is based on their sexuality or gender identity; as I found, white gay men were the most likely to view their violent experiences as homophobic, while LGBT people of color expressed less certainty, particularly when a white man perpetrated the violence, because they could not be certain whether racism or sexism had also played a role. As Dominique, a twenty-three-year-old Black transgender woman, said, "When I'm called a fag or a freak by a white person, I have a hard time telling if they hate me because I'm trans or because I'm Black." Kimberlé Crenshaw (1989) has argued that antidiscrimination laws are frequently ineffective in helping Black women, who must position their discriminatory experiences as either racist or sexist, even when they are both of these things. LGBT people of color are similarly helped less by hate crime laws than white gay men, given that the former experience forms of violence that often cannot be easily classified as homophobic because they are rooted in racism and sexism in addition to homophobia or antitransgender prejudice.

Hate crimes are also not the forms of violence that most LGBT people experience, much less the forms confronting lesbians, LGBT people of color, and transgender people. Indeed, police brutality, sexual assault, and state-sanctioned violence are seldom viewed as part of "hate crime." Although lesbian and transgender women experienced forms of sexual assault from strangers, these forms of stranger-based violence are not what people think of when hearing about anti-queer violence. These omissions are due largely to the male-centered nature of much of the advocacy and scholarly work concerned with reducing homophobic abuse. The goal is not to include more forms of stranger-based violence in these narratives, but to shift the focus away from public attacks on the street and toward private and institutionalized forms of violence, including those experienced by lesbians in the home, by transgender people under state control, and by LGBT people of color from the police. Further, efforts to reduce anti-queer violence will accomplish little without addressing the social problems that arise along with concentrated poverty; any strategy that fails to reduce economic marginalization and improve the social safety net is bound to leave in place the violence confronting LGBT people in low-income neighborhoods.

More recently, narratives concerning anti-queer violence have expanded beyond hate crime to include bullying in schools. Initially, I found great promise in these discussions—after all, bullying indicates the degree to which LGBT people face violence and discrimination at a relatively young age—but as the advocacy work progressed, the very same tropes emerged. The victims of bullying have repeatedly been positioned as white gay men— frequently at college campuses—and the case receiving the most media attention involved an Indian American college student, Dharun Ravi, facing charges for driving a white gay man, Tyler Clementi, to commit suicide. Some of the facts of the case were hidden: although it was widely reported that Clementi was closeted, he was actually "out" at the time of the suicide (Parker 2012). The reason for this misrepresentation is in part because normative conceptions of lesbians and gay men establish "the closet" as a site of suffering, but the act of "coming out" as emancipatory, where queer lives are supposedly bound to improve. Nevertheless, many LGBT people's lives are not made "easier" upon disclosing their sexuality or gender identity.

More important than the facts of the Clementi case are the reasons it received widespread media attention at this particular moment in time. Many LGBT people commit suicide every year in the United States, and yet this case was among the very few that received national media exposure. Scholarship has pointed to Ravi's ethnicity as a contributing factor, as the United States has increasingly come to position itself as exceptional in its tolerance toward homosexuality (Puar 2012). Although Ravi is American, his ethnicity positions him as foreign, as "other," in the mind of many, largely white, people in the United States. Thus, the case served dominant U.S. goals: in comparison to other implicitly "backwards" countries, the United States is supposedly "more tolerant"; the implication is then that other countries need to become more like the United States. These narratives not only justify U.S. mistreatment of other countries but also gloss over the many forms of anti-queer violence facing LGBT people in the United States. As a result, ideas of American exceptionalism must be resisted in the hope of reducing anti-queer violence. Allowing these narratives to continue privileges the United States, and, implicitly, white heterosexual Americans as the epitome of tolerance. Focusing on the experiences of multiply marginalized LGBT people, including LGBT people of color, is one of the ways to challenge these arguments. Indeed, LGBT people of color experience violence at the hands of relatively powerful white and middle-class men, including police officers, intimate partners, and supervisors at work.

Conservative race, class, and gender politics remain deeply entrenched in much of the mainstream gay rights movement; work attempting to reduce anti-queer violence is but one example.[3] Indeed, although this dichotomy simplifies LGBT advocacy work, queer organizing has divided between dominant, mainstream organizations that focus primarily on providing acceptance for normative middle-class lesbians and gay men and those serving LGBT people marginalized based on race, class, and gender, in addition to sexuality (Mogul, Ritchie, and Whitlock 2011; Spade 2011; Ward 2004). The Human Rights Campaign (HRC) has the most funding of any gay rights organization in the United States, and yet its politics, while certainly center-left, are arguably the least progressive of any mainstream gay rights organization (Ghaziani 2011; Walters 2014). In pushing LGBT organizations to take race, class, and gender more seriously, those who can afford to do so must invest time and money in those organizations serving marginalized LGBT people.

Although real and important changes have taken place over the last twenty years—from increasing media representations to medical, inheritance, and immigration benefits for married gay couples—real dangers lie ahead for LGBT organizing that views these changes as sufficient. Conservative gay rights activist Andrew Sullivan famously stated, "Following legalization of same-sex marriage and a couple of other things, I think we should have a party and close down the gay rights movement for good" (Groff 1997, quoting Sullivan). To emphasize the persistence of inequality, LGBT advocates must challenge these statements implying complete social progress. Narratives of undisputed advancement ignore the many ways in which progress has not been made, and how some social conditions have even worsened, including a growing wealth divide between the rich and the poor and the rapid expansion of the U.S. prison population, which has disproportionately affected low-income people of color (Harvey 2005; Western 2006). As Black LGBT people, particularly Black transgender women, have been harmed by increasing criminalization policies, many LGBT people's lives have not "gotten better" over the last thirty years. Public expressions of homophobia have arguably decreased, but more pervasive heteronormative social conditions have certainly remained intact.

Equal rights have also sometimes failed to produce equality, as legal discrimination has simply been replaced by less formal, unequal practices. Although many Americans concluded that formal legal equality has eliminated the problem of discrimination following the civil rights movement and the abolition of Jim Crow, widespread racial disparities still exist throughout American society: from housing and employment to education and the criminal justice system. The feminist movement has been similarly dismissed as only relevant to the past, even though women continue to make only three-fourths as much as men (Faludi 2006). In this regard, laws outlawing discrimination do not necessarily limit its occurrence; short of proof—documentation that can be shown in court of an employer admitting to firing a person based on race or gender—discrimination continues to occur because those in powerful positions are still free to favor some groups and discriminate against others as long as they do not formally admit to doing so (Spade 2011). Discrimination, that is, continues to occur even though prohibitions against it are written into the law. The LGBT rights movement should take seriously the limits of formal equality, as sexuality and gender identity are bound to remain fundamental ways of dividing people in the United States, despite any legal gains that are made.

Pointing to societal differences between LGBT people and heterosexual people is likely to become exceedingly difficult as the mainstream gay rights movement has downplayed these differences. In advocating for gay marriage, the mainstream gay rights movement has frequently used the phrase "love is love"—a nonsensical phrase if ever there was one—to advance the idea that lesbian and gay couples love each other just as heterosexual couples do.[4] Such phrases are classically assimilationist—that is, a strategy whereby minority groups emphasize their similarities to the mainstream in the hope of gaining acceptance.[5] The problem with assimilation in this way is that it reinforces rather than challenges dominant norms (Walters 2014). A particular type of heterosexual love, and all of the familial tropes that implies, remains ideal. Yet, even among heterosexual people, not all forms of love are viewed equally, as some are granted considerable more esteem than others, and LGBT people should not have to insist "we're just like you" to avoid discrimination.

With regard to race, narratives that purport to be neutral have been described as colorblindness—when individuals ignore racial hierarchies, remaining "blind" to the effects of race, and yet the structures of society continue to work in favor of white people (Bonilla-Silva 2006; Carbado 2013; Gallagher 2003). As a result of colorblindness, people of color are discouraged from pointing out racism they encounter in their daily lives and white people are encouraged to overlook the privilege they gain from their racial identity, while simultaneously reaping the rewards. I have noticed a similar shift in discussions of sexuality, which I have described as "sexuality blindness." With gay marriage increasingly becoming accepted in the United States, norms have shifted in such a way that differences based on sexuality are supposed to be ignored. During my adolescence, in the late 1990s, most of my high school classmates would not have been offended at being accused of homophobia—some even wore it as a badge of honor—and yet if someone mentioned the existence of homophobia, nearly everyone would have acknowledged its presence. Conversely, in my sexualities classes now, students rarely admit to having homophobic thoughts, while at the very same time these students are frequently invested in downplaying ideas that heterosexuality remains privileged in such a way that homosexuality is not. According to these perspectives, lesbians and gay men can get married now; it's time to move on.[6]

These arguments downplaying the persistence of discrimination must be resisted: after all, one need look no further than the rates of LGBT youth being kicked out of their homes and becoming homeless to see that prejudice and discrimination against queer people continues. Low-income lesbian and gay youth, and especially transgender adolescents, remain considerably more likely to become homeless than heterosexual, cisgender people (Cochran et al. 2002; Gibson 2011). Discrimination based on sexuality and gender identity remains in many areas of social life, and attempts to limit LGBT people's rights have increasingly been advanced under the guise of "religious freedom." In 2014, proposed legislation in states such as Arizona and Kansas would have allowed Christian businesses the right to refuse service to LGBT customers; in 2015 similar legislation was controversially passed and revised in Indiana. Further, the current version of the Employment Non-Discrimination Act (ENDA), an attempt to prohibit discrimination against LGBT people in the workplace, exempts religious organizations, including not only churches but also religiously affiliated hospitals and schools, effectively allowing them to discriminate against LGBT people. Currently, without the passage of ENDA, an act that that would federalize these employment protections, it is legal to fire people based on sexual orientation in twenty-nine states and based on gender identity in thirty-two states.

Employment protections, however, do not prevent discrimination from continuing in modified, less overt, ways. Indeed, these protections do nothing to prevent the familial rejection experienced by the LGBT people in this study. Thus, legal parity, while important in some ways, must not be viewed as equivalent to genuine equality, as heterosexual and cisgender people continue to enjoy a myriad of privileges, including routine familial acceptance, that LGBT people do not. It does little good, then, to ignore these realities, and the LGBT rights movement must challenge narratives that emphasize sexuality blindness. Notions of "personal responsibility" must also be resisted, as U.S. social norms increasingly position unequal social conditions as the product of individual "choice." Focusing on marginalized LGBT people's experiences is a good way to resist these ideas, as their lives reveal how homophobic and antitransgender discrimination persist in the United States.

Hate crime discourse has helped to downplay societal discrimination by associating anti-queer violence with the actions of a highly prejudiced person. The danger of this idea is that it reproduces notions that homophobic violence occurs because an individual person "hates" lesbians or gay men, not because social conditions are set up in such a way that homosexuality is stigmatized. A more productive analysis would focus on the social structures that make anti-queer violence possible instead of viewing it as socially decontextualized, individual pathology. These ideas also define prejudice in individualistic ways. In U.S. media, discrimination is most frequently discussed as the property of individuals, with emphasis being placed on whether one person has said or done something racist, sexist, or homophobic. These discussions not only prevent analysis of more important matters concerning social inequality but also distort the more subtle and pervasive ways that discrimination operates, where nothing "hateful" is said but the act has lasting, discriminatory consequences. Discrimination frequently operates through reflexive favoritism rather than aggressive "hate": a white boss who routinely favors white applicants for a job—passing over the vast majority of Black candidates—or a transgender woman who cannot find housing because landlords ignore her application.[7] Nothing explicitly hateful is said in these situations, but they are undoubtedly discriminatory.

I worry that in focusing only on calling out individual racist, sexist, and homophobic language that we simply push these acts behind closed doors, while simultaneously making ourselves feel better. Opposing public expressions of bigotry can be productive, of course, but more large-scale changes are also necessary, as systems of inequality are resilient and slow to change. Attempts to emphasize "straight pride" and to attach homosexuality with notions of "political correctness" are part of this conservative resistance to LGBT people in public arenas. The notion that a heterosexual person has to be "politically correct" around a lesbian or gay person—something I have heard much more frequently over the past five years than before this time—reframes heterosexual people as the "true victims" of sexuality norms in the United States. This line of thinking contends that heterosexual people are being prevented from saying something they really think instead of saying what is true. As a result, these ideas shift attention from a lesbian or gay person's experiences of homophobia to a heterosexual person's experience of being labeled homophobic, reinforcing ideas that it is more difficult to be accused of homophobia than to experience it.

Although I have little tolerance for the "politically correct" label, it is important to push beyond challenging only individual acts of discrimination. Pointing to something racist, sexist, or homophobic, while potentially useful in revealing the larger social forces at work, keeps the focus on individuals rather than social structures. Under individualistic understandings of prejudice, anyone can be bigoted; according to this line of thought, some Black people dislike white people, just as some white people dislike Black people. Of course, prejudice against Black and white individuals is not equal, and experiments generally show that people across racial lines hold unconscious prejudice against Black women and men (Ziegert and Hanges 2005). Still, sociological analyses of inequality throw out questions of who is the "most racist." Under societal understandings, these individualistic determinations have little relevance: Black people are more likely than white people to live in poor neighborhoods, attend bad schools, and work in low-wage jobs. Whether or not one person has prejudicial thoughts tells us nothing about these societal dynamics. Inequality is a collective process, not an individual one.

Social forces also establish hierarchies within communities, not only between them. In LGBT communities, lines have increasingly been drawn between mainstream lesbians and gay men—those who want to get married and raise children, for example—and less normative queer people. This divide, often described as "homonormativity" in which heteronormative ideals are incorporated into gay communities, has been viewed as one between the "good gay" and the "bad queer" (Duggan 2003; Seidman 2002; Williams, Giuffre, and Dellinger 2009). These divisions are inevitably bound up in race, class, and gender, as white and middle-class gay men have greater access to normative dimensions of gayness, while those who do not have these necessary identity markers—much less the age, weight, and attractiveness requirements—will find it considerably more difficult to pass as a "good gay." The problem with these distinctions, then, is that many queer people are being left behind by mainstream gay rights advocacy, as issues such as homelessness or police violence have remained largely absent from the mainstream gay rights agenda. In this sense, LGBT advocacy has not benefited all queer people equally. Gay marriage does not substantially improve the lives of most homeless LGBT people; certainly, some low-income queer people benefit from gay marriage, but their needs have not guided the agenda. Instead, much of gay rights advocacy has served lesbians and gay men who are well-off financially, assuming that benefits and privileges will trickle down to less privileged queer people.

With regard to violence, divisions among LGBT people become problematic to the extent that they reproduce ideas that some queer people "deserve" protection. By implication, other LGBT people are less worthy—or, more aggressively, this idea would translate into they "get what they deserve." I have noted many examples of LGBT people facing these ideas throughout this book; transgender sex workers confronted suggestions from the police that they were somehow deserving of violence because of their involvement in sex work. Lesbian, bisexual, and transgender women who experienced sexual assault sometimes faced similar ideas based on what they had done before the assault, as if they somehow brought it on themselves. In contrast, privileged representations of anti-queer violence have frequently focused on the "gay kiss" (Haritaworn 2010). Although many respondents in this study experienced violence after public displays of affection, the acts were usually less normative and more in your face than a single kiss. The "gay kiss" has likely received such widespread attention because the assumption is that no one—"not even" a queer person—deserves to experience violence for engaging in such an act. Still, the gay kiss narrative is associated with lesbians and gay men of a particular race and social class standing; a Black transgender woman kissing her Latina butch lesbian girlfriend is likely to be read very differently than two white, conventionally attractive lesbians or gay men kissing on the street. Both the act and the identities of the people involved shape whether the public display of affection will be viewed as deserving or undeserving of violence. As gay marriage becomes more normative, conventional forms of romance, including kissing and holding hands in public, as well as marriage and monogamous coupling, are likely to be viewed as even more worthy of protection, while other queer formations, including being single, sexual, or nonmonogamous may be afforded even less protection.

These divisions privilege the experiences of the "good gay," and thereby paint very broad strokes with regard to LGBT people, focusing overwhelming attention on a relatively small percentage of queer people. While white lesbians and Black gay men with social class privilege figure in some mainstream media representations, the needs and concerns of low-income queer people have rarely been discussed publicly. Mainstream gay rights organizations have paid little attention to social class inequality in part because of alliances that have been created between corporations and LGBT activist groups (Walters 2014; Ward 2008; Whitehead 2011). Any gay pride parade serves as an advertisement for a multitude of corporations. In one specific example of this trend, in 2012 an antigay group called One Million Moms protested Ellen DeGeneres's role as the new spokesperson for JC Penney. Ellen, as well as gay rights organizations, called for lesbians and gay men to show their support by shopping at JC Penney, thereby undermining antigay groups. If this action—giving money to a corporation—is what gay rights activism has come to, then the movement is in serious trouble. Supporting LGBT rights should involve giving time or money to an organization that supports LGBT rights, not a corporation that cares primarily about making a profit.

These alliances with corporations diminish much of the radical potential of LGBT activist work. Indeed, gay marriage has become accepted by much of U.S. society at the same time as laws have been enacted in U.S. states criminalizing people for not disclosing an HIV-positive status to their sexual partners (Hoppe 2013); mainstream gay rights groups have been largely silent in mobilizing against these policies. Sex workers' rights have been similarly ignored by the mainstream gay rights movement, which has not fought against criminalization policies targeting transgender sex workers, many of whom remain isolated from the formal economy due to widespread job discrimination (Grant et al. 2011; Spade 2011). Moreover, my concern with hate crime discourse is that mainstream gay rights movements have become complicit in blaming poor people for social problems rather than working to fix the social conditions that lead to them. In particular, by advocating in favor of hate crime laws, gay rights groups have helped make the criminal justice system even more punitive, allowing prosecutors to charge defendants with extraordinarily harsh sentences in the hope of securing plea bargains. Hate crime laws, after all, are a strategy of criminalization, not prevention (Mogul, Ritchie, and Whitlock 2011; Moran 2001; Reddy 2011). Reducing anti-queer violence cannot possibly be accomplished by simply imprisoning more poor people; moreover, because of biases in the criminal justice system, people of color are bound to be disproportionately harmed as a result of harsher criminalization policies.

Although some mainstream gay rights organizations will undoubtedly continue to serve the interests of a relatively narrow group of LGBT people, resistance can occur not only by supporting the organizations that aid low-income queer people but also by challenging assimilationist ideals that encourage queer people to be "normal." Race and class are fundamental to notions of normalcy, yet LGBT people are divided into "good" and "bad" camps in many other ways as well, including HIV status, age, religion, immigration status, and, increasingly, marital and relationship standing. Gender is also deeply implicated in these divisions: among gay men, femininity remains devalued, and mainstream representations of gay men have increasingly incorporated traditional aspects of masculinity. Frank Bruni, who became the first openly gay op-ed columnist for the *New York Times* in 2011, regularly writes about his affection and love for sports. These mainstream media representations were not around ten years ago, much less twenty or thirty. One of the consequences of these representations is that they have granted privileges to gay men who present themselves as similar to heterosexual men (Carbado 2013). Gay men face new pressures to present themselves as "normal," as just like heterosexual men, save for that one little thing that is different—their sexuality.

Lesbians face these pressures as well, although it is perhaps a bit more complicated, since women sometimes increase in status by performing masculinity: standards of normalcy for lesbians, then, are less likely to require them to repudiate masculinity in the same way that gay men are encouraged to reject femininity (Denissen and Saguy 2014; Kazyak 2012). At the same time, lesbians in this study frequently confronted violence for appearing as butch in their gender presentation of self. Although lesbians gain status for performing masculinity in some contexts, they are punished for gender nonconformity and masculine gender performances in others.

A lot of the changes that have taken place over the past twenty years have certainly been positive, but hierarchies based on gender performance continue. Gender conformity remains privileged over gender nonconformity, and LGBT people who adhere to gender norms are increasingly becoming accepted into the mainstream, while LGBT people who discard traditional gender displays continue to be stigmatized. The point is not necessarily that conditions are better or worse now, even though they are different, but that it is as important as ever to pay attention to how gender is policed. Although I am not arguing that gender is more important than sexuality, the United States has hardly become a paradise for butch lesbians and feminine "sissy boys." Considerable evidence suggests that feminine gay men, often not valued in LGBT communities, experience significant negative mental health consequences when others insult their gender identities (Rieger and Savin-Williams 2012; Sandfort, Melendez, and Diaz 2007). Queer challenges to these processes must not merely encourage tolerance of homosexuality but also emphasize the value of gender-nonconforming presentations of self. Narratives that emphasize social progress typically overlook these gendered components, ignoring how gender nonconformity is culturally devalued. Public tolerance of homosexuality has become increasingly common, yet it is much more debatable as to whether this tolerance has benefited gender-nonconforming queer people.

Focusing on gender, as well as race and social class, helps to move beyond strategies that simply benefit LGBT people who are already the most privileged. The phrase "LGBT people" is even quite simplistic, as I have highlighted many differences in how lesbians, gay men, and transgender people experience violence. Thus, while using the phrase "LGBT people" is useful for highlighting the challenges confronting individuals who experience discrimination based on gender and sexuality, the phrase can become problematic when it is used to gloss over differences and to stand in for the experiences of a very small group of relatively privileged LGBT people. At the very least, then, it remains important to emphasize the differences among individuals who belong to this extraordinarily broad category— LGBT people—or else work will inevitably reinforce homonormativity by privileging the most normative gay subjects. While other scholarship may find it useful to abandon this phrase altogether—focusing instead on the differences among transgender people or among lesbians—emphasizing some similarities among LGBT people can be productive. Still, what is needed is an analysis of LGBT people's experiences that takes power and inequality seriously, exploring how social forces unequally distribute life chances. Such an analysis then allows for work to improve the conditions of LGBT people in the broadest way possible, while also not harming other marginalized groups. After all, improving the position of LGBT people at the expense of Black, Muslim, or Latino Americans reinforces racism and Islamophobia; given that many LGBT people are Black, Muslim, and Latino, such strategies harm queer people of color. Thus, in opposing anti-queer prejudice and discrimination, it is essential to avoid challenges that also reinforce regressive race, class, and gender politics.

Descriptions of violence often end on a hopeful or uplifting note, as if to suggest it can all be overcome. While hoping to avoid such a narrative here, I maintain that LGBT people's violent experiences will be better understood by focusing not only on homophobia and heteronormativity but also on other dimensions of inequality. By perpetually emphasizing sexuality, we continue to favor the experiences of the most privileged LGBT people—those who need the least help—and marginalize the experiences of the most disadvantaged. I have perhaps been short on solutions and long on problems, but the implication of my analysis is that scholarly and advocacy work should begin with the experiences of marginalized LGBT people rather than starting with the experiences of the most privileged subjects and assuming that benefits granted to them will trickle down to less privileged queer people. By doing so, scholarship and activism concerned with anti-queer violence can benefit the widest possible range of LGBT people, including the most marginalized.

APPENDIX
Methods

I interviewed forty-seven people from 2006 through 2011, recruiting participants from a wide range of organizations in New York City, many of which provide services for LGBT people of color. At these organizations, recruitment flyers were placed on a bulletin board or in a waiting room. The flyer read: "Have you experienced violence because you are (or were perceived to be) lesbian, gay, bisexual or transgender?" People interested in participating in the study then contacted me. Given the sensitive nature of this study—asking LGBT people to share their experiences of violence with a stranger—the recruitment process was relatively slow, as I sometimes had to wait several weeks before a person would call me. This process made it difficult to interview a lot of people, but also gave me plenty of time to sharpen and refine the questions I asked—what qualitative researchers describe as their "interview protocol"—and allowed me to analyze the data at the same time as I was interviewing people.

Many LGBT people who experience violence would never respond to a recruitment flyer, and the people I interviewed are probably overrepresented in experiencing normative forms of anti-queer violence such as public attacks on the street. Lesbian, bisexual, and transgender women who had experiences of sexual assault may have been particularly hesitant to participate, especially given that the name on the recruitment flyer was male. Moreover, as public discussions of anti-queer violence have changed since 2006–2011, participants were probably particularly likely to contact me if they had experiences of homophobic street violence, while now, in 2014, LGBT people might be more likely to respond to the same flyer if they had experiences of antigay bullying. Qualitative research is rarely generalizable—my results here cannot be viewed as representative of all LGBT people's experiences of violence—and yet qualitative work is useful for revealing the context of people's lived experiences, as well as their perceptions of those experiences, and for providing in-depth, nuanced data.

During the interview, I asked respondents to describe their experiences in detail and to explain their understanding of violence more generally. I conducted what qualitative social scientists refer to as "semistructured, in-depth interviews," which means that I had some questions prepared, while also asking different follow-up questions depending on how participants responded to my initial questions. Respondents were asked a variety of questions: how they defined violence, how they perceived physical and verbal abuse, and what they thought the person committing the violence was trying to accomplish. They were also asked to explain any possible racial implications and to describe how they determined that the violence was based on their sexuality or gender identity. The interviews lasted from approximately one to three hours; the median interview was 104 minutes.

Studies of homophobic hate crime have typically used survey or questionnaire methods to examine LGBT people's evaluations of their violent experiences (see Herek, Gillis, and Cogan 1999; Rose and Mechanic 2002), yet some social scientists have argued that an interview method is more useful for capturing the ways in which respondents create meaning (Holstein and Gubrium 1995). Moreover, interview studies examining anti-LGBT violence have generally employed highly structured interviews with each respondent asked a uniform (but small) number of questions (see Herek et al. 1997). This method allows for a large sample size, but it prevents respondents from actively constructing their own narratives (Holstein and Gubrium 1995). In contrast, I employed a less structured approach, allowing respondents to guide much of the discussion and to describe their violent experiences in detail.

My social position as a white gay man undoubtedly shaped what respondents said: white respondents sometimes felt comfortable making arguably racist statements and gay men occasionally shared sexist thoughts with me. Conversely, LGBT people of color generally focused on homophobia, perhaps suspicious of how their experiences of racism would be described by a white, male academic. My analysis of the data is also inevitably immersed in power dynamics: although I have tried not to reinforce hierarchies of race, class, and gender, larger social structures undoubtedly shape sociological research, including my own. Despite these political concerns, I asked respondents to describe their experiences of racism and misogyny, which they often outlined in detail; the frequency with which LGBT people of color described such experiences—even under conditions, with a white gay man, where they might have felt uncomfortable sharing such incidents—demonstrates the importance of race and gender norms in shaping many forms of anti-queer violence.

Following the interviews, I analyzed the interview data by using the qualitative coding software program ATLAS.ti. I transcribed each interview and sorted what respondents said into different "codes," or conceptual categories. These codes—for example, "respondents' perceptions of physical violence"—were broad initially, but then became more specific as I continued interviewing. The code "respondents' perceptions of physical violence" became a series of narrower codes: "connections between physical and sexual violence" and "perceptions of physical violence as more severe than verbal abuse," among others.

Respondents' demographic characteristics are presented in a table on the following pages; after the interview, participants completed a short questionnaire providing this information. In total, I interviewed twenty women, seventeen men, and ten transgender people. All of the men identified as gay and fifteen of the women identified as lesbian; three women identified as heterosexual and two as bisexual. Eight of the transgender people identified as male-to-female (MTF), one as female-to-male (FTM), and one as intersex. Participants ranged from twenty to sixty-two years old; the median age was forty-three. Concerning race and ethnicity, twenty-one participants identified as Black or African American, sixteen as white, eight as Latina or Latino (five identified as Puerto Rican, two as Mexican, and one as Colombian), and two as Asian (one identified as Chinese and one as Vietnamese). I have used the phrase "LGBT people of color" to denote Black, Latino, and Asian participants. As twenty-one of these respondents identified as Black, and eight identified as Latina or Latino, this research project focuses primarily on the experiences of Black LGBT people, and to a lesser extent on the experiences of Latino participants.

I did not quantify respondents' social class positions, but I did ask about their job histories, as well as what their parents did for a living; on the questionnaire, respondents were also asked to report their income and their highest educational degree. Most respondents belonged to one of two broad social class groups: (1) they experienced considerable financial strain, which sometimes included extreme poverty or homelessness and typically involved cycling in and out of temporary, low-wage work; or (2) they held professional, upper-middle-class jobs, coming from relatively well-off, albeit not wealthy, backgrounds. Since respondents received twenty dollars for their participation, this financial compensation attracted a fair number of poor LGBT people; conversely, several upper-middle-class respondents said that they did not need to be financially compensated for their time. This difference led to a partially bifurcated sample with middle-class respondents, most of whom were upper middle class, and low-income participants, about half of whom had experienced long-term unemployment or homelessness. Thus, throughout *Violence against Queer People*, I have used the categories of "low income" and "middle class" to describe some differences among respondents; although these categories are imperfect, they reflect social class differences among the people in this study. Race, ethnicity, and social class also intersected in some important ways: most white respondents described working primarily in professional or high-income jobs and most Black and Latino participants described working in low-income occupations or said they were unemployed. This division along race and class lines arose in part from my sampling technique: most of the organizations where I placed flyers appeared to serve either a largely middle-class white population or a predominantly low-income Black and Latino population.

Respondents' Demographic Characteristics and Experiences of Violence

Gender and sexuality (with pseudonyms)	Age	Race/ ethnicity	Education	Occupation	Forms of anti-queer violence experienced
Lesbians					
Diamond	51	Black	High school diploma	Unemployed	Physical, verbal, sexual assault
Tamika	53	Black	High school diploma	Unemployed	Physical, verbal
Jetta	28	Black	High school diploma	Unemployed, unpaid volunteer work	Physical, verbal
Jasmine	44	Black	High school diploma	Security guard	Physical, verbal
Latoya	50	Black	College degree	Balloon decorator	Physical, verbal, sexual assault
Aisha	53	Black	College degree	Dental assistant	Physical, verbal
Page	45	Latina	High school diploma	Unemployed, recently quit the police force	Physical, verbal, sexual assault

Gender and sexuality (with pseudonyms)	Age	Race/ ethnicity	Education	Occupation	Forms of anti-queer violence experienced
Tina	21	Latina	Some college	College student	Physical, verbal
Judy	43	Latina	College degree	Unemployed, unpaid nonprofit work	Physical, verbal, sexual assault
Maria	26	Latina	College degree, MA student	Graduate student/ adjunct college teacher	Physical, verbal
Martha	54	White	Some college	Nursing assistant	Physical, verbal
Dorothy	49	White	College degree	Security guard and auxiliary police officer	Physical, verbal
Jill	49	White	College degree	Kindergarten teacher	Verbal
Catherine	46	White	Graduate degree	Professor/activist (nonprofit work)	Verbal
Julia	28	White	Graduate degree	Pediatrician	Verbal
Bisexual Women					
Leslie	50	Black	High school diploma	Unemployed	Physical, verbal
Ling	29	Asian	College degree	Temporary office jobs	Physical, verbal
Heterosexual Women					
Anne	41	Black	8th Grade	Unemployed	Physical, verbal
Lisa	36	Latina	College degree	Homemaker	Physical, verbal
Emily	55	White	Some college	Salesclerk	Verbal
Gay Men					
Walter	24	Black	9th Grade	Unemployed	Physical, verbal
Cole	33	Black	High school diploma	Part-time cook	Physical, verbal
Gideon	25	Black	High school diploma	Unemployed	Physical, verbal

(continued)

Gender and sexuality (with pseudonyms)	Age	Race/ethnicity	Education	Occupation	Forms of anti-queer violence experienced
Jayvyn	33	Black	High school diploma	Secretary	Physical, verbal
Daniel	26	Black	Some college	Receptionist	Physical, verbal
Andre	24	Black	Some college	College student	Physical, verbal, sexual assault
Kevin	62	Black	College degree	Coordinator for a nonprofit	Physical, verbal
Frankie	48	Latino	10th Grade	Unemployed—occasional janitorial work	Physical, verbal
Thomas	41	Asian	College degree	Marketing consultant	Physical, verbal
Bill	51	White	College degree	Auxiliary police officer	Physical, verbal
George	45	White	College degree	Adjunct college teacher	Physical, verbal
Greg	43	White	College degree	Paralegal	Physical, verbal
Mark	46	White	College degree	Paralegal, public interest law	Physical, verbal
Paul	57	White	College degree	Corporate/marketing work	Physical, verbal
Bob	54	White	College degree	High school teacher	Verbal
Ted	33	White	Graduate degree	Corporate lawyer	Physical, verbal
Jacob	40	White	Graduate degree	Medical doctor	Physical, verbal
Male-to-Female Transgender Women					
Lakeisha	38	Black	8th Grade	Unemployed, unpaid volunteer work	Physical, verbal
Ebony	20	Black	11th Grade	Sex worker	Physical, verbal, sexual assault
Lela	48	Black	High school diploma	Unemployed	Physical, verbal

Gender and sexuality (with pseudonyms)	Age	Race/ ethnicity	Education	Occupation	Forms of anti-queer violence experienced
Eva	46	Black	High school diploma	Receptionist	Physical, verbal, sexual assault
Dominique	23	Black	Some college	Unemployed, occasional sex work	Physical, verbal, sexual assault
Kayla	36	Black	Some college	Unemployed	Physical, verbal
Carol	39	Latina	High school diploma	Nonprofit work	Physical, verbal, sexual assault
Mary	47	White	Graduate degree	Physician	Verbal
Female-to-Male Transgender Men					
William	29	Latino	High school diploma	Temporary clerical work	Physical, verbal
Intersex					
Nevada	36	White	High school diploma	Unemployed	Physical, verbal

NOTES

CHAPTER 1 INTRODUCTION

1. Pseudonyms are used throughout to respect respondents' confidentiality.

2. Studies of LGBT hate crime victims and social movements concerned with preventing anti-queer violence have focused overwhelmingly on homophobia and heterosexism, revealing the psychological costs of homophobic violence (Dunbar 2006; Herek, Gillis, and Cogan 1999; Jenness and Broad 1994). Anti-queer violence, however, can typically be explained not only by sexuality but also by gender, as many of its forms occur when LGBT people "do gender" inappropriately (Perry 2001; West and Zimmerman 1987). Nevertheless, with a few notable exceptions (see Mason 2001, 2002; Perry 2001), studies of LGBT hate crime victims have typically neglected the gendered implications of anti-queer violence, overlooking how gender and sexuality are simultaneously implicated in LGBT people's violent experiences (Mason 2002). Herek (1990), for example, notes that lesbians and gay men both experience violence for violating gender norms, yet conceptualizing homophobic hate crime as emanating from "cultural heterosexism" ignores the role of sexism and misogyny in shaping forms of antilesbian violence (see Herek et al. 1997).

3. Studies typically assume or imply that transgender people experience more violence than LGB people, even though these groups are not usually compared (Kosciw 2012; Lombardi et al. 2002; Perry and Dyck 2014; Stotzer 2009). Nevertheless, data from advocacy groups shows alarmingly high rates of violence and discrimination experienced by transgender people, especially transgender women of color (Ahmed and Jindasurat 2014; Grant et al. 2011). Moreover, the National Coalition of Anti-Violence Programs found that 72 percent of all anti-LGBT homicide victims in 2013 were transgender women, even though the number of lesbians and gay men in the United States is undoubtedly larger; thus, transgender women are murdered at higher rates than lesbians and gay men, due in large part to antitransgender prejudice (Ahmed and Jindasurat 2014).

4. Savage (2008) attaches homophobia to Black heterosexual Americans. See Puar (2007) for an analysis of how homophobia has been attached to people of color, especially Muslim populations, to justify racist and colonial practices. Puar's (2007) widely cited concept of homonationalism contends that gay rights have frequently been co-opted for other aims, as the United States has positioned itself as exceptional in its tolerance toward homosexuality as a way of justifying the Iraq War and the detention of Muslim Americans.

5. For exceptions, see Moran (2000, 2001), Richardson and May (1999), and Tomsen (2006). The exclusion of social class from scholarship on anti-queer violence reflects broader trends, as intersectionality theory has tended to focus on the overlap of sexuality with race and gender more than with social class (Choo and Ferree 2010).

CHAPTER 2 MORE THAN HOMOPHOBIA

1. Respondents' gender presentations of self should be viewed as situational accomplishments, as West and Zimmerman's (1987) well-known concept of "doing gender" suggests that individuals continually perform gender through interaction. For further discussion of gender as something one does, rather than simply who one is, see West and Zimmerman (2009).

2. Miller (2001) suggests that women who violate gender norms are often characterized in such negative ways, becoming stereotyped as overly aggressive or emotionally weak.

3. For feminist debates on lesbians' gender presentations, as well as the terms "butch" and "femme," see Moore (2006) and Nestle (1992).

4. Moore (2011) has pointed to differences between Black and white lesbians in their gender presentations of self. While white lesbians have frequently been immersed in lesbian-feminist efforts to replace butch and femme gender displays with androgyny, low-income Black lesbians have more often felt liberated by explicitly masculine gender displays, presenting themselves as "aggressive" to emphasize how they are in control of their own sexuality. Thus, although dichotomous understandings of lesbian sexuality are frequently too simplistic, it remains important not to condemn lesbians for identifying as "masculine" or "feminine," since evidence suggests that low-income lesbians of color are the most likely to adopt masculine presentations of self.

5. While research has found race and gender differences with regard to the likelihood of confronting anti-LGBT violence, these studies have generally not focused on social class (see Dunbar 2006; Herek 2009). Thus, although scholarship remains limited on the relationship between social class and the likelihood of experiencing anti-LGBT violence, it seems likely that low-income LGBT people would encounter these forms of abuse more frequently than their middle-class counterparts given that low-income people are more likely to confront violence than people from other social classes (Britton 2011; Moran 2000).

6. Research suggests that population density rather than macroeconomic conditions correlates most strongly with antigay hate crime, yet research has generally not compared the likelihood of low-income LGBT people encountering violence with the likelihood of LGBT people from other social groups (Green et al. 2001).

7. Randall Collins (2008) theorizes that contrary to traditional understandings that make violence appear smooth and uncomplicated, violence is a rare, uneasy, and disorderly process that is fraught with tension, and the product of the situation rather than the internal characteristics of an individual.

8. Abrajano (2010) also found that increased Black and Latino turnout did not result in the passage of Proposition 8, but she did find that Black voters were more likely than white voters to favor the ban.

9. Puar (2007) argues that emphasizing the persecution of LGBT people has been used to reinforce racism and Islamophobia, perpetuating violence against Black and Muslim Americans and promoting attacks against countries in the Middle East.

10. Hannah Arendt's (1970) classic work *On Violence* provides an important contrast here, as she argues that even though violence and power seem concurrent, violence generally occurs when power is slipping away. For Arendt, violence is not the ultimate expression of power, but the product of its decline.

11. Gender norms construct women's violence as especially deviant, as performing masculinity through violence is sometimes applauded, while such behavior is much more frequently viewed as inappropriate for women (Messerschmidt 2012; Meyer 2009).

12. More generally, Lewis (2013) argues that hate crime perpetrators are frequently demonized as a way of constructing social inequality as "un-American," even though the United States remains profoundly unequal.

13. McCormack's (2012) research suggests that in the United Kingdom homophobia is largely on the decline, as many male adolescents no longer feel compelled to emphasize their masculinity through homophobia. His research contrasts, in many ways, with Pascoe's (2007) research in the United States.

CHAPTER 3 "I'M MAKING BLACK PEOPLE LOOK BAD"

1. Despite the universalizing tendencies of the mainstream gay rights movement— where the differences among LGBT people are glossed over in the name of presenting a unified, homogenous front—considerable research indicates that LGBT people do not have uniform interests, but rather interests differentiated along race and social class lines (Carbado 2013; Moore 2006; Ward 2008).

2. Representations of LGBT people of color have increased in recent years, with positive portrayals in the film *Pariah* and the television shows *The Wire, True Blood,* and *Orange Is the New Black.* Still, these representations remain infrequent and most of them have focused on Black LGBT people, as Latino and Asian LGBT people have not been presented quite as often. For critiques of media representations of LGBT people—many of which have been of affluent white men—see Avila-Saavedra (2009).

3. See Kearney (2004) for a review of research on how welfare affects fertility rates. She suggests that most scholarship has not found a causal relationship between welfare and pregnancy; some studies have found a relationship among some racial groups, but not among others. Kearney's own research examined the effects of welfare family caps, which prohibit families from receiving additional assistance if a child is born into a family already on welfare. She found that welfare family caps did not reduce birth rates.

4. For analyses of how these representations affect perceptions of lesbian and female sexuality, see Jackson and Gilbertson (2009) and Webber (2013).

5. Gray (2009), Moran (2000), and Ward (2008) are among the few researchers to focus explicitly on the experiences of white, low-income LGBT people. As they argue, the needs and concerns of low-income LGBT people have remained largely absent from mainstream sexualities scholarship.

6. Several scholars have placed these pressures in the context of a "politics of respectability" that Black LGBT people confront, whereby they are encouraged to present themselves in a "respectable" way, and therefore discouraged from disclosing their homosexuality (Collins 2004; Moore 2011). Still, research suggests that LGBT people of color have frequently resisted a politics of respectability, challenging their invisibility in white LGBT communities and heterosexual communities of color (Cohen 1999; Meyer 2012; Thomas 2001).

7. Schilt and Westbrook (2009) found that media representations of antitransgender murders frequently present transgender people as "lying" about their gender, which the authors describe as the "deception frame" for legitimizing antitransgender violence.

8. For a parallel examination of how women in a domestic violence shelter resisted the staff's attempts at control, see Gengler's (2012) astute analysis.

9. The heterosexual men in Bridges's (2014) study also distance themselves from traditional standards of masculinity, but his research suggests that they do so by concealing the benefits they gain from gender and sexual inequality. In contrast, Asencio's (2011) research on Puerto Rican gay men suggests that some gay men feel pressured to distance themselves from femininity to gain status in queer communities and the larger society.

10. Some of the participants in Moore's (2011, 148) study encountered similar pressures around motherhood and the politics of respectability, as she found that "claiming a lesbian identity makes the mothers in my study particularly sensitive to whether they are being seen as 'good mothers' by others."

CHAPTER 4 GENDERED VIEWS OF SEXUAL ASSAULT, PHYSICAL VIOLENCE, AND VERBAL ABUSE

1. Most research focusing on LGBT hate crime victims does not address sexism and misogyny (see D'Augelli and Grossman 2001; Herek, Cogan, and Gillis 2002; Levin 2010). For work that gives gender more serious consideration, see Mason (2001), Perry (2001), and Tomsen and Mason (2001).

2. See Herek (1990) and Herek et al. (1997).

3. Perry's (2001) work is an important exception here, as she persuasively analyzes the role of gender in forms of anti-LGB violence, although arguably to the point of downplaying heteronormativity.

4. Gibson (2011) and Spade (2011) mention this gap and give considerable attention to homelessness among LGBT people.

5. This understanding of anti-queer violence as shaped primarily by gender and sexism has informed subsequent work, as Perry (2001, 110) conceptualizes "gay-bashing as a response to doing gender inappropriately," making little reference to homophobia and heterosexism.

CHAPTER 5 RACE, GENDER, AND PERCEPTIONS OF VIOLENCE AS HOMOPHOBIC

1. Gail Mason (2001, 2002) and Stephen Tomsen (2006) further examine the intersection of gender and sexuality regarding anti-queer violence (see also Tomsen and Mason 2001).

2. Herek and colleagues outline the importance of contextual cues in how lesbians and gay men determine the causes of their violent experiences (Herek et al. 1997; Herek, Cogan, and Gillis 2002). These studies found that lesbians and gay men often examine their perpetrators' statements to determine whether violence is based on their sexuality. In these situations, lesbians and gay men confront explicit, unambiguous homophobic remarks, while at other times they identify incidents as antilesbian or antigay by examining the context. For instance, victims perceive violence as rooted in homophobia when it occurs near a gay-identified location or when it occurs after public displays of affection between same-sex couples (Herek et al. 1997; Herek, Cogan, and Gillis 2002).

3. For further elaboration of my critique of hate crime laws, see Meyer (2014), which situates the laws in their historical development and critiques the legislation through intersectionality theory and a leftist, queer perspective. Lewis (2013) provides even more detail on how the laws developed in relation to leftist and conservative political movements. In some of my previous work, I have used the phrase "hate crime victim," which I would now avoid because I worry that using this discourse reinforces notions of "stranger danger" and reproduces power imbalances based on race and social class (Meyer 2008, 2010).

CHAPTER 6 "NOT THAT BIG OF A DEAL"

1. For further information concerning respondents' social class positions, see the appendix. In Meyer (2010), I also provide more detail on respondents' social class positions and how their evaluations should be viewed in light of previous scholarship.

2. These differences between middle-class white respondents and low-income people of color correspond with research indicating that middle-class people frequently convey a sense of entitlement (Lareau 2003; Williams 2006). Indeed, white, middle-class LGBT people often expressed entitlement concerning rights to their personal space, highlighting violations of these rights as reasons for viewing their violent experiences as severe. Low-income people of color, in contrast, less frequently described their rights as being violated.

3. Future research is needed to examine possible racial differences among groups of LGBT people who are similarly positioned based on social classes. Middle-class white respondents emphasized the severity of their violent experiences more than the few middle-class LGBT people of color in this study, which suggests that race, in addition to social class, may affect the degree to which individuals view violence as severe.

4. Many hate crime studies have privileged the effects of hate-motivated physical violence, constructing this abuse as the most severe, while also overlooking the importance of social class (D'Augelli and Grossman 2001; Herek, Gillis, and Cogan 1999; Rose and Mechanic 2002).

CHAPTER 7 THE HOME AND THE STREET

1. Stark's (2007) concept of "coercive control" is particularly relevant here, as he theorized that domestic violence is not simply a matter of physical abuse but also entails a myriad of emotional attacks, such as intimidation, humiliation, and isolation, designed to disempower the person experiencing the abuse (for further analysis of the role of gendered power relations in coercive control, see Anderson 2009; Stark 2009).
2. This tendency reflects the value accorded to therapeutic language in the United States, which tends to focus on the power of the individual to overcome their biases. Alyson Cole (2007) argues that therapeutic language problematically "tends to preserve the status quo . . . [as] attention shifts from evaluating social circumstances to focusing on individual character. The struggle for power becomes an exercise in self-help" (138).
3. Walters (2014) is even less accepting of tolerance as a goal for LGBT politics, as she refers to it as a "trap" and argues that it is a conservative approach of "accepting" difference rather than a more radical embrace of queerness.
4. Gender-neutral pronouns, such as "ze" or "hir," are often used for intersex people. Ze is used as an alternative to "she" or "he," and hir (pronounced "here") is used in place of her/his and her/him. Nevada referred to herself as "she" throughout the interview; thus, here I have used the same gender pronouns that she used.
5. Several of the transgender men in Schilt's (2011) study encountered similar comments.

CHAPTER 8 CONCLUSION

1. The deterrent argument in favor of the laws rests on the faulty assumption that offenders would not feel deterred by punishment for the underlying crime, but would feel deterred by the additional sentence enhancements that hate crime laws specify. Given that the statutes likely have no deterrent effect, the laws are not an effective means to reduce anti-queer violence, and LGBT people must concern themselves with other prevention strategies (Franklin 2001; Mogul, Ritchie, and Whitlock 2011; Moran 2001).
2. As LGBT people of color, particularly those in low-income neighborhoods, are most likely to be harmed as a result of increased police surveillance, the role of hate crime laws in further subsidizing and expanding law enforcement harms many LGBT people (Reddy 2011; Spade 2011). Quality of life policing strategies such as arresting homeless people and sex workers reveal the costs of providing greater funding and more discretionary power to the police, as transgender women and low-income LGBT people kicked out of their homes are disproportionately harmed as a result of these policies (Mogul, Ritchie, and Whitlock 2011; Spade 2011).

3. See Carbado (2013) for an analysis of gay rights advocacy challenging the military policy, "Don't Ask, Don't Tell." Such advocacy work incorporated elements of colorblindness, whereby advocates emphasized the harm done to white gay men, even though Black lesbians and Black gay men were disproportionately harmed by the policy.

4. For further critiques of LGBT social movements' privileging gay marriage, see Conrad (2010), Walters (2014), and Warner (1999), all of whom point to the assimilation in such a politics and argue that it dilutes the more radical potential of activism around gender and sexuality. Bernstein and Taylor's (2013) edited volume complicates those critiques and provides further evidence of the many ways gay marriage has been debated within LGBT communities. Further, Stone (2012) examines the historical development of anti-gay-marriage ballot initiatives, while Kimport (2013) reveals the multifaceted and seemingly contradictory ways that queer people can view their own marriages.

5. Steinbugler (2012) suggests that popular ideas of love that suggest that "we are all just people" align with colorblindness and encourage assimilation by implying that love can make oppression and group differences seem trivial.

6. Bridges (2014) and Smith and Shin (2014) examine how heterosexual men deal with these changing constructions of gender and sexuality, as they distance homophobia from ideal expressions of heterosexuality, while simultaneously disassociating their heterosexual identities from privilege.

7. Pager's (2007) research reveals how employers favor white men over Black men, but may nevertheless be unaware of their biases. Her study shows significant differences based on race and criminal record, with her most surprising finding indicating that white men with a criminal record were more likely than Black men without one to receive callbacks for a job interview, even when the two groups were equally qualified.

REFERENCES

Abbey, Antonia, Lisa Thomson Ross, Donna McDuffie, and Pam McAuslan. 1996. "Alcohol and Dating Risk Factors for Sexual Assault among College Women." *Psychology of Women Quarterly* 20(1): 147–169.

Abrajano, Marisa. 2010. "Are Blacks and Latinos Responsible for the Passage of Proposition 8? Analyzing Voter Attitudes on California's Proposal to Ban Same-Sex Marriage in 2008." *Political Research Quarterly* 63(4): 922–932.

Ahmed, Osman, and Chai Jindasurat. 2014. "Lesbian, Gay, Bisexual, Transgender, Queer, and HIV-Affected Hate Violence in 2013." New York: National Coalition of Anti-Violence Programs.

Alexander, Michelle. 2010. *The New Jim Crow: Mass Incarceration in the Age of Colorblindness.* New York: New Press.

Anderson, Eric. 2002. "Openly Gay Athletes: Contesting Hegemonic Masculinity in a Homophobic Environment." *Gender & Society* 16(6): 860–877.

Anderson, Kristin. 2009. "Gendering Coercive Control." *Violence Against Women* 15(12): 1444–1457.

Anderson, Kristin, and Debra Umberson. 2001. "Gendering Violence: Masculinity and Power in Men's Accounts of Domestic Violence." *Gender & Society* 15(3): 358–380.

Arendt, Hannah. 1970. *On Violence.* New York: Harcourt, Brace and World.

Asencio, Marysol. 2011. "'Locas,' Respect, and Masculinity: Gender Conformity in Migrant Puerto Rican Gay Masculinities." *Gender & Society* 25(3): 335–354.

Avila-Saavedra, Guillermo. 2009. "Nothing Queer about Queer Television: Televized Construction of Gay Masculinities." *Media, Culture & Society* 31(5): 5–21.

Badgett, M. V. Lee. 2003. *Money, Myths, and Change: The Economic Lives of Lesbians and Gay Men.* Chicago: University of Chicago Press.

Barton, Bernadette. 2012. *Pray the Gay Away: The Extraordinary Lives of Bible Belt Gays.* New York: New York University Press.

Beckett, Katherine, and Theodore Sasson. 2004. *The Politics of Injustice: Crime and Punishment in America.* Thousand Oaks, CA: Sage.

Berns, Nancy. 2001. "Degendering the Problem and Gendering the Blame: Political Discourse on Women and Violence." *Gender & Society* 15(2): 262–281.

Bernstein, Mary. 1997. "Celebration and Suppression: The Strategic Uses of Identity by the Lesbian and Gay Movement." *American Journal of Sociology* 103(3): 531–565.

Bernstein, Mary, and Verta Taylor, eds. 2013. *The Marrying Kind? Debating Same-Sex Marriage within the Lesbian and Gay Movement.* Minneapolis: University of Minnesota Press.

Best, Joel. 1999. *Random Violence: How We Talk about New Crimes and New Victims.* Berkeley: University of California Press.

Blee, Kathleen. 2002. *Inside Organized Racism: Women in the Hate Movement.* Berkeley: University of California Press.

Bonilla-Silva, Eduardo. 2006. *Racism without Racists: Color-Blind Racism and the Persistence of Racial Inequality in the United States*. Lanham, MD: Rowman & Littlefield.

Boykin, Keith. 2005. *Beyond the Down Low: Sex, Lies, and Denial in Black America*. New York: Carroll & Graff.

Bridges, Tristan. 2014. "A Very 'Gay' Straight? Hybrid Masculinities, Sexual Aesthetics, and the Changing Relationship between Masculinity and Homophobia." *Gender & Society* 28(1): 58–82.

Britton, Dana. 2011. *The Gender of Crime*. Lanham, MD: Rowman & Littlefield.

Bryant, Karl, and Salvador Vidal-Ortiz. 2008. "Introduction to Retheorizing Homophobias." *Sexualities* 11(4): 387–396.

Campbell, Rebecca, and Sheela Raja. 1999. "Secondary Victimization of Rape Victims: Insights from Mental Health Professionals Who Treat Survivors of Violence." *Violence and Victims* 14(3): 261–275.

Carbado, Devon. 2013. "Colorblind Intersectionality." *Signs* 38(4): 811–845.

Choo, Hae Yeon, and Myra Marx Ferree. 2010. "Practicing Intersectionality in Sociological Research: A Critical Analysis of Inclusions, Interactions, and Institutions in the Study of Inequalities." *Sociological Theory* 28(2): 129–149.

Cochran, Bryan, Angela Stewart, Joshua Ginzler, and Ana Mari Cauce. 2002. "Challenges Faced by Homeless Sexual Minorities: Comparison of Gay, Lesbian, Bisexual, and Transgender Homeless Adolescents with Their Heterosexual Counterparts." *American Journal of Public Health* 92(5): 773–777.

Cohen, Cathy. 1997. "Punks, Bulldaggers, and Welfare Queens: The Radical Potential of Queer Politics?" *GLQ: A Journal of Lesbian and Gay Studies* 3(4): 437–465.

———. 1999. *The Boundaries of Blackness: AIDS and the Breakdown of Black Politics*. Chicago: University of Chicago Press.

Cole, Alyson. 2007. *The Cult of True Victimhood: From the War on Welfare to the War on Terror*. Palo Alto, CA: Stanford University Press.

Collier, Kate, Gabriël van Beusekom, Henny Bos, and Theo Sandfort. 2013. "Sexual Orientation and Gender Identity/ Expression Related Peer Victimization in Adolescence: A Systematic Review of Associated Psychosocial and Health Outcomes." *Journal of Sex Research* 50 (3–4): 299–317.

Collins, Patricia Hill. 1998. "The Tie That Binds: Race, Gender, and US Violence." *Ethnic and Racial Studies* 21(5): 917–938.

———. 2000. *Black Feminist Thought: Knowledge, Consciousness and the Politics of Empowerment*. 2nd ed. New York: Routledge.

———. 2004. *Black Sexual Politics: African Americans, Gender, and the New Racism*. New York: Routledge.

Collins, Randall. 2008. *Violence: A Microsociological Theory*. Princeton, NJ: Princeton University Press.

Comstock, Gary David. 1991. *Violence against Lesbians and Gay Men*. New York: Columbia University Press.

Confessore, Nicholas. 2012. "Anti-Gay-Marriage Group Recommends Creating Tension between Gays and Blacks." *New York Times*, March 27, 2012, http://thecaucus

.blogs.nytimes.com/2012/03/27/anti-gay-marriage-group-recommends-creating -tension-between-gays-and-blacks (accessed June 1, 2012).

Connell, R. W. 1995. *Masculinities*. Berkeley: University of California Press.

Conrad, Ryan (ed.). 2010. *Against Equality: Queer Critiques of Gay Marriage*. Lewiston, ME: Against Equality Press.

Crenshaw, Kimberlé. 1989. "Demarginalizing the Intersection of Race and Sex: A Black Feminist Critique of Antidiscrimination Doctrine, Feminist Theory, and Antiracist Politics." *University of Chicago Legal Forum*: 139–167.

———. 1991. "Mapping the Margins: Intersectionality, Identity Politics, and Violence against Women of Color." *Stanford Law Review* 43(6): 1241–1299.

Cvetkovich, Ann. 2003. *An Archive of Feelings: Trauma, Sexuality, and Lesbian Public Cultures*. Durham, NC: Duke University Press.

D'Augelli, Anthony, and Arnold Grossman. 2001. "Disclosure of Sexual Orientation, Victimization, and Mental Health among Lesbian, Gay, Bisexual Older Adults." *Journal of Interpersonal Violence* 16(10): 1008–1027.

Davis, Angela. 2003. *Are Prisons Obsolete?* New York: Seven Stories Press.

DeKeseredy, Walter, and Martin Schwartz. 2009. *Dangerous Exits: Escaping Abusive Relationships in Rural America*. New Brunswick, NJ: Rutgers University Press.

Denissen, Amy, and Abigail Saguy. 2014. "Gendered Homophobia and the Contradictions of Workplace Discrimination for Women in the Building Trades." *Gender & Society* 28: 381–403.

De Rosa, Christine, Susanne Montgomery, Michele Kipke, Ellen Iverson, Joanne Ma, and Jennifer Unger. 1999. "Service Utilization among Homeless and Runaway Youth in Los Angeles, California: Rates and Reasons." *Journal of Adolescent Health* 24(3): 190–200.

Duggan, Lisa. 2003. *The Twilight of Equality? Neoliberalism, Cultural Politics, and the Attack on Democracy*. Boston: Beacon Press.

Dunbar, Edward. 2006. "Race, Gender, and Sexual Orientation in Hate Crime Victimization: Identity Politics or Identity Risk?" *Violence and Victims* 21(3): 323–337.

Egan, Patrick J., and Kenneth Sherrill. 2009. "California's Proposition 8: What Happened, and What Does the Future Hold?" Washington, DC: National Gay and Lesbian Task Force.

Elizabeth, Vivienne, Nicola Gavey, and Julia Tolmie. 2012. "The Gendered Dynamics of Power in Disputes over the Postseparation Care of Children." *Violence Against Women* 18(4): 459–481.

England, Paula. 2010. "The Gender Revolution: Uneven and Stalled." *Gender & Society* 24(2): 149–166.

Espiritu, Yen Le. 2005. "'Americans Have a Different Attitude': Family, Sexuality, and Gender in Filipina American Lives." In *Gender through the Prism of Difference*, 3rd ed., edited by Pierrette Hondagneu-Sotelo, Maxine Baca Zinn, and Michael Messner, 233–241. New York: Oxford University Press.

Faludi, Susan. 2006. *Backlash: The Undeclared War against American Women*. 15th anniversary ed. New York: Three Rivers Press.

Farrow, Kenyon. 2010. "Is Gay Marriage Anti-Black?" In *Against Equality: Queer Critiques of Gay Marriage,* edited by Ryan Conrad, 21–31. Lewiston, ME: Against Equality Press.

Feinberg, Leslie. 1999. *Trans Liberation: Beyond Pink or Blue.* Boston: Beacon Press.

Ferber, Abby. 1998. *White Man Falling: Race, Gender, and White Supremacy.* Lanham, MD: Rowman & Littlefield.

Franklin, Karen. 2002. "Good Intentions: The Enforcement of Hate Crime Penalty-Enhancement Statutes." *American Behavioral Scientist* 46(1): 154–172.

Gallagher, Charles. 2003. "Color Blind Privilege: The Social and Political Functions of Erasing the Color Line in Post-Race America." *Race, Gender and Class* 10(4): 22–37.

Garcia, Lorena. 2012. *Respect Yourself, Protect Yourself: Latina Girls and Sexual Identity.* New York: New York University Press.

Garfield, Gail. 2010. *Through Our Eyes: African American Men's Experiences of Race, Gender, and Violence.* New Brunswick, NJ: Rutgers University Press.

Garland, David. 2001. *The Culture of Control: Crime and Social Order in Contemporary Society.* Chicago: University of Chicago Press.

Gates, Gary J., and Frank Newport. 2012. "Special Report: 3.4% of U.S. Adults Identify as LGBT: Inaugural Gallup Findings Based on More Than 120,000 Interviews." *Gallup Politics.* http://www.gallup.com/poll/158066/special-report-adults -identify-lgbt.aspx (accessed November 10, 2012).

Gengler, Amanda. 2012. "Defying (Dis)Empowerment in a Battered Women's Shelter: Moral Rhetorics, Intersectionality, and Processes of Control and Resistance." *Social Problems* 59(4): 501–521.

Ghaziani, Amin. 2011. "Post-Gay Collective Identity Construction." *Social Problems* 58(1): 99–125.

Gibson, Kristina. 2011. *Street Kids: Homeless Youth, Outreach, and Policing New York's Streets.* New York: New York University Press.

Giddens, Anthony. 1984. *The Constitution of Society: Outline of the Theory of Structuration.* Berkeley: University of California Press.

Grant, Jaime, Lisa Mottet, Justin Tanis, Jack Harrison, Jody Herman, and Mara Keisling. 2011. "Injustice at Every Turn: A Report of the National Transgender Discrimination Survey." Washington, D.C.: National Center for Transgender Equality and National Gay and Lesbian Task Force.

Gray, Mary. 2009. *Out in the Country: Youth, Media, and Queer Visibility in Rural America.* New York: New York University Press.

Green, Adam Isaiah. 2007. "Queer Theory and Sociology: Locating the Subject and the Self in Sexuality Studies." *Sociological Theory* 25(1): 26–45.

Green, Donald, Dara Strolovitch, Janelle Wong, and Robert Bailey. 2001. "Measuring Gay Populations and Antigay Hate Crime." *Social Science Quarterly* 82(2): 281–296.

Groff, David, ed. 1997. *Out Facts: Just about Everything You Need to Know about Gay and Lesbian Life.* New York: Universe.

Halberstam, Judith. 2005. *In a Queer Time and Place: Transgender Bodies, Subcultural Lives.* New York: New York University Press.

Hancock, Ange-Marie. 2004. *The Politics of Disgust: The Public Identity of the Welfare Queen.* New York: New York University Press.

———. 2007. "Intersectionality as a Normative and Empirical Paradigm." *Politics & Gender* 3(2): 248–254.

Hanhardt, Christina. 2013. *Safe Space: Gay Neighborhood History and the Politics of Violence.* Durham, NC: Duke University Press.

Haritaworn, Jin. 2010. "Queer Injuries: The Racial Politics of 'Homophobic Hate Crime' in Germany." *Social Justice* 37(1): 69–89.

Harvey, David. 2005. *A Brief History of Neoliberalism.* New York: Oxford University Press.

Herek, Gregory. 1990. "The Context of Anti-Gay Violence: Notes on Cultural and Psychological Heterosexism." *Journal of Interpersonal Violence* 5(3): 316–333.

———. 2000. "The Psychology of Sexual Prejudice." *Current Directions in Psychological Sciences* 9(1): 19–22.

———. 2009. "Hate Crimes and Stigma-Related Experiences among Sexual Minority Adults in the United States: Prevalence Estimates from a National Probability Sample." *Journal of Interpersonal Violence* 24(1): 54–74.

Herek, Gregory, Jeanine Cogan, and J. Roy Gillis. 2002. "Victim Experiences in Hate Crimes Based on Sexual Orientation." *Journal of Social Issues* 58(2): 319–339.

Herek, Gregory, J. Roy Gillis, and Jeanine Cogan. 1999. "Psychological Sequelae of Hate Crime Victimization among Lesbian, Gay, and Bisexual Adults." *Journal of Consulting and Clinical Psychology* 67(6): 945–951.

Herek, Gregory, J. Roy Gillis, Jeanine Cogan, and Eric Glunt. 1997. "Hate Crime Victimization among Lesbian, Gay, and Bisexual Adults: Prevalence, Psychological Correlates, and Methodological Issues." *Journal of Interpersonal Violence* 12(2): 195–215.

Hlavka, Heather. 2014. "Normalizing Sexual Violence: Young Women Account for Harassment and Abuse." *Gender & Society* 28(3): 337–358.

Holstein, James, and Jaber Gubrium. 1995. *The Active Interview.* Thousand Oaks, CA: Sage.

Hoppe, Trevor. 2013. "Controlling Sex in the Name of 'Public Health': Social Control and Michigan HIV Law." *Social Problems* 60(1): 27–49.

Horn, Stacey, Joseph Kosciw, and Stephen Russell. 2009. "Special Issue Introduction: New Research on Lesbian, Gay, Bisexual, and Transgender Youth: Studying Lives in Context." *Journal of Youth and Adolescence* 38(7): 863–866.

Hull, Gloria, Patricia Bell-Scott, and Barbara Smith, eds. 1982. *All the Women Are White, All the Blacks Are Men, but Some of Us Are Brave.* New York: Old Westbury.

Iganski, Paul. 2001. "Hate Crimes Hurt More." *American Behavioral Scientist* 45(4): 626–638.

Jackson, Sue, and Tamsyn Gilbertson. 2009. "'Hot Lesbians': Young People's Talk about Representations of Lesbianism." *Sexualities* 12(2): 199–224.

Jakobsen, Hilde. 2014. "What's Gendered about Gender-Based Violence? An Empirically Grounded Theoretical Exploration from Tanzania." *Gender & Society* 28(4): 537–561.

Johnson, Michael. 2006. "Conflict and Control Gender Symmetry and Asymmetry in Domestic Violence." *Violence Against Women* 12(11): 1003–1018.

Johnson, Patrick. 2001. *Appropriating Blackness: Performance and the Politics of Authenticity.* Durham, NC: Duke University Press.

Jones, Nikki. 2010. *Between Good and Ghetto: African American Girls and Inner-City Violence.* New Brunswick, NJ: Rutgers University Press.

Kazyak, Emily. 2012. "Midwest or Lesbian? Gender, Rurality, and Sexuality." *Gender & Society* 26(6): 825–848.

Kearney, Melissa Schettini. 2004. "Is There an Effect of Incremental Welfare Benefits on Fertility Behavior? A Look at the Family Cap." *Journal of Human Resources* 39(2): 295–325.

Kenagy, Gretchen, and Wendy Bostwick. 2005. "Health and Social Service Needs of Transgender People in Chicago." In *Transgender Health and HIV Prevention: Needs Assessment Studies from Transgender Communities across the United States,* edited by Walter Bockting and Eric Avery, 57–66. Binghamton, NY: Haworth Medical Press.

Kimmel, Michael. 2001. "Masculinity as Homophobia: Fear, Shame, and Silence in the Construction of Gender Identity." In *The Masculinities Reader,* edited by Stephen Whitehead and Frank Barrett, 266–287. Cambridge: Polity Press.

———. 2002. "'Gender Symmetry' in Domestic Violence A Substantive and Methodological Research Review." *Violence Against Women* 8(11): 1332–1363.

Kimport, Katrina. 2013. *Queering Marriage: Challenging Family Formation in the United States.* New Brunswick, NJ: Rutgers University Press.

King, Deborah. 1988. "Multiple Jeopardy, Multiple Consciousness: The Context of a Black Feminist Ideology." *Signs* 14(1): 42–72.

Klein, Jessie. 2012. *The Bully Society: School Shootings and the Crisis of Bullying in America's Schools.* New York: New York University Press.

Kosciw, Joseph, Emily Greytak, Mark Bartkiewicz, Madelyn Boesen, and Neal Palmer. 2012. "The 2011 National School Climate Survey: The Experiences of Lesbian, Gay, Bisexual and Transgender Youth in Our Nation's Schools." New York: Gay, Lesbian and Straight Education Network (GLSEN).

Lacy, Karyn. 2007. *Blue-Chip Black: Race, Class, and Status in the New Black Middle Class.* Berkeley: University of California Press.

Lareau, Annette. 2003. *Unequal Childhoods: Class, Race, and Family Life.* Berkeley: University of California Press.

Lawrence, Frederick. 1999. *Punishing Hate: Bias Crimes under American Law.* Cambridge, MA: Harvard University Press.

Levin, Jack. 2010. *The Violence of Hate: Confronting Racism, Anti-Semitism, and Other Forms of Bigotry.* Boston: Allyn and Bacon.

Lewis, Clara. 2013. *Tough on Hate? The Cultural Politics of Hate Crimes.* New Brunswick, NJ: Rutgers University Press.

Lewis, Gregory. 2003. "Black-White Differences in Attitudes toward Homosexuality and Gay Rights." *Public Opinion Quarterly* 67(1): 59–78.

Loffreda, Beth. 2000. *Losing Matt Shepard: Life and Politics in the Aftermath of Anti-Gay Murder.* New York: Columbia University Press.

Lombardi, Emilia, Riki Anne Wilchins, Dana Priesing, and Diana Malouf. 2002. "Gender Violence: Transgender Experiences with Violence and Discrimination." *Journal of Homosexuality* 42(1): 89–101.

Lorde, Audre. 1981. "An Interview with Audre Lorde." *Denver Quarterly* 16(1): 10–27.

———. 1984. *Sister Outsider.* Trumansburg, NY: Crossing Press.

Madriz, Esther. 1997. *Nothing Bad Happens to Good Girls: Fear of Crime in Women's Lives.* Berkeley: University of California Press.

Mahoney, Martha. 1994. "Victimization or Oppression? Women's Lives, Violence, and Agency." In *The Public Nature of Private Violence*, edited by Martha Albertson Fineman and Roxanne Mykitiuk, 59–92. New York: Routledge.

Maier, Shana. 2012. "The Complexity of Victim-Questioning Attitudes by Rape Victim Advocates Exploring Some Gray Areas." *Violence Against Women* 18(12): 1413–1434.

Mardorossian, Carine. 2014. *Framing the Rape Victim: Gender and Agency Reconsidered.* New Brunswick, NJ: Rutgers University Press.

Mason, Gail. 2001. "Body Maps: Envisaging Homophobia, Violence, and Safety." *Social & Legal Studies* 10(1): 23–44.

———. 2002. *The Spectacle of Violence: Homophobia, Gender and Knowledge.* New York: Routledge.

McCorkel, Jill. 2013. *Breaking Women: Gender, Race, and the New Politics of Imprisonment.* New York: New York University Press.

McCormack, Mark. 2012. *The Declining Significance of Homophobia: How Teenage Boys Are Redefining Masculinity and Heterosexuality.* New York: Oxford University Press.

McDevitt, Jack, Jennifer Balboni, Luis Garcia, and Joann Gu. 2001. "Consequences for Victims: A Comparison of Bias- and Non-Bias-Motivated Assaults." *American Behavioral Scientist* 45(4): 697–713.

McIntosh, Peggy. 2004. "White Privilege: Unpacking the Invisible Knapsack." In *Race, Class, and Gender in the United States*, edited by Paula Rothenberg, 188–192. New York: Worth Publishers.

McLean, Kirsten. 2007. "Hiding in the Closet? Bisexuals, Coming Out, and the Disclosure Imperative." *Journal of Sociology* 43(2): 151–166.

Merton, Robert. 1957. *Social Theory and Social Structure.* New York: Free Press.

Messerschmidt, James. 2012. *Gender, Heterosexuality, and Youth Violence: The Struggle for Recognition.* Lanham, MD: Rowman & Littlefield.

Meyer, Doug. 2008. "Interpreting and Experiencing Anti-Queer Violence: Race, Class, and Gender Differences among LGBT Hate Crime Victims." *Race, Gender & Class* 15(3–4): 262–282.

———. 2009. "'She Acts Out in Inappropriate Ways': Students' Evaluations of Violent Women in Film." *Journal of Gender Studies* 18(1): 63–73.

———. 2010. "Evaluating the Severity of Hate-Motivated Violence: Intersectional Differences among LGBT Hate Crime Victims." *Sociology* 44(5): 980–995.

———. 2012. "An Intersectional Analysis of Lesbian, Gay, Bisexual, and Transgender (LGBT) People's Evaluations of Anti-Queer Violence." *Gender & Society* 26(6): 849–873.

———. 2014. "Resisting Hate Crime Discourse: Queer and Intersectional Challenges to Neoliberal Hate Crime Laws." *Critical Criminology* 22(1): 113–125.

Meyer, Doug, and Eric Anthony Grollman. 2014. "Sexual Orientation and Fear at Night: Gender Differences among Sexual Minorities and Heterosexuals." *Journal of Homosexuality* 61(4): 453–470.

Miller, Jody. 2001. *One of the Guys: Girls, Gangs, and Gender.* New York: Oxford University Press.

———. 2008. *Getting Played: African American Girls, Urban Inequality, and Gendered Violence.* New York: New York University Press.

Mogul, Joey, Andrea Ritchie, and Kay Whitlock. 2011. *Queer (In)Justice: The Criminalization of LGBT People in the United States.* Boston: Beacon Press.

Moore, Mignon. 2006. "Lipstick or Timberlands? Meanings of Gender Presentation in Black Lesbian Communities." *Signs* 32(1): 113–139.

———. 2011. *Invisible Families: Gay Identities, Relationships, and Motherhood among Black Women.* Berkeley: University of California Press.

Moraga, Cherrie, and Gloria Anzaldúa, eds. 1983. *This Bridge Called My Back: Writings by Radical Women of Color.* Latham, NY: Kitchen Table Press.

Moran, Leslie. 2000. "Homophobic Violence: The Hidden Injuries of Class." In *Cultural Studies and the Working Class: Subjects to Change,* edited by Sally Munt, 206–218. London: Cassell.

———. 2001. "Affairs of the Heart: Hate Crime and the Politics of Crime Control." *Law and Critique* 12(3): 331–344.

Moran, Leslie, and Andrew Sharpe. 2004. "Violence, Identity and Policing: The Case of Violence against Transgender People." *Criminal Justice* 4(4): 395–417.

Mottet, Lisa, and John Ohle. 2006. "Transitioning Our Shelters: Making Homeless Shelters Safe for Transgender People." *Journal of Poverty* 10(2): 77–101.

Munoz-Plaza, Corrine, Sandra C. Quinn, and Kathleen A. Rounds. 2002. "Lesbian, Gay, Bisexual, and Transgender Students: Perceived Social Support in the High School Environment." *High School Journal* 85(4): 52–63.

Nagel, Joane. 2003. *Race, Ethnicity, and Sexuality: Intimate Intersections, Forbidden Frontiers.* New York: Oxford University Press.

Namaste, Viviane. 2000. *Invisible Lives: The Erasure of Transsexual and Transgendered People.* Chicago: University of Chicago Press.

———. 2006. "Genderbashing: Sexuality, Gender and the Regulation of Public Space." In *The Transgender Studies Reader,* edited by Susan Stryker and Stephen Whittle, 584–600. New York: Routledge.

Nestle, Joan, ed. 1992. *The Persistent Desire: A Femme-Butch Reader.* New York: Alyson Books.

Pager, Devah. 2007. *Marked: Race, Crime, and Finding Work in an Era of Mass Incarceration*. Chicago: University of Chicago Press.

Parker, Ian. 2012. "The Story of a Suicide." *New Yorker,* February 6, 37–51.

Pascoe, C. J. 2007. *Dude, You're a Fag: Masculinity and Sexuality in High School.* Berkeley: University of California Press.

Pattillo-McCoy, Mary. 2000. *Black Picket Fences: Privilege and Peril among the Black Middle Class.* Chicago: University of Chicago Press.

Perry, Barbara. 2001. *In the Name of Hate: Understanding Hate Crimes.* New York: Routledge.

Perry, Barbara, and Ryan Dyck. 2014. "'I Don't Know Where It Is Safe': Trans Women's Experiences of Violence." *Critical Criminology* 22(1): 49–63.

Pharr, Suzanne. 1998. *Homophobia: A Weapon of Sexism.* Little Rock, AR: Chardon Press.

Provine, Doris Marie. 2007. *Unequal under Law: Race in the War on Drugs.* Chicago: University of Chicago Press.

Puar, Jasbir. 2007. *Terrorist Assemblages: Homonationalism in Queer Times.* Durham, NC: Duke University Press.

———. 2012. "Coda: The Cost of Getting Better Suicide, Sensation, Switchpoints." *GLQ: A Journal of Lesbian and Gay Studies* 18(1): 149–158.

Reddy, Chandan. 2011. *Freedom with Violence: Race, Sexuality, and the US State.* Durham, NC: Duke University Press.

Renzetti, Claire. 1992. *Violent Betrayal: Partner Abuse in Lesbian Relationships.* Thousand Oaks, CA: Sage.

Richardson, Diane, and Hazel May. 1999. "Deserving Victims? Sexual Status and the Social Construction of Violence." *Sociological Review* 47(2): 308–331.

Richie, Beth. 1996. *Compelled to Crime: The Gender Entrapment of Battered Black Women.* New York: Routledge.

Rieger, Gerulf, and Ritch C. Savin-Williams. 2012. "Gender Nonconformity, Sexual Orientation, and Psychological Well-Being." *Archives of Sexual Behavior* 41(3): 611–621.

Rios, Victor. 2011. *Punished: Policing the Lives of Black and Latino Boys.* New York: New York University Press.

Ristock, Janice. 2002. *No More Secrets: Violence in Lesbian Relationships.* New York: Routledge.

Roberts, Dorothy. 1997. *Killing the Black Body: Race, Reproduction, and the Meaning of Liberty.* New York: Vintage Books.

Rose, Suzanna, and Mindy Mechanic. 2002. "Psychological Distress, Crime Features, and Help-Seeking Behaviors Related to Homophobic Bias Incidents." *American Behavioral Scientist* 46(1): 14–26.

Runciman, Walter Garrison. 1966. *Relative Deprivation and Social Justice: A Study of Attitudes to Social Inequality in Twentieth-Century England.* New York: Routledge.

Rust, Paula Rodriguez, ed. 2000. *Bisexuality in the United States: A Social Science Reader.* New York: Columbia University Press.

Sandfort, Theo G. M., Rita M. Melendez, and Rafael M. Diaz. 2007. "Gender Non-conformity, Homophobia, and Mental Distress in Latino Gay and Bisexual Men." *Journal of Sex Research* 44 (2): 181–189.

Savage, Dan. 2008. "Black Homophobia." *The Stranger.* November 5, 2008. http://slog .thestranger.com/2008/11/black_homophobia (accessed December 1, 2009).

Schilt, Kristen. 2011. *Just One of the Guys? Transgender Men and the Persistence of Gender Inequality.* Chicago: University of Chicago Press.

Schilt, Kristen, and Laurel Westbrook. 2009. "Doing Gender, Doing Heteronormativity: 'Gender Normals,' Transgender People, and the Social Maintenance of Heterosexuality." *Gender & Society* 23(4): 440–464.

Scully, Diana. 1994. *Understanding Sexual Violence: A Study of Convicted Rapists.* New York: Routledge.

Seidman, Steven. 2002. *Beyond the Closet: The Transformation of Gay and Lesbian Life.* New York: Routledge.

Semaan, Ingrid, Jana Jasinski, and Anne Bubriski-McKenzie. 2013. "Subjection, Subjectivity, and Agency: The Power, Meaning, and Practice of Mothering among Women Experiencing Intimate Partner Abuse." *Violence Against Women* 19(1): 69–88.

Smith, Dorothy. 1987. *The Everyday World as Problematic: A Feminist Sociology.* Boston: Northeastern University Press.

Smith, Lance, and Richard Shin. 2014. "Queer Blindfolding: A Case Study on Difference 'Blindness' toward Persons Who Identify as Lesbian, Gay, Bisexual, and Transgender." *Journal of Homosexuality* 61(7): 940–961.

Soss, Joe, Richard Fording, and Sanford Schram. 2011. *Disciplining the Poor: Neoliberal Paternalism and the Persistent Power of Race.* Chicago: University of Chicago Press.

Spade, Dean. 2011. *Normal Life: Administrative Violence, Critical Trans Politics, and the Limits of Law.* Cambridge, MA: South End Press.

———. 2013. "Intersectional Resistance and Law Reform." *Signs* 38(4): 1031–1055.

Spade, Dean, and Craig Willse. 2000. "Confronting the Limits of Gay Hate Crimes Activism: A Radical Critique." *UCLA Chicano-Latino Law Review* 21:38–52.

Stark, Evan. 2007. *Coercive Control: How Men Entrap Women in Personal Life.* New York: Oxford University Press.

———. 2009. "Rethinking Coercive Control." *Violence Against Women* 15(12): 1509–1525.

Steinbugler, Amy. 2012. *Beyond Loving: Intimate Racework in Lesbian, Gay, and Straight Interracial Relationships.* New York: Oxford University Press.

Stone, Amy. 2012. *Gay Rights at the Ballot Box.* Minneapolis: Minnesota University Press.

Stotzer, Rebecca. 2008. "Gender Identity and Hate Crimes: Violence against Transgender People in Los Angeles County." *Sexuality Research & Social Policy* 5(1): 43–52.

———. 2009. "Violence against Transgender People: A Review of United States Data." *Aggression and Violent Behavior* 14(3): 170–179.

Thomas, Kendall. 2001. "'Ain't Nothin' Like the Real Thing': Black Masculinity, Gay Sexuality, and the Jargon of Authenticity." In *Traps: African American Men on*

Gender and Sexuality, edited by Rudolph P. Byrd and Beverly Guy-Sheftall, 327–341. Bloomington: Indiana University Press.

Tolman, Deborah L. 1994. "Doing Desire: Adolescent Girls' Struggles for/with Sexuality." *Gender & Society* 8(3): 324–342.

Tomsen, Stephen. 2006. "Homophobic Violence, Cultural Essentialism, and Shifting Sexual Identities." *Social & Legal Studies* 15(3): 389–407.

Tomsen, Stephen, and Gail Mason. 2001. "Engendering Homophobia: Violence, Sexuality, and Gender Conformity." *Journal of Sociology* 37(3): 257–273.

Van Leeuwen, James, Susan Boyle, Stacy Salomonsen-Sautel, D. Nico Baker, J. T. Garcia, Allison Hoffman, and Christian Hopfer. 2006. "Lesbian, Gay, and Bisexual Homeless Youth: An Eight-City Public Health Perspective." *Child Welfare* 85(2): 151–170.

von Schulthess, Beatrice. 1992. "Violence in the Streets: Anti-Lesbian Assault and Harassment in San Francisco." In *Hate Crimes: Confronting Violence against Lesbians and Gay Men,* edited by Gregory Herek and Kevin Berrill, 65–75. Newbury Park, CA: Sage.

Wacquant, Loïc. 2009. *Prisons of Poverty.* Minneapolis: University of Minnesota Press.

Walters, Mikel, Jieru Chen, and Matthew Breiding. 2013. "The National Intimate Partner and Sexual Violence Survey (NISVS): 2010 Findings on Victimization by Sexual Orientation." Atlanta: National Center for Injury Prevention and Control, Centers for Disease Control and Prevention.

Walters, Suzanna. 2014. *The Tolerance Trap: How God, Genes, and Good Intentions Are Sabotaging Gay Equality.* New York: New York University Press.

Ward, Jane. 2004. "'Not All Differences Are Created Equal': Multiple Jeopardy in a Gendered Organization." *Gender & Society* 18(1): 82–102.

———. 2008. *Respectably Queer: Diversity Culture in LGBT Activist Organizations.* Nashville, TN: Vanderbilt University Press.

Warner, Michael. 1991. "Introduction: Fear of a Queer Planet." *Social Text* 9(4): 3–17.

———. 1999. *The Trouble with Normal: Sex, Politics, and the Ethics of Queer Life.* Cambridge, MA: Harvard University Press.

Webber, Valerie. 2013. "Shades of Gay: Performance of Girl-on-Girl Pornography and Mobile Authenticities." *Sexualities* 16(1–2): 217–235.

Weitzer, Ronald. 2012. *Legalizing Prostitution: From Illicit Vice to Lawful Business.* New York: New York University Press.

West, Candace, and Don H. Zimmerman. 1987. "Doing Gender." *Gender & Society* 1(2): 125–151.

———. 2009. "Accounting for Doing Gender." *Gender & Society* 23(1): 112–122.

Western, Bruce. 2006. *Punishment and Inequality in America.* New York: Russell Sage.

Whitbeck, Les, Xiaojin Chen, Dan Hoyt, Kimberly Tyler, and Kurt Johnson. 2004. "Mental Disorder, Subsistence Strategies, and Victimization among Gay, Lesbian, and Bisexual Homeless and Runaway Adolescents." *Journal of Sex Research* 41(4): 329–342.

Whitehead, Jaye Cee. 2011. *The Nuptial Deal: Same-Sex Marriage and Neo-Liberal Governance.* Chicago: University of Chicago Press.

Wilkins, Amy. 2008. *Wannabes, Goths, and Christians: The Boundaries of Sex, Style, and Status*. Chicago: University of Chicago Press.

Williams, Christine. 2006. *Inside Toyland: Working, Shopping, and Social Inequality*. Berkeley: University of California Press.

Williams, Christine, Patti A. Giuffre, and Kirsten Dellinger. 2009. "The Gay-Friendly Closet." *Sexuality Research & Social Policy* 6(1): 29–45.

Ziegart, Jonathan and Paul Hanges. 2005. "Employment Discrimination: The Role of Implicit Attitudes, Motivation, and a Climate for Racial Bias." *Journal of Applied Psychology* 90(3): 553–562.

INDEX

adultery, gender and, 126–127
alcohol use, 81
assimilationist strategies, 149, 155, 173n5
autonomy, lesbians' focus on, 57–58, 59–61, 69, 70

bisexual people, 38, 79, 128
bisexual women, 161, 163; domestic violence against, 36, 123, 125, 127–128, 129–130; victim blame of, 153
"bitch" (term), 3, 74, 75, 141–142
Black men, 9; hypersexuality stereotypes about, 49; racial profiling of, 2–3, 87. *See also* gay men, Black and Latino
Blackness: heterosexuality associated with, 3, 26; as marked, 45–47; masculinity and, 49, 58–59; performance of, 62. *See also* whiteness
Blacks. *See* LGBT people, Black and Latino
Blacks' homophobia, stereotypes about, 8–9, 32–34, 52–53, 54–55, 95–96, 167n4
Black women: hypersexuality stereotypes about, 49. *See also* lesbians, Black and Latina
Boys Don't Cry (film), 131
bullying, 5, 28, 42, 66–67, 123, 147

cisgender people, 37, 79, 88, 139, 144. *See also* transgender people
civil rights movement, 149
class. *See* perception of severity of violence, social class and; social class; social class/ sexuality overlap in violent acts
classism, 8, 102, 139–141, 142, 144. *See also* social class
Clementi, Tyler, 5, 9–10, 123, 147
Cole, Alyson, 172n2
college campuses, 28
Collins, Patricia Hill, 116
colorblindness, 7–8, 150, 173n3
"coming out," 147; family reactions to, 121,
134, 135; violence following, 85, 110, 123–124, 125
Crenshaw, Kimberlé, 102, 146
crime rates, 29

date rape, 12, 64–65, 75, 77, 80
DeGeneres, Ellen, 154
dehumanizing language/violence: against intersex people, 136–137; against transgender people, 10, 35–37, 69, 79, 143–144
discrimination: denial of feelings of, 133; elimination of legal, 149; employment, 137–138, 150–151, 173n7; of marked aspects, 47; routine forms of, 41–42; as social vs. individual phenomenon, 133, 134–135; subtlety of, 118, 151–152
domestic violence, 12–13, 123–132, 141, 172n1; against bisexual women, 36, 123, 125, 127–128, 129–130; gender performance and, 134, 135–136; against lesbians, 36, 123–130, 143; mothers and, 128–129; perpetrators of, 126, 129; social class/sexuality overlap and, 30, 123, 125–126, 143; against transgender women, 35–36, 129–131; verbal, 15, 122–123
"Don't Ask, Don't Tell" policy, 173n3
"down low" men, 55
downward mobility, 136
"dyke" (term), 3, 69, 75

Egan, Patrick J., 33
employment: discrimination in, 137–138, 150–151, 173n7; middle-class LGBT people and, 143; transgender people's difficulty finding, 137–138, 144
Employment Non-Discrimination Act (ENDA), 150–151
equal rights, 149
escalation of violence, 27–28

"faggot" (term), 66–67, 69, 95, 101

187

ABOUT THE AUTHOR

DOUG MEYER is a visiting instructor at the University of Virginia in the Women, Gender & Sexuality Studies Program and holds a PhD in sociology from the Graduate Center of the City University of New York (CUNY). His work has been published in *Gender & Society, Sociology, Critical Criminology,* and *Race, Gender & Class.* He has received an emerging diversity scholar citation from the National Center for Institutional Diversity and a graduate student paper award from the Race, Gender, and Class section of the American Sociological Association; one of his articles has been reprinted in Margaret Andersen and Patricia Hill Collins's *Race, Class, & Gender.* His research interests include intersectionality theory, sociological approaches to violence, and feminist and queer studies.

CPSIA information can be obtained at www.ICGtesting.com
Printed in the USA
LVOW07s2044210916

505628LV00002B/257/P